Soul Hunters

Soul Hunters

Hunting, Animism, and Personhood among the Siberian Yukaghirs

Rane Willerslev

UNIVERSITY OF CALIFORNIA PRESS
Berkeley · Los Angeles · London

University of California Press, one of the most
distinguished university presses in the United States,
enriches lives around the world by advancing scholar-
ship in the humanities, social sciences, and natural
sciences. Its activities are supported by the UC Press
Foundation and by philanthropic contributions from
individuals and institutions. For more information,
visit www.ucpress.edu.

University of California Press
Berkeley and Los Angeles, California

University of California Press, Ltd.
London, England

Library of Congress Cataloging-in-Publication Data

Willerslev, Rane, 1971–
    Soul hunters : hunting, animism, and personhood
among the Siberian Yukaghirs / Rane Willerslev.
        p.   cm.
    Includes bibliographical references and index.
    ISBN 978-0-520-25216-5 (cloth : alk. paper) —
ISBN 978-0-520-25217-2 (pbk. : alk. paper)
    1. Yukaghir—Hunting—Russia (Federation)—
Siberia.   2. Animism—Russia (Federation)—Siberia.
3. Yukaghir—Russia (Federation)—Siberia—Folklore.
4. Ethnology—Russia (Federation)—Siberia.
5. Siberia (Russia)—Social life and customs.
I. Title.
DK759.Y8W55   2007
305.89'46—dc22   2006035803

15   14   13   12   11   10   09   08   07
10   9   8   7   6   5   4   3   2   1

To Akulina and Gregory Shalugin
in friendship and gratitude

Contents

Illustrations

Preface

This book is based on a total of eighteen months' field research among the Upper Kolyma Yukaghirs, a small group of indigenous Siberian hunters living in the village of Nelemnoye on the Yasachnaya River in the Russian Republic of Sakha (Yakutia). In 1993 I visited the Yukaghirs for the first time as a member of an interdisciplinary Danish-Russian expedition (R. Willerslev 1995).[1] My task was to collect ethnographic artifacts from both the Upper and Lower Kolyma Yukaghirs for an exhibition at a museum in Denmark. In 1997 I returned to the Upper Kolyma Yukaghir settlement of Nelemnoye on two separate occasions to shoot ethnographic films about hunting and trapping (Willerslev and Høgel 1997; Willerslev 1997). In 1998 I was sent back to the village by a Danish NGO to establish a cooperative society with the aim of promoting and assisting the sale of Yukaghir-produced sable furs directly on the world market (Willerslev and Christensen 2000; Willerslev 2000a, 2000b). These various visits, amounting to a total of about six months, provided me with the basic language skills and personal contacts that facilitated my one-year-long doctoral fieldwork among Yukaghir hunters, which I carried out in 1999 and 2000. During this prolonged stay I came to participate as a hunter myself, and much of the material analyzed in this book is based on my participation in this role.

My initial interest in the Yukaghirs came from reading Jochelson's classic 1926 monograph, *The Yukaghir and the Yukaghized Tungus*, which is still by far the most complete work on these people. Jochelson was a Russian intellectual and revolutionary who, first as an exile in Yakutia and later as a member of the American Museum of Natural History's famous Jesup North Pacific Expedition (1897–1902), carried out fieldwork among both the Upper and Lower Kolyma Yukaghirs at the turn of the twentieth century.[2] Here he made wide-ranging studies of Yukaghir culture and religious life, with a particular interest in their shamanic practices and spiritual beliefs. As was customary at the time, he interpreted those beliefs as an early form of religion in the evolutionary passage from savagery to civilization, according to Tylor's concept of "animism." Since Jochelson, only a few studies on the Yukaghirs have been published, all in the Russian language and most building on Jochelson's data rather than on the living voices of contemporary Yukaghirs.[3] Thus, when I arrived in the village of Nelemnoye in the summer of 1999 to do fieldwork, it was with Jochelson's work in the back of my mind and with a great interest in finding out what had happened in the intervening hundred years. Were the Yukaghirs still the bearers of the kind of traditional spiritual knowledge that Jochelson had described so vividly, or had these ideas been altogether transformed or lost? What I did not realize at the time, however, was that my research would lead me to rethink the complex phenomena that Tylor denoted as "animism." Nor did I know that Yukaghir hunting would become the framework through which I would come to do this.

My fieldwork soon took an uneasy turn, however, which was decisive for the way in which my research would be carried out. Because of my involvement in promoting and assisting in the sale of Yukaghir-produced sable furs on the world market, I came under attack from the powerful Yakutian fur company Sakhabult, which, since the collapse of the Soviet Union, has monopolized the Republic's fur trade. When the company realized that I was helping the Yukaghirs collect and send their furs directly to the European fur-auction houses, it sent the police to Nelemnoye to arrest me on charges of "illegal" trade and poaching. Consequently, I had to flee the village and seek refuge among hunters in the forest. My fate, however, was much preferable to that of my Russian associate in Yakutsk, a fur specialist and trader who drowned under mysterious circumstances (Willerslev and Christensen 2000).

Thus, for almost six months I stayed with "Old" Spiridon Spiridonov and his group of hunters, including his two adult sons Yura and Peter and his grandson Stephan, on the Omulevka, a precipitous mountain river that enters the Yasachnaya River about a hundred kilometers south of Nelemnoye. Despite the physical hardships of forest life, which occasionally involved a shortage of food, frostbite, and even a bear attack, I truly came to enjoy my stay. When the other hunters saw that I was prepared to work hard, I was largely absorbed into the group. Each day we went hunting together or alone, and over time I became quite successful at it. I was given my equal share of the meat and the furs produced, which I sent back to my acquaintances in Nelemnoye whenever a hunter from our group returned to the village. This enforced exile in the forest allowed me not only to observe matters such as the different phases of the hunting process and various practical and magical techniques for dealing with prey and spirits, but also, through my participation in day-to-day routines, to become personally immersed in the hunters' mode of existence. Gradually, I started to experience their environment as they do: whenever I was out hunting, my every sinew would be straining to distinguish tracks and other signs of prey, and during my nightly dreams it occasionally happened that some spiritual being approached me with tokens of hunting luck.

However, it was not until I returned to Nelemnoye from my forest refuge that I realized how deeply life in the forest had affected me. Like most other hunters, I found the monotony of life in the village almost intolerable. In addition, the young village women, with their elegant leather boots and Russian-style clothes, seemed alien to me. When I was not interviewing teachers, administrators, and retired people, I killed time by hitting the bottle with the other hunters. It was only when Akulina and Gregory Shalugin, an elderly Yukaghir couple with whom I had developed a particularly warm friendship, dragged me along to the forest that my condition improved. From that point on, however, I avoided village life as much as I could and spent the rest of my time in the field with Spiridon's group and other groups of hunters in the forest.

My point is that I cannot claim to represent all Yukaghirs, or even all the Yukaghirs of Nelemnoye. Therefore, when I use the terms *Yukaghir, the Yukaghirs,* or *the Yukaghir people,* I resort to ethnographic shorthand for those individuals among the Yukaghir population whom I know the best (see Atkinson 1989: 5). These are predominantly hunters, and also people of the older generation. Because of my time spent in the forest, I did not have much opportunity to talk to younger Yukaghir women in the village. My work reflects that fact: for better or worse, this book is written mainly from a hunter's perspective. This is mostly, but not exclusively, a male perspective. Traditionally, gender differences were not pronounced among the Yukaghirs. Men and women performed similar roles during the hunting seasons, and although women faced some taboos—such as, for example, prohibition from participating in hunting during menstruation and right after childbirth (Jochelson 1926: 146)—it was by no means unusual for women to go hunting alone or together with the men. Even today, there are elderly women renowned for their hunting prowess, and who are known even for hunting bears. However, since the 1960s this has all changed. The women have settled permanently in the village of Nelemnoye and are employed in institutions such as the residential school, the kindergarten, and the hospital. The men, for their part, stayed on the land to hunt for fur—especially sable—which was an important source of wealth for the Soviet state (Willerslev 2000a). Today the majority of Yukaghir men still spend eight months or more of the year deep in the forest hunting for elk and sable. It is this universe of hunters with which this book is concerned, and although it includes some women, it describes primarily a male world.

Acknowledgments

Many people have participated in the completion of this book. My greatest debt is to the population of Nelemnoye and the hunters for their unstinting help and hospitality. In particular, I would like to thank Akulina and Gregory Shalugin, Alexandra and Ivan Danilov, Spiridon, Yuri, Peter, and Konstantin Spiridonov, Vyacheslav Sinitskiy, Vyacheslav Shadrin, Nikolai Shalugin, Vasili Shalugin, and Nikolai Likhachev.

The final form of this book was greatly influenced by critiques and comments generously offered by several readers. I am especially indebted to my former supervisors Caroline Humphrey and Piers Vitebsky, and to my Ph.D. thesis examiners, Tim Ingold and Stephen Hugh-Jones. The reports of my two reviewers, Nikolai Ssorin-Chaikov and Peter Schweitzer, and the editorial board committee reports by James Clifford and Joel Robbins also have been enormously helpful. In addition, I would like to thank my former fellow students and friends in Cambridge for their critical comments: Rebecca Empson, Sari Wastell, James Suzman, Martin Holbraad, Morten Pedersen, Lars Højer and Mette Holm, Vera Skvirskaja, Olga Ulturgasheva, Agnieszka Halemba, Katie Swancut, Janne Flora, Signe Gundersen, and Karoline Normann. My former colleagues in the Department for Social Anthropology at the University of Manchester—especially Alberto Corsín Jiménez, Karen Sykes, Stef Jansen, Soumhya Venkatesan, Sarah Green, Cathrine Degnen, and Penny Harvey—have been very generous with comments and criticisms as well. In Denmark, I would like to thank Torben Vestergaard,

Lotte Meinert, Nils Bubandt, and Ton Otto from the University of Aarhus, and Ida Nicolaisen, Esther Fihl, Inger Sjørslev, and Kirsten Hastrup from the University of Copenhagen.

I gratefully acknowledge the work of Mads Salicath, Marie Carsten Pedersen, and Jens Kirkeby from the Moesgaard Museum, who kindly produced the line drawings of ethnographic items used in this book. I would also like to thank Coilín ÓhAiseadha and Khadidjah Mattar for proofreading earlier drafts, and Anne Dunbar-Nobes, Sharron Wood, and Jacqueline Volin for providing editorial advice and for helping to prepare the final text for publication.

My research would never have been completed had it not been for generous awards from the following institutions: the Independent Research Councils of Denmark, the Economic and Social Research Council (UK), Her Royal Majesty the Queen of Denmark Margaret's and Prince Henrik's Fund, the Committee for Nature and Peoples of the North in Denmark, Girton College, and the William Wyse Fund in Cambridge.

Finally, I thank Blackwell Publishing for permission to use part of my article "Not Animal, Not Not-Animal: Hunting, Imitation, and Empathetic Knowledge among the Siberian Yukaghirs," *Journal of the Royal Anthropological Institute* 10 (2004): 629–52, in chapter 5. I also thank Sage Publications for permission to reprint part of my article "Spirits as 'Ready to Hand': A Phenomenological Analysis of Yukaghir Spiritual Knowledge and Dreaming," *Journal of Anthropological Theory* 4 (4): 395–418 (Sage Publications Ltd., 2004), in chapter 7.

CHAPTER I

Animism as Mimesis

Watching Old Spiridon rocking his body back and forth, I was puzzled whether the figure I saw before me was man or elk. The elk-hide coat worn with its hair outward, the headgear with its characteristic protruding ears, and the skis covered with an elk's smooth leg skins, so as to sound like the animal when moving in snow, made him an elk; yet the lower part of his face below the hat, with its human eyes, nose, and mouth, along with the loaded rifle in his hands, made him a man. Thus, it was not that Spiridon had stopped being human. Rather, he had a liminal quality: he was not an elk, and yet he was also not *not* an elk. He was occupying a strange place in between human and nonhuman identities.

A female elk appeared from among the willow bushes with her offspring. At first the animals stood still, the mother lifting and lowering her huge head in bewilderment, unable to solve the puzzle in front of her. But as Spiridon moved closer, she was captured by his mimetic performance, suspended her disbelief, and started walking straight toward him with the calf trotting behind her. At that point he lifted his gun and shot them both dead. Later he explained the incident: "I saw two persons dancing toward me. The mother was a beautiful young woman and while singing, she said: 'Honored friend. Come and I'll take you by the arm and lead you to our home.' At that point I killed them both. Had I gone with her, I myself would have died. She would have killed me."

Lifting us into an animated world, this passage sets the scene for this book, which is about the Yukaghirs, a small group of indigenous hunters on the Upper Kolyma River in northeastern Siberia. For us in the West, it is customary to assume that attributes of personhood, with all this entails in terms of language, intentionality, reasoning, and moral awareness, belong exclusively to human beings. Animals are understood to be wholly natural beings, and their behavior is typically explained as automatic and instinctive. Among the Yukaghirs, however, a different assumption prevails. In their world, persons can take a variety of forms, of which a human being is only one. They can also appear in the shape of rivers, trees, souls, and spirits, but above all it is mammals that Yukaghirs see as "other-than-human persons" (Hallowell 1960: 36). Moreover, humans and animals can move in and out of different species' perspectives by temporarily taking on each other's bodies. Indeed, among the Yukaghirs, as we shall see later, this capacity to take on the appearance and viewpoint of another being is one of the key aspects of being a person.

The traditional term for this set of beliefs, whereby nonhuman animals (and even nonanimals such as inanimate objects and spirits) are endowed with intellectual, emotional, and spiritual qualities paralleling those of human persons, is *animism*. Animism is one of anthropology's earliest concepts, if not the first. It was introduced by Tylor (1929a [1871]: 424) as a way of characterizing the simplest form of religious belief, "the belief in spiritual beings," but it is a term that anthropologists today use with caution, if at all. The reason for this is summarized well by Descola, who writes, "modern anthropology has been extremely reticent on the topic of animism . . . perhaps out of an implicit fear of drawing undue attention to an apparently irrational aspect of the life of archaic societies" (1992: 114). It is certainly true that anthropologists have tended to give little credence to accounts, such as that of Old Spiridon, that differ radically from what we would consider "normal." In the early days of the discipline, Victorian scholars would say that if the old hunter were not actually lying, then he must be suffering from delusions of some sort and would be incapable of telling fact from fantasy, or reality from dreams. Other, more recent, anthropologists, by temperament and training inclined to be rather more sympathetic to the indigenous viewpoint, would accept the hunter's story by adding an "as if" to his account—so instead of talking nonsense, the hunter is deemed to be speaking in metaphors, constructing figurative parallels between the two separate domains of nature and culture. However, to say that the hunter is talking "as if" animals were persons is to say that his story should not be taken in a literal way but instead seen as a symbolic statement. The "metaphor model," which has roots in Durkheim's sociology, is to be found everywhere in modern studies of hunter-gatherers. For both models, however, the result remains essentially the same: animals are not *really* persons, but exist as such only in the mind of the hunter, whose account is therefore not to be taken seriously as founded in reality. By this move, indigenous metaphysics appears to pose no challenge to our ontological certainties, and the anthropologist can get on with his job without having to worry about whether there is any foundation in reality for what people have to say.

In this book, however, I wish to reverse the primacy of Western metaphysics over indigenous understandings and to follow the lead of the Yukaghirs in what they are saying about the nature of spirits, souls, and animal persons. Only in this way can we hope to develop a framework that takes their viewpoints on these matters seriously. This does not imply exoticizing the Yukaghirs as being somehow more knowledgeable or wiser than us. Nor does it imply adopting their beliefs or accepting these beliefs without question. Rather, it involves an honest effort to draw attention to complex patterns of common features and differences between Yukaghirs and ourselves by placing their animistic beliefs and practices in a critical dialogue with our theories of knowledge. The remaining part of this chapter is mostly devoted to sketching out this new approach to the animism "problem." However, before we can embark on this task, which will bring us up against both philosophy and anthropological theory, I need to introduce the people with whom this book is concerned.

THE YUKAGHIRS

The name *Yukaghir* (alternative spellings: *Iukagir, Yukagir, Yukagiry,* and *Yukagirskiy*) is considered to be a generic name of Evenki origin, which was adopted by the Russians in the seventeenth century.[1] The meaning of the name has not been firmly established, although it has been suggested that it could mean "the icy or frozen people" (Ivanov 1999: 153). In their own language the Upper Kolyma Yukaghirs call themselves *Odul*, which means "strong" or "powerful." Although this name is widely known among these people, hardly anyone uses it. Instead, they refer to themselves as *Yukaghirs*, which is why I refer to them by this name.

Roughly speaking, the Yukaghirs consist nowadays of two groups who speak mutually incomprehensible dialects of the Yukaghir language: the Upper Kolyma group, whose main settlement is the village of

Nelemnoye in Verkhne Kolymsk Ulus; and the Lower Kolyma group, who live in Nizne Kolymsk Ulus (see the map of the Yukaghirs' territory). It is the former group with whom I have worked, and it is they who are the focus of this book. The most remarkable difference between the two groups is that while the Lower Kolyma group lives mainly from reindeer herding (which they are thought to have adopted in relatively recent times from the Evenki), members of the Upper Kolyma group have remained hunters and fishermen, and even today the dog is their only domesticated animal.[2]

At the time of the Russian conquest of northeastern Siberia in the mid-seventeenth century, Yukaghir-speaking groups occupied a vast territory (about 1.5 million square kilometers) stretching from the lower reaches of the Lena River in the west to the Anadyr Basin in the east, and from the shores of the Arctic Ocean in the north to the upper reaches of the Yana, Indigirka, and Kolyma rivers in the south. They consisted of a large number of separate groups, such as the Chuvantsy, Khodyntsy, Anauls, and Omoks, who, although they spoke kindred languages, had no political unity. It is estimated that the Yukaghirs numbered about five thousand in the years before Russian contact (Zukova, Nikolaeva, and Dëmina 1993). However, during the first three centuries of Russian rule the Yukaghirs underwent the most rapid decline ever recorded among northern Siberian peoples. The 1859 census recorded some 2,500 Yukaghirs, the 1897 census 1,500, and the 1927 census only 443. Wars with invading neighboring reindeer-breeding peoples, including the Evenki, Evens, Koryaks, Chukchi, and Sakha (horse and cattle breeders), greatly reduced the population.[3] The introduction of European diseases also had a disastrous impact, with very large numbers of Yukaghirs dying during smallpox and measles epidemics (Jochelson 1926: 54–55).

The practice of changing one's ethnic membership to avoid paying fur tribute (yasak) also may have contributed to the steady decline in the number of Yukaghirs (Morin and Saladin d'Anglure 1997: 168). Censuses for the purpose of fur tribute were undertaken infrequently, and the size of the tribute was calculated on the basis of the number of people counted in the previous census, so the Yukaghirs, with their population rapidly declining, often found themselves paying tribute for dead men. By identifying themselves as members of one of the demographically expanding groups, such as the Sakha (Yakuts) and Chukchi, they could ease their tax burden. Such "manipulation of ethnicity" is apparent even today. According to the 1989 census, there were a total of 1,112 Yukaghirs, of whom approximately half belonged to the Upper Kolyma

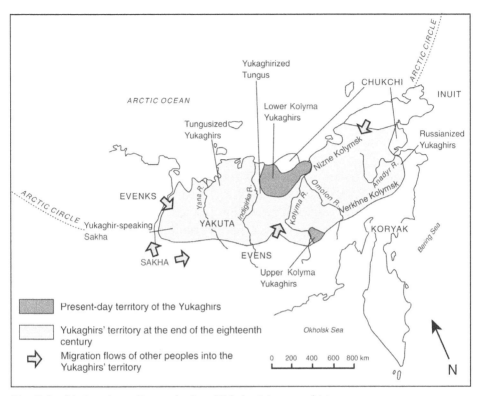

The Yukaghirs' territory. Drawn by Jens Kirkeby, Moesgaard Museum.

group. Strikingly, the 1979 census gives a figure of only 500 Yukaghirs total. The reason for this remarkable increase is mostly that people from different ethnic backgrounds register themselves as Yukaghir in order to qualify for a variety of welfare entitlements, such as special hunting and fishing rights, for which only Yukaghirs are eligible (Derlicki 2003: 123). Likewise, most children born of mixed parentage are today being registered as Yukaghirs. At present, Nelemnoye's population numbers 307, of which 146 are registered as Yukaghirs. In addition to a few Evens, most of the remaining population is listed as either Sakha or Russian.

It is important to note, however, that these ethno-administrative categories (Rus. *Natsional'nost'*) tell us very little about the local population's actual sense of belonging. For example, there are a number of elderly people in Nelemnoye who regard themselves as Yukaghirs and speak the Yukaghir language but who in their youth were registered as Sakha or Russians. Moreover, for many local people, being a Yukaghir person is not so much an identity that one is born with or born to, but a quality that is obtained through one's occupation and territory of residence. An elderly man thus explained to me that although his parents were Yukaghirs, he registered as an Even when he moved to the mountains to work with reindeer herders, and then became a Yukaghir again when he returned to Nelemnoye to take up hunting. Likewise, a man who was born in the neighboring village of Verkhne Kolymsk and listed as a Yakut assured me that after twenty years of residence in Nelemnoye, he is now more Yukaghir than Sakha because he is "living, eating, and working like a Yukaghir." Anderson calls this phenomenon a "relational identity," a way of accounting for the situational and fluid nature of identity formation in northeastern Siberia, where it is quite common for a single individual to move from one ethnic identity to another within a life span or even hold several identities simultaneously (Anderson 2000: 91). Indeed, as we shall see throughout this book, this relational quality of identity extends into the human-nonhuman domain as well: humans become animals, animals become humans, and one class of spirits turns into another. There are no fixed identities here, only continuous transformations of one class of beings into another.

The Yukaghir language belongs to the so-called Paleo-Asiatic group, where it occupies a special place. It is conventionally considered a genetically isolated group, yet it can probably be affiliated with the Uralic superfamily, consisting of the Finno-Ugric and Samoedian languages (Shnirelman 1999: 119). Until recently, multilingualism was widespread in Nelemnoye, with the Yukaghir, Even, and Sakha languages serving as alternative modes of intercultural communication (Maslova and Vakhtin 1996: 999). Although this is still the case among the oldest people (those over sixty), the long-term survival of the Yukaghir language is under threat from Russian, which since the late 1960s has become the dominant language. This, as I shall discuss in chapter 7, is mainly the result of the Soviet boarding school system, which removed Yukaghir children from their families. Today only the oldest generation is competent in the indigenous language; for everyone under the age of sixty, the primary language is Russian or Sakha, although for many of them the mother tongue is Yukaghir (Vakhtin 1991).

In 1931, during the Soviet era, the Yukaghirs were organized into a collective farm (kolkhoz) called Shining Life (Svetlaya zhizn), whose center was located in Nelemnoye, which was originally an old Yukaghir camp called Nungeden aNil', situated where the Yasachnaya River meets the Rassokha River. Between 1956 and 1958, Shining Life was merged with the mainly Sakha collective farm called the Soviet Constitution to form the *kolkhoz* named Yukaghir. However, just two years later this collective farm was subsumed into the much larger state farm *(sovkhoz)* called Verkhne Kolymsk, and Nelemnoye was moved downriver, about 70 kilometers from the district center of Zyrianka.[4]

During the Soviet period, Nelemnoye's hunters were subject to the region's official planning regimes; they were set target figures for the number of sable skins they were required to deliver to the *sovkhoz,* in return for which they received cash payments. Subsistence hunting remained vital for local people until the mid-1960s. Thereafter, however, the village was increasingly incorporated into the Soviet state economy, with its wage employment and centralized delivery of consumer goods, and subsistence hunting came to constitute a supplementary rather than a central activity.

However, since the collapse of the state farm in 1991 and the economic crises that followed, people have largely returned to a subsistence-based lifestyle. Virtually no wages have been paid since 1993, yet prices of essential goods have risen several hundred percent. Consequently, the great majority of Nelemnoye's population are now totally dependent on hunting and fishing for their survival, and apart from bread, tea, and tobacco, no imported food products are consumed on a daily basis. This movement back to a subsistence existence is also reflected in the steady increase in the number of registered "full-time" or "professional" hunters (Rus. *kadrovye okhotniki*) through the 1990s. In 1991 there were twenty-two professional hunters in Nelemnoye (about 44 percent of the able-bodied male population), whereas there are now thirty-nine (about 78 percent). What is more, in comparison with the Soviet period, little time is spent hunting for sable today. Instead people focus mainly on subsistence. Old people, women, and children set nets for fish (white fish, trout, pike, and turbot), gather berries (cloudberries, great bilberries, and red bilberries), and set hoop snares for white grouse and hares near the village, while the men travel deep into the forest to hunt for big game, especially elk.

The Yukaghirs' history and present situation raise at least two interesting questions. First, to what extent are these people—who have undergone centuries of demographic decline, virtually lost their indigenous language, and lived through all the vicissitudes of Sovietization—still the bearers of old beliefs about spirits, souls, and animal persons? Moreover, what happens to these beliefs in times of total economic collapse, when subsistence and survival have again become critical issues? In

Figure 1. Hunters with dead elk. Photo by Rane Willerslev.

chapters 6 and 7, which deal with Yukaghir shamanism and spiritual knowledge, I shall suggest some answers to these questions, but a few remarks are needed at this point.

Although I call the Yukaghirs "animists," this does not imply that they dogmatically attribute personhood to everything in the world around them. One of the reasons that recent anthropologists have called for the term *animism* to be abandoned is its liberal use in the past to brand as primitive superstition systems of beliefs that supposedly attribute personhood freely to things that to any rational, thinking person are obviously mere objects of nature (Ingold 2000: 106). Animism among the Yukaghirs, however, is not an explicitly articulated doctrinal system for perceiving the world, nor does it hold that all natural objects and phenomena are endowed with personhood all the time. In fact, quite the opposite is true. The personhood of animals and things is, as we shall see, something that emerges in particular contexts of close practical involvement, such as during hunting. Outside these particular contexts, Yukaghirs do not necessarily see things as persons any more than we do, but instead live in a world of ordinary objects in which the distinction between human subjects and nonhuman objects is much more readily drawn.

Yet if Yukaghir animism does not resemble anything like a formally abstracted and articulated philosophy about the world, but is instead essentially pragmatic and down-to-earth, restricted to particular contexts of activity and experiences, then what is it? My overall argument is that it is a practice—or at least it contains within it the traces of a practice. This practice, I suggest, is mimesis.

MIMESIS

Mimesis is usually regarded as a literary theory, a theory of interpretation. Only recently has this theory been extended to the realm of anthropology (Jackson 1983: 330–39; Taussig 1993; Koester 2002; Cox 2003; Roepstorff and Bubandt 2003: 9–30; Harrison 2005; Willerslev 2004a, 2006; Santos-Granero forthcoming). However, as Cox points out, "The concept of mimesis has undergone so many changes in the history of its usage, from Plato and Aristotle to Auerbach and Adorno, that one cannot properly talk of it as a coherent theory" (2003: 106). I shall discuss mimesis in its more limited sense as the meeting place of two modes of being-in-the-world—"engagement" and "reflexivity"—while also including other members of the mimetic family such as "sameness" and "difference," "self" and "other," "me" and "not me." In so doing, I shall draw upon Taussig's (1993) anthropological reinterpretation of mimesis, whose primary inspiration comes from the German cultural critic Benjamin. Benjamin sees in mimesis not a theory but a "faculty," which, like the body, is an inherent part of the human condition. In modern times this faculty has resulted in a world filled to overflowing with images and simulacra, so that nothing seems real any more, but its origin, Benjamin argues, can be traced back to a primitive compulsion to imitate, thereby fostering similarity with the world and with others: "Nature creates similarities. One need only think of mimicry. The highest capacity for producing similarities, however, is man's. His gift of seeing similarities is nothing other than a rudiment of the powerful compulsion in former times to become and behave like something else. Perhaps there is none of his higher functions in which his mimetic faculty does not play a decisive role" (Benjamin cited in Taussig 1993: 19).

Taussig, in his Benjaminesque analysis, takes up this notion of a mimetic faculty, which he defines as "the nature that culture uses to create *second nature,* the faculty to copy, imitate, make models, explore difference, yield into and become Other" (1993: xiii; my emphasis). What are we to understand by "second nature"? Taussig does not tell us, but I shall try to make a suggestion on his behalf toward the end of this chapter. However, let me begin with Taussig's own account. He proposes a two-layered notion of mimesis that involves both "copying" and "sensuous contact." Mimesis is a form of representation, an expression that involves copying. However, there is also a decisively corporal, physical, and tangible aspect to mimesis, which is its second layer, that of sensuous contact (1993: 21). This notion of mimesis is drawn from Frazer's two classes of "sympathetic magic," discussed in *The Golden Bough* (1993 [1922]): "magic of contact" and "magic of similarity or imitation." Taussig argues that Frazer's idea of the copy in magical practices is compelling in its power to affect "the original to such a degree that the representation shares in or acquires the properties of the represented" (1993: 47). He illustrates this with a number of different examples, mostly from the colonial milieu, in which colonial subjects mimic their European "masters" as a means of manipulating and controlling them.

Taussig's description of "colonial mimicry" finds certain parallels in recent anthropological writings on the relationship of Siberian indigenous peoples with the former Soviet state. Ssorin-Chaikov (2003), for example, describes how the Evenki of the 1930s reclothed themselves in the state's image (copy) by putting on Soviet-style clothing, wore medals (contact), and even let themselves be persecuted for engaging in shamanism in humiliating trials of self-confession, all in an attempt to "embody certain state politics, if not the state itself" (Ssorin-Chaikov 2003: 115). Likewise, Grant (1995) describes how the Nivkhi willingly traded their traditional culture for pan-Soviet symbols and ideals, and Bloch (2004: 108) reveals how many Evenki women allied themselves with the Soviet state's attempt at modernizing them "and in this process gained a sense of belonging to it." These are all examples of how Siberian indigenous peoples, through acts of mimicry, have attempted to incorporate the Soviet state's version of modernity into their own selves in order to assume its character and power.

During my fieldwork, however, I saw nothing of this sort of colonial mimicry. In fact, I was struck by the almost complete absence of the former Soviet state. I saw no statues of Lenin—or any other statesmen, for that matter—no helicopters, no money, and almost no imported food products. Virtually all the well-known symbols of the state's presence and power had vanished, and it was quite hard to imagine these people ever having been an integral part of the Soviet empire. What is more, because of the general economic crisis, many had returned to a subsistence lifestyle, and questions about state politics and ideology were generally of little or no interest to them. All the same, the ability to see similarities and invent correspondences with the surrounding world is, as we shall see, an enduring trait among Yukaghirs. In fact, their entire cosmos is in effect a hall of mirrors, as various dimensions of reality are conceived as replicas or reflections of others. Thus, the world of the dead is, as we shall see, conceived as a shadowy mirror image of the world of the living, populated with the souls of people, animals, and objects found in this world. Similarly, humans and animals are locked in a pattern of mutual replication. Animals and their associated spiritual beings are thus said to take on human shapes and live lives analogous to those of humans when in their own lands and households. Likewise, when the hunter seeks to bring an elk out into the open by mimicking its bodily movements, he is inevitably put into a paradoxical situation of mutual mimicry. As a result, the bodies of the two blend to a point that makes them of the same kind. In sum, the world of the Yukaghirs is by and large a "mimeticized" world: everything is paired with an almost endless number of mimetic doubles of itself, which extend in all directions and continually mirror and echo one another.

However, as with Taussig's colonial subjects, there is more to this than mere copying. Yukaghirs imitate significant and powerful others not simply to represent them, but also to exercise power over them. The question, then, is in what way does the copy have to resemble the original in order for the copy to take power over what it is a copy of? Taussig himself observes that a copy is rarely perfect: "It is logical to expect that the form such an imaginary gratification would take is one of 'the greatest possible resemblance to the original' so as to increase, in the case of magic, the efficacy of the charm. . . . But no! This is not the case. Instead, 'primitive man who avails himself of dolls and drawings in order to bewitch is generally quite indifferent to the lifelike character of his magical instruments'" (1993: 51).

Remember Old Spiridon mimicking the elk? He was a strange "elk" indeed, with a human face, two legs, and a gun. His imitation is in no way a perfect doubling, and the differences between the two are quite striking—in some ways more striking than their likenesses. Why is the hunter ambiguous, at once similar to and manifestly different from the animal he is imitating? I shall argue that it is because what we are dealing with in the seemingly identical mirror world of Yukaghirs are not "full identifications" but "partial ones" (Pedersen 2001). It is by means of their *difference* from the world impersonated that they can hold power over it. Without difference, the imitator and imitated would collapse into each other, would become one, making any exercise of power impossible. Thus, although the basic movement of mimesis is, as

Benjamin describes it, toward similarity (what Taussig calls sensuous contact), it always depends on the opposite—that is, difference. As we shall see in chapter 5, when I return to hunters' mimetic encounters with animal prey, it is the "copiedness" of mimesis, its lack of realism, so to speak, that secures this strikingly necessary difference because it forces the imitator to turn back on himself. It reverses his dominant and "natural" directedness toward the object of imitation back toward his own awareness as imitating subject, thus preventing him from achieving unity with the object imitated. Such turning back upon oneself is what we understand by reflexivity. In this sense we can talk about a kind of "depth reflexivity" built into mimesis, a certain withholding or nongiving of the self. If, in fact, mimesis becomes totalizing, and the imitator loses himself in what he imitates, we are no longer talking about mimesis but metamorphosis: nothing is left to imitate when the difference between the copy and the original is totally gone. Mimesis, therefore, is situated and defined through difference as much as through similarity. As imitator, one must move in between identities, in that double negative field, which I, using Schechner's words (1985), will call "not me, *not* not-me."

The world of the Yukaghirs is, as we shall see, just like this. People here are betwixt and between: their souls are both substance and nonsubstance; they are both their bodies and their souls, their selves and reincarnated others; hunters are both humans and the animals they hunt, both predators and prey, and so on. This condition of fundamental liminality or in-betweenness seems to have no ending. People must constantly steer a difficult course between analogy and identity and tread a fine line between transcending difference and maintaining identity: they can and do transform themselves into various others, both human and nonhuman, but must avoid total participation and confusion.

Now, this idea that something can be both X and not X at the same time plays serious havoc with established Western dualisms and dichotomies. The notion that a human being can be both himself and a deceased relative, let alone that he can transform himself into various animals, is simply inconceivable within canonical Western thought. The reaction of anthropologists, as we shall see, has been to neutralize the challenge that this set of ideas presents to our own mode of thinking by imposing a comparative framework, which a priori presupposes the primacy of the Western dichotomies and the falsity of indigenous attempt to reject them. In other words, the comparison between their understandings and ours has been on our terms, creating conditions under which animism can be nothing but a false epistemology (Bird-David 1999). In what follows, I shall illustrate this by singling out for inspection a sample of anthropological accounts in the study of animism. In doing this, I do not attempt to chronologically outline the entire history of the animism debate within anthropology, which is huge and obviously cannot be dealt with here. Rather, my aim is to reevaluate what I take to be certain Cartesian presumptions commonly underlying the anthropological models of explanation. The most basic of these assumptions is that an impermeable barrier exists between the human mind or consciousness on the one hand, and things and objects in the world on the other, such that the perceiver can make the world available to himself only by means of mentally representing it in his mind through some kind of cognitive processing. However, not only shall I argue that the terms of such a mind-world dichotomy make it impossible to take the animism phenomenon seriously, but I also intend to show that it provides an almost entirely distorted account of the nature of human perception. As an alternative, I shall suggest a radically different approach, one that holds that perception is firmly situated within the practical contexts of people's ongoing engagement with the world. This, as we shall see, allows us to work from a Yukaghir understanding of personhood, which rather than being something that is "added on" to animals and things by the human mind is instead immanent in particular relational contexts of involved activity. However, let me begin my discussion by attending to Descartes himself, who in a fundamental way has shaped the already established anthropological theories on animism, but who also in a strange way plays a key role in my own line of argument.

THE CARTESIAN LEGACY

A prominent feature of the Western intellectual tradition has been the need to keep humans and nonhumans apart by constructing a diverse yet interrelated set of dichotomies, each along a different axis of a dualistic opposition. The dichotomy between humanity and animality has thus been arranged next to those between subject and object, person and thing, mind and body, intentionality and instinct, and, above all, culture and nature (Ingold 2000: 41). These hierarchically ordered dualisms largely arose from Cartesian metaphysics some three centuries ago and have had a potent and lasting impact on how we think about ourselves in relation to nonhuman animals.

Descartes sought to arrive at a basis for certainty of knowledge by doubting everything that could possibly be doubted, including his own body and the very existence of the world. He concluded, as we know, that he was a mind, a thinking thing *(res cogitas)*, because his ability to think was the only thing that he could not doubt and because doubting is a form of thinking (Descartes 1996: 19). He then moved from the proposition that he could doubt the existence of his body and the external world to the conclusion that he could exist without them: "I was a substance whose whole essence or nature is solely to think, and which does not require any place, or depend on any material thing, in order to exist. . . . the soul by which I am what I am—is entirely distinct from the body" (Descartes 1988: 36). The overriding implication of this was a radical dualism, separating mind from body and self from world. The body, Descartes argued, was merely a vessel—a machine, he called it—in which the self, made up only of mind, was situated, and this disembodied self was totally self-sufficient, with no need for the mediation of the real world of things and people for its existence.

So what did this do for the way we think about nonhuman animals? In his writings, Descartes is blunt:

> Primitive man probably did not distinguish between, on the one hand, the principle by which we are nourished and grow and accomplish without any thought all the other operations which we have in common with the brutes, and, on the other hand, the principle in virtue of which we think. He therefore used the single term "soul" to apply to both. . . . I, by contrast, realizing that the principle by which we are nourished is wholly different—different in kind—from that in virtue of which we think, have said that the term "soul," when it is used to refer to both the principles, is ambiguous. . . .
> I consider the mind not as part of the soul but as the thinking soul in its entirety. (1984: 246)

Thus, although humans and animals are physically the same, that is, machines, they are mentally wholly different. Animals lack the thing that makes humans distinct from mere machines: they lack mind, and because mind and soul are absolutely inseparable, animals do not possess souls either. Animals, he claims, are merely self-moving machines, which, like a clock or an artificial fountain or mill, have the power to operate purely in accordance with their own internal principles, depending solely on the dispositions of the relevant organs (Descartes 1984: 161).

This separation of mind and matter, which is so central to Cartesian philosophy, and the denial of a rational mind to animals fed into the world of science at large. Although a few bio-behavioral scientists, as I shall describe in chapter 5, kept challenging this purely mechanistic conception of animal behavior, the vast majority accepted Descartes' doctrine of the "beast-machine" as a "fact of nature" (see, for example, Skinner 1938; Kennedy 1992). It comes as no surprise, therefore, that anthropology as an intellectual product of the Cartesian tradition has tended to see indigenous claims about the existence of nonhuman persons as a particular cultural construct, intensely intriguing and interesting perhaps, but without any foundation in reality.

THE ANTHROPOLOGICAL TRADITION

At first, this view was proposed under the banner of social evolutionism. Victorian scholars such as Tylor and his protégé Frazer read cognitive underdevelopment into the animism concept, arguing that because of their inadequately developed scientific reasoning, "primitive" peoples attempted to explain the world to themselves by "ascribing personality and life not to men and beasts only, but to things" (Tylor 1929a: 477). The expression "ascribing" at a stroke downgraded indigenous ideas about nonhuman persons to the category of "mistake," and this was indeed the crux of their argument. Animism was understood as a "magical" philosophy about the workings of the world, akin to a scientific theory but grounded in error.[5] It was based on the "association of ideas," a faculty that Tylor saw as lying "at the very foundation of human reason" (1929a: 116). But, said Tylor, instead of moving from fact to thought, from things to image (as in the Western sciences), the "primitive" reversed the flow, "thus mistaking an ideal connection for a real connection" (1929a: 116). In other words, analogy—such as when the Yukaghir hunter imitates his prey as a means to kill it—was mistakenly taken as a causal connection. However, as we shall see in the discussion of Yukaghir imitation of prey in chapter 5, there is in fact considerable causal power in just such analogical production of resemblances. For Tylor, however, this analogical thinking was taken as a sign that the "primitive" was incapable of making a rigid distinction between imagination and reality, and between subjective and objective realms of being (1929a: 445). He went on to speculate how the "primitive" had come to these erroneous ideas. He suggested that dreams of dead relatives and friends had led the "primitive" to believe in the existence of "ghost-souls," a conviction that was extended to explain causality throughout all of nature as well, so that the entire universe became endowed with animated souls (1929b: 356). Now, it turns out that Tylor might have been right in treating dream experience as the ultimate source of spiritual beliefs. In fact, I shall propose an argument not unlike Tylor's in chapter 8. However, the problem with his and Frazer's speculations was that they were just that, based neither on fieldwork nor on other kinds of empirical research, but merely on secondary accounts provided by missionaries, administrators, travelers, and other people from the colonial establishment. Whether or not their speculations were at all what the natives themselves had in mind or could acknowledge as the real forces behind their animistic convictions was not considered an issue. On the contrary, it was argued that the indigenous peoples did not understand the real grounds of their own convictions and that the job of the anthropologist was to explain (or correct) the natives' faulty explanations and replace them with his own. As Frazer put it to an audience of anthropologists some 150 years ago, "It is to be observed that the explanations, which I give of many of the following customs are not the explanations offered by the people who practice these customs. Sometimes people give no explanation of their customs, sometimes (much oftener than not) a wrong one" (Frazer quoted in Stocking 1996: 131).

The naturalistic and mentalist stance of evolutionist theory has seen a recent revival in the work of Guthrie (1993, 1997). Attempting a solution to the question of why living creatures, ranging from frogs to human beings, animate the world around them and do it so pervasively, Guthrie has employed a "cognitive and game-theoretical model," suggesting that animistic thinking is "pre-programmed" into our hereditary makeup through natural selection because it has proved to be useful for survival in an uncertain world: "In the face of chronic uncertainty about the nature of the world, guessing that some thing or event is humanlike or has a human cause constitutes a good bet. It is a bet because, in a complex and ambiguous world, our knowledge always is uncertain. It is a good bet because if we are right, we gain much by correct identification, while if we are wrong, we usually lose little" (Guthrie 1997: 55–56).

However, if, as Guthrie argues, it holds true that uncertainty is what drives animistic thinking, why is it that the more regularly and closely we engage with nonhuman entities and the less doubtful we become about them, the more we are inclined to see in them anthropomorphic qualities? This, as we shall see, is true of the Yukaghir hunter's conception of his prey, which becomes gradually more personlike the closer and more intimately he engages with it. But it is equally true of our own cars, computers, and other mechanical devices, which we, through regular and consistent involvement, come to experience as intentional persons with minds of their own (Gell 1998: 18–19).[6] In addition, one could ask how

Guthrie would explain the fact that animistic ideas and practices not only survive but continue to flourish among indigenous peoples like the Yukaghirs (a problem that he shares with Tylor and Frazer). If the Yukaghirs retrospectively recognize their animistic interpretations as mistakes, why should they let these mistakes remain as a centerpiece of their cosmology? Indeed, the consequence of Guthrie's argument, as one of his critics has pointed out, is that "it further downgrades indigenous cognitive ability, for now they cannot do even what frogs can do, namely, 'after the fact' recognise their 'mistakes'" (Bird-David 1999: 71). However, as will become apparent below, the mistake might well be Guthrie's assumption that the world is divided a priori between the non-human and the human, and his assumption that the world has to be "grasped" conceptually within the terms of an imposed mental design as a precondition for meaningful action.[7]

For now, however, I shall turn to another grand tradition in the study of animism, that of symbolic anthropology. The term *symbolic anthropology* of course fails to differentiate between the diverse writings of this field, but I use it very schematically to refer to the congeries of theories that identify animistic thinking as inherently metaphoric or symbolic, being generated by human society. Although this tradition at first appears to be rather more respectful of indigenous understandings, as we shall see, it points to roughly the same conclusion: that animism is essentially an erroneous mental operation. Consider, for instance, the following statement by Århem with regard to the Makuna of the Colombian Amazon: "Animal communities are organised along the same lines as human societies, and human interaction with animals is *modelled* on the interaction among different groups of people in the human life world" (1996: 190; my emphasis).

Thus, the Makuna are said to call upon their experiences of relations in the human social domain in order to model their relations with animals, because the latter, it is assumed, cannot really possess powers of intentionality, awareness, and sociality. "Socio-centric" models, like that of Århem, which see animist ideas as symbolic reflections or representations of human social relations, have provided the theoretical framework of much modern hunter-gatherer research (see, for example, Leach 1965; Tanner 1979; Bird-David 1992, 1993) and can be traced back to the sociology of Durkheim (1976 [1912]). In his classic studies on totemism (a term that encompasses aspects of animism), Durkheim thus expressed his main argument in symbolist terms, namely that totemism was best understood as "metaphorical and symbolic," and that the concrete and living reality that it expressed was the social group.[8] In other words, totemism was not really what it purported to be about, that is, nonhuman persons and agencies and their relationships with humans. For Durkheim, totemic concepts and beliefs constituted a symbolic representation of the human social order, which they served to enforce. That the natives themselves did not realize this fact was, Durkheim claimed, due to their fundamentally irrational feelings about the force of the social: "It is natural that the impressions aroused by the clan in individual minds . . . should fix themselves on the idea of the totem rather than that of the clan: for the clan *is too complex a reality to be represented clearly in all its complex unity by such rudimentary intelligences*" (1976: 251–52; my emphasis).

At this point we see that Durkheim's argument runs parallel to that of Tylor. In both instances, the analyst finds it necessary to replace the indigenous peoples' own animistic explanations of relevant occurrences with his own, because the natives, it is assumed, do not speak the literal truth in their statements about nonhuman persons.

Although few anthropologists today would put it as crudely as Durkheim did, his main argument, that the human social domain is the fundamental reality from which all representations of the natural environment are derived, is still commonly held. Bird-David (1993) is a case in point. In a recent article she proposes the existence of four distinctive animistic constructs, each of which she claims is expressed by a "core metaphor." While the Nayaka, Mbuti, and Batek draw extensively on an "adult-child" metaphor in representing their relationship with the environment, the Canadian Cree draw on a "sexual" metaphor, Western Australian Aborigines on a "procreational" metaphor, and the San Bushmen on a "namesake" metaphor (1993: 112). However, as Ingold (2000: 43–46) has shown, the notion of "metaphor" or "social modeling of nature" escapes evolutionist reductionism only to fall into a nature-culture dualism. This is because the notion of metaphor supposes a prior distinction between a domain in which social relations are constitutive and literal (the social world of humans) and another in which they are representational and metaphorical (the natural world of animals). Consequently, Bird-David ends up with the very same dichotomy—between human society and nature—as Durkheim does. Thus, with regard to, for example, the Nayaka, Mbuti, and Batek, she argues that their "adult-child" metaphors, drawn from the human social domain, provide them with a cultural framework that enables them to make sense of their environment, even though "they may not be normally aware of [the metaphors]" (1990: 190). In other words, when the Nayaka, Mbuti, and Batek say that the forest is a parent who shares with them, Bird-David claims that they are indulging in metaphor, for nature cannot really share with people. Although they themselves assert the contrary—that they share with humans and nonhumans on an equal footing—we are told that this is because the practice of sharing within their own human communities is so deeply embedded in their thought that they fail to distinguish metaphor from reality (Ingold 2000: 76). However, Bird-David insists that *she* can, and she implies on this ground that the hunter-gatherers have gotten it wrong.

It seems we are pretty much back to Descartes, who by means of his method of radical doubt drew the initial lines between true and false knowledge on the one hand and humans and animals on the other. Three hundred years later, the same dichotomies lie at the heart of the anthropological thesis on animism. Now, it appears that the indigenous peoples themselves do not endorse these dualisms. As Bird-David herself notes, hunter-gatherers "do not inscribe into the nature of things a division between the natural agencies and themselves as we do with our 'nature: culture' dichotomy. They view their world as an integrated entity" (1992: 29–30). A nondualistic perspective is also evident among the Yukaghirs, who, as we shall see, do not even have a word corresponding to our term "nature."

THE PHENOMENOLOGICAL ALTERNATIVE

So, whom should we believe? The various theorizing anthropologists, who argue that animism is best understood as either "erroneous thinking" or as "symbolic constructions of nature," and that its real significance operates behind the backs of its indigenous practitioners? Or the Yukaghirs, who, along with other hunter-gatherers, hold that animals and other nonhumans possess qualities paralleling those of human selves or persons, qualities that come into view in the context of close mutual engagement? The anthropological accounts take the Cartesian division between humanity and animality as axiomatic—"Personhood as a state of being is not open to non-human animal kinds" (Ingold 2000: 48)— but must necessarily be "added on" or "superimposed" upon them through an alternative construction—what Tylor, Durkheim, and Bird-David would call "culture" and Guthrie describes as naturally encoded structures of the mind. For the Yukaghirs, however, animals and other nonhumans are conceived as persons, not because personhood has been bestowed upon them by some kind of cognitive processing, but because they reveal themselves as such within relational contexts of real-life activities, such as during hunting.

The question is not so much *whom* we are to believe (as if the Yukaghirs had chosen to participate in this debate about the true nature of their animistic convictions), but *what* we are to believe.[9] Are we to believe that people come to know what is "out there" in the world by mentally representing it in their minds, prior to any attempt at engagement with it? This is what the anthropological accounts presume—for people, it is supposed, can neither know nor act upon the world directly, but only indirectly through imposing some kind of "mental design" upon it, whether this design is provided by culture (Tylor, Durkheim, and Bird-David) or is naturally built into the human brain (Guthrie). As we have seen, this assumption has its roots in the Cartesian mind-world dichotomy, which lies deep in Western thinking. Or, as an alternative, could it be that meaning is inherent in the relational contexts of peoples' direct perceptual engagement with the world, so that mental representations or cognition instead of being primary is derived from a practical background of involved activity? This is what the Yukaghirs seem to hold when they argue that animals are persons because they are experienced as such during subsistence-related activities.

I take the second view to be both more accurate as an ethnographic description and heuristically more valuable in understanding the nature of perception. In doing so, I join not only the Yukaghirs, but also certain recent figures in Western thought, all with a broadly phenomenological bent. These include, above all, Heidegger, but also various other scholars firmly based in the phenomenological tradition, such as Merleau-Ponty, Sartre, Schultz, Dillon, and Ingold.

Although all of these thinkers belong to different disciplines—philosophy, sociology, and anthropology—they share a common urge to overcome the Cartesian rift between mind and world as two totally independent realms of reality. Thus, all take as their starting point the view that notions of the world and of human reality are ontologically inseparable—an idea conveyed in Heidegger's well-known phrase "being-in-the-world" (1962: 107). The hyphenation of this expression signals that our everyday involvement with the various components that make up the world implies that we cannot regard them as a purely objective and value-free set of things, waiting, as it were, for our mental construction to render them meaningful. Rather, things with which we deal have meaning for us in the immediacy of our dealings with them. This, however, does not imply that such dichotomies as "sub-ject" versus "object," "self" versus "world," or "culture" versus "nature" are altogether false or useless, but rather that they are deriv-ative modes of being. Our practical involvement with things is prior to the cogitating ego, confronting an external world "out there," and that which is revealed through involved activity is ontologically more fun-damental than the context-free properties revealed by detached con-templation.

Now what does this do for the way we might think about person-hood? If the person or self is, before all else, a being-in-the-world, caught up in the everyday activities of living a life, it follows that *world* in this sense is not something that the self can get outside or stand beside as a self-contained Cartesian "mind." This is because, first, a self that is *in*-the-world is necessarily embodied. Only someone who is firmly based in some corporal physicality can have a place in it (Merleau-Ponty 1998 [1962]: 408). Second, no matter how much we may reflect and abstract, we are already in a direct and immediate relationship with the world. Thus, we cannot think of self and world in terms of external contact between two separate domains. Rather, self and world are always from the outset inextricably intertwined, and one cannot be without the other. As Heidegger puts it, "Self and world belong together in the single entity . . . self and world are not two entities, like subject and object . . . rather self and world are . . . in the unity of the structure of being-in-the-world" (1982 [1927]: 297).

The critical consequence of all of this is that personhood, rather than being an inherent property of people and things, is constituted in and through the relationships into which they enter. Personhood is, so to speak, a potentiality of their being-in-the-world, which might or might not be realized as a result of their position within a relational field of activity. An animal therefore can be just that, or it can be a subject-per-son with a mind of its own. The relational context in which it is placed and experienced determines its being. This considerably reduces the havoc caused by indigenous peoples like the Yukaghirs attributing per-sonhood freely to nonhuman animals, for not only does it reveal that ani-mals and things are not self-sufficient persons, and gain personhood only in and through textures of close practical involvement with others (most notably humans), but it also explains what anthropologists since Tylor could not help noticing, namely that indigenous peoples do not endow all things with personhood all the time, but only ascribe personhood to cer-tain things and only every so often.

THE PROBLEM OF ENGAGEMENT VERSUS REFLEXIVITY

Have we then, with Heidegger's theory of being-in-the-world, finally found a suitable framework for analyzing the animism problem in a way that takes its indigenous practitioners seriously? The theory certainly has several advantages. First, it reverses the ontological priorities of anthropological analysis by convincingly showing that everyday practical life is the crucial foundation upon which so-called "higher" activities of mental representation or cognition are firmly premised. Moreover, by taking seriously the actual experience of those indigenous practitioners, the theory allows anthropologists, for the first time, to analyze animistic beliefs in a way that is compatible with the indigenous peoples' own accounts, which tend to be based on hands-on experience with animals and things rather than on abstract philosophical contemplation. Ingold points to exactly this when he writes, "I shall argue that hunter-gatherers do *not*, as a rule, approach their environment as an external world of nature that has to be 'grasped' conceptually. . . . indeed the separation of mind and nature has no place in their thought and practice. . . . I wish to suggest that we . . . follow the lead of hunter-gatherers in taking the human condition to be that of being immersed from the start . . . in an active, practical and perceptual engagement with the constituents of the dwelled-in world" (Ingold 2000: 42; emphasis in the original).

Ingold's careful and nuanced view of perception, expressed in his use of the Heideggerian term "dwelling," is foundational to all that follows in the argument of this book about indigenous animism. Indeed, no other scholar has exerted a greater influence on my thinking. It is not only the profundity with which he engages with the hunter-gatherer literature from which I draw inspiration, but also, and even more so, the clarity of his theoretical challenge to anthropology's Cartesian tradition. However, although I adhere to Ingold's attempt at turning hunter-gatherer studies away from abstract Cartesian dualisms and back to the concrete and solid ground of practical and perceptual engagement with the world, I believe that his approach runs headlong into a dualism of its own, which seriously distorts our understanding of the "human condition" of perception in general and the animism problem in particular. What I am pointing to here is the stark dichotomy that the Heideggerian model draws between "practical" and "reflexive" states of being. For Heidegger, these two modes are seen as mutually exclusive: either you are absorbed in the world of involved activity or you step back and become an "onlooker," conceptually reflecting upon the world and your relations with it. You cannot, Heidegger seems to hold, be "world-involved" and "self-involved" at once. Indeed, for him the reflexive mode is simply seen as a derivative state of being, which may or may not follow from our practical and prereflexive types of engagements with the world. Ingold conveys exactly this idea when he asserts, "Imagination [i.e., reflection] is not a necessary *prelude* to our contact with reality, but rather an *epilogue* and an optional one at that. We do not have to think the world in order to live in it, but we do have to live in it in order to think it" (1996: 118, emphasis in the original; see also Ingold 1992: 52–53).

I find such a contrast problematic, at least when it is made in such stark terms as defined by Ingold. I do agree that people often carry out tasks without interpreting or reflecting upon their meanings in the abstract, and that for the most part meaning already inheres in the relational properties of the subject's practical engagement with the world. This is, in fact, my point in chapter 7, where I argue that during everyday rituals such as "feeding the fire," Yukaghirs simply perceive spirits as tools, "ready-to-hand," which they employ in an immediate and matter-of-fact fashion. Still, I find it hard to accept that our practical involvement in the world, no matter how absorbed our coping with things and people around us might be, does not involve some self-referential mode of awareness. It holds true that consciousness by its very nature actively transcends itself, what in phenomenological theory goes by the name of "intentionality." Consciousness is always and necessarily directed outside oneself and has no inner content. We cannot therefore retreat into a self-enclosed subjectivity in which we doubt the existence of the external world, as did Descartes, since even our awareness of our own subjectivity is possible only if we are also aware of a world that transcends it. Subject and object of experience are inseparably bound together, and our being is and must therefore be a being-in-the-world.

Still, there is an element of truth to Descartes' claim that our experience of the world requires as a starting point our awareness of ourselves as subjects. As Dillon writes, "To perceive a thing is *not* to coincide with it, to be it. The presencing of a phenomenon requires *a distantiation,* a space between the *here* of perception and the *there* of the phenomenon; and there *has* to be an awareness, albeit tacit, of the *here* for the *there* to appear *as such*" (1988: 103; my emphasis).

In other words, we can only have an experience of the world if we ourselves are conscious subjects of experience that somehow distinguish between ourselves as subjects and a world that transcends our subjective experience of it. Merleau-Ponty also draws attention to precisely this point: "All thought of something is at the same time self-consciousness, in the absence of which it could have no object" (1998 [1962]: 371). Thus it cannot be, as Heidegger argues, that the being-in-the-world of our everyday practical involvement with things and people carries with it a sense of *being absorbed in the world*" (Heidegger 1962: 80; my emphasis), a situation in which "self and world merge . . . so that one cannot say where one ends and the other begins" (Ingold 2000: 169). If this were the case, then the experienced and the experiencer would conflate, would become one, thereby making any experience of the world impossible. Such a state of fusion or perfect continuity between self and world is, as I shall argue in chapter 3, something akin to stumbling into death or the total dissolution of the self. There must therefore be a reflexive awareness of the "I" as distinct from the world built into experience from the very start.

This insight is, I shall argue, of paramount importance when it comes to understanding animism, which, although it rejects the Cartesian principle of absolute differences between self and world, is anxious about drawing differences nevertheless. Let me begin my argument by quoting Pedersen, who defines animism in terms of "partial" rather than "absolute" identifications with the world: "Since animism conceptualises a continuity between human and non-humans . . . a logic of endless substitutions seems intrinsic to animist thought, the principle that every element . . . can be interchanged with another. There are no radical discontinuities here, only continuous substitutions of Same becoming Other, and vice versa. The fundamental animist principle I therefore propose is one of *analogous identification*. I use 'analogous identification' to stress that we are *not* faced with full identifications here, but only *partial* ones" (2001: 416; my emphasis).

In Cartesian dualistic thinking, identity and difference are, so to speak, correlates: a thing can be what it is only by dint of its total difference from other things. Indeed, this was the Cartesian view of the *cogito* as a special kind of "inner" object, clearly distinguishable from all "outer" objects in mere flux by being both unified and fully transparent to itself. However, the moment we accept that the self is caught up in a world that transcends it, our selfhood cannot take the kind of unified transparency that Descartes attributed to it. As a being-in-the-world, the self cannot be fully identical with itself because it is, as we have seen, not self-sufficient, but needs the "otherness" of the world as a condition of its possibility. Indeed, without the mediation of the world of others, there would be no conception of self as such. However, the self is not truly identical with the world either, because a germ of self-awareness—the self as a subject standing apart from the world—is built into experience from the very start. Thus, the world can never furnish the self with an integrated or coherent being in the way that Ingold seems to suggest when he writes, "self and world merge . . . so that one cannot say where one ends and the other begins" (2000: 169). Rather, the otherness of the world, its difference from the self, is part of the meaning it has on the most primordial and prereflexive levels of experience.

This condition of being like and not like, the same and different from oneself and from the world, is what Lacan (1989 [1966]) brings together in his account of the "imaginary," a mode of being in which no absolute distinction between subject and object is apparent; the self identifies with the world, feeling at once *within* and *apart* from it, so that the two glide ceaselessly in and out of each other in a sealed circuit. I shall return to discuss Lacan's theory in detail in chapter 3 as part of my account of Yukaghir soul conceptions. What I want to convey at this point is that animism can be seen as the example par excellence of seeing personhood in terms of this enigma of "dissimilar similarity." Thus, the Yukaghir world is, as we have already seen, very much like Pedersen's (2001: 416) description, "a logic of endless substitutions" in which "every element can be interchanged with another" and "no radical discontinuities are apparent"—all of which points to a state of fundamental similitude between self and world. Taking a closer look, however, "we are not faced with full identifications here, but only partial ones." Thus, rather than being at one with the world, the Yukaghir self is in a state betwixt and between: its soul is both substance and nonsubstance; it is its body and its soul, itself and a reincarnated other; it is both human and the animal hunted; it is both predator and prey, and so on. In this world, in which everyone is never solely themselves but always at the same time something else as well, and anyone can transform into virtually anything else, much everyday activity is not just routine and unreflexive practice. Rather, here everyday practical life demands a kind of "depth reflexivity" as a form of defense mechanism against the dissolution of the self, which faces a real risk that identification with the world of other bodies, things, and people will become so complete that all differences will appear to vanish and an irreversible metamorphosis will occur. Reflexivity and engagement, therefore, rather than being mutually exclusive, constitute each other, and neither is amenable to prioritization. What this means, then, is that if we are to take animism seriously, we need to single out that mode of being-in-the-world, which is capable of accommodating both "self-involvedness" and "world-involvedness" within a unitary and coherent view of human experience. This mode of being is mimesis. Mimesis, as we have seen, puts the imitator in contact with the world of other bodies, things, and people, and yet separates him from them by forcing him to reflexively turn in on himself. Indeed, this is why the Yukaghirs attach such tremendous importance to mimesis as a source of power, because as imitator, one can enter into relations with significant and powerful others and be transformed, but without necessarily losing oneself in the process.

SECOND NATURE

Perhaps we are now in a position to suggest what is meant by mimesis being "the nature that culture uses to create *second nature*" (Taussig 1993: xiii; my emphasis). "Second nature" is nature that is reflexively aware of itself as standing somewhat *apart from* nature. We are, however, not talking about a disembodied Cartesian *cogito* that turns in on itself in passive isolation from the world. Second nature reflects upon itself in activity, and it is through its mimetic encounter with other things and bodies that it acquires its self-awareness of standing apart from them. This, as we shall see in chapter 3, is backed up by much physiological research, which gives mimesis a central role in the constitution of the self. The very young child has no sense of differentiation from the world of others, but must learn this by mimetically incorporating an other into the self, which then comes to be experienced as both "me" and "not me." In this way the child assumes a duality or doubling of perspectives, which allows it to see itself as another would see it from an external vantage—that is, it comes to observe itself reflexively.

While nonhuman animals can imitate others (e.g., insects imitating leaves) and might even possess self-awareness to some degree (Noske 1997: 131), mimesis reaches its highest capacity, as Benjamin notes, in human beings. Yukaghir animism, as we shall see, exploits this capacity to its fullest. By means of mimicry, the Yukaghir hunter assumes the viewpoint, senses, and sensibilities of his prey while still remaining aware of himself as a human hunter with the intention of killing it. Likewise, the Yukaghir person is intertwined with the deceased relative of whom he is considered a reincarnation, sharing the same name, personality, and knowledge. Yet, he also retains a personhood of his own and is capable of individual agency and intention. These are all events that could not be achieved without the intervention of the mimetic faculty and its power to "dance between the very same and the very different . . . registering both sameness and difference, of being like and of being Other" (Taussig 1993: 129). If animism is defined by "analogous identification," not "full identifications" but "partial ones" (Pedersen 2001: 416), then mimesis is what calls animism into action. Mimesis is the practical side of the symbolic world of animism—its necessary mode of being-in-the-world.

BOOK OUTLINE

With these considerations in mind, let me sketch out the structure of the book. The next chapter examines the ethnography of the hunters and their relationship to the animals they seek to kill, with a particular focus on their ideas about animal rebirth. I ask if there is any connection between hunters' belief in reincarnation and their apparently "aggressive" subsistence practices, in which more animals are killed than can be transported and eaten. Chapter 3 continues the discussion of reincarnation, but with a focus on its implications for relations within the human lifeworld. I show how reincarnation, which emphasizes the continuity rather than the finality of personal relationships, is important as a model for dealing with grief. However, I also reveal how a person's relation to the soul of his previous incarnation is problematic. The dead ancestor may work with or against the person, sometimes helping him but also occasionally sabotaging him by taking control of parts of his body and making them work against his intentions. I relate this notion of the fragmented body to Lacan's theory of the "mirror stage" and discuss the complex pattern of common features and differences between their and our understanding of the self and embodiment.

Chapter 4 returns us to the issue of human-animal relations. I describe Yukaghir ideas about species and personhood and reveal that they can be ascribed to what has been called a "perspectival ontology," in which all creatures—humans and nonhumans—see themselves as humans and everyone else as prey and predators (Viveiros de Castro 1998). In chapter 5 I suggest a possible grounding if not origin of perspectivism in the mimetic encounter between hunter and prey. Moreover, I suggest how we are to understand animal personhood, which opposes both anthropological and biological models. Chapter 6 discusses shamanism. I argue that shamanism among the Yukaghirs, rather than being seen as "mysticism" under the control of a particular religious elite, is to be understood as a much more broadly based activity practiced to varying degrees by ordinary hunters. Chapter 7 shifts the focus toward the spirit world. The

Yukaghirs rarely give names to spirits and have no neatly ordered system of classification. Drawing on Heidegger's philosophy, I develop an argument that relates this to the nature of Yukaghir practical experience, going beyond the widespread view of knowledge as a matter of linguistic representations or cognition. Chapter 8 looks at hunters' storytelling, learning, and dreaming. I argue against theories of the "mental map," which sees storytelling as a medium for transmitting knowledge. Instead I show how Yukaghirs learn through nonverbal means, and how hunters' narratives serve as a tool for "humanizing" them when they return from the forest. Moreover, drawing on recent findings in cognitive science, which show that concepts can and do exist independently of language, and that dreaming shares basic cognitive structures and processes with waking life, I suggest that it is possible that children, before they learn to talk, could develop prototypical concepts of spirits through dream experiences. In the concluding chapter, I revisit the animism debate and suggest how mimesis might help us in taking animism seriously.

CHAPTER 2

To Kill or Not to Kill

Rebirth, Sharing, and Risk

HUNTING AND ANIMAL REBIRTH

The subarctic environment of the Upper Kolyma Yukaghirs is part of the vast and largely unpopulated larch forest that is popularly known as the taiga. The climate is sharply continental, with permafrost and long, icy, cloudless winters, when the temperature can fall as low as minus 63° Celsius. Winter starts with the first snowfall in early October and persists into late May. In fact, there are only seventy to eighty frost-free days in the course of the whole year (Ivanov 1999: 153). Midwinter is dominated by darkness. The sun rises above the horizon for only an hour in late December, but twilight extends the day to six or seven hours. Despite the cold and darkness, people continue to hunt and ice fish throughout the winter. Spring brings very rapid changes in both the light cycle and temperatures, as the sun stays above the horizon eight or ten minutes longer each day. From mid-April until mid-August the sun never goes far enough below the horizon to cause real darkness, and the temperature in summer can reach as high as 43° Celsius.

Among all the animals of the taiga, the elk is by far the most important in the present-day economy and lifestyle of the population of Nelemnoye.[1] Its meat is distributed among village families as a key expression of community ties and is exchanged for fuel and other necessities in the district center of Zyrianka. Elk meat is also considered to be food par excellence, the focal dish of feasts and family meals. Because it

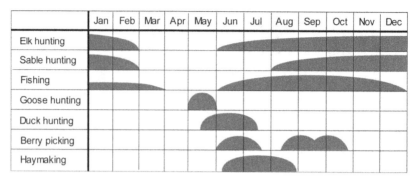

Figure 2. The annual subsistence cycle. In the state-farm era, some Yukaghirs were hired as wage laborers during the haymaking months to feed the cows in Verkhne Kolymsk village. However, this type of work ceased completely with the collapse of the state farms. Drawing by Jens Kirkeby, Moesgaard Museum.

comes from large, strong animals, it is thought to be a source of strength and is the preferred diet of hunters who themselves rely on physical strength. This general passion for elk meat, however, along with the growing importance of subsistence hunting, has put an enormous pressure on the elk population, which has undergone a catastrophic decline over the past decade. Old Spiridon's hunting group alone kills an average of forty to fifty elk a year. In comparison, the same group killed only five or six elk yearly during the state farm period. At that time, people had money to buy the imported meat of domestic animals, and elk meat was a delicacy for many families rather than a staple food. I would estimate that today elk meat accounts for 50 percent or more of the total intake of calories in Nelemnoye.

I once voiced the opinion to members of Old Spiridon's group that overhunting was surely the main reason for the decline of the elk population. The hunters, to my surprise, responded that they did not regard the elk population as having declined at all. The animals, they assured me, had simply "gone elsewhere." Later, a group of biologists from Zyrianka undertook a survey by helicopter of the number of elk in the district. They reported that the population had dropped by more than 30 percent since 1990, when there was an average of two thousand elk, and said that this was the result of a combination of overhunting and a growth in the wolf population. At a public meeting in Nelemnoye a government official *(okhotoved)* urged the hunters to reduce the scale of their killings in order to conserve the rapidly declining elk population. The hunters sat in silence and listened to the government official prove his point with one statistic after another. Afterward, however, I heard them talking among themselves, saying that the biologists had simply got it wrong: there were no fewer elk now than there had been in the past. The animals had simply gone elsewhere for the time being and would soon come back.[2] At first I regarded their explanation as an incredibly naive attempt to legitimize their large-scale killings. However, I later came to realize that their point is a different one—one rooted in a completely different perspective on the cycle of life and death. As explained to me by an elderly Yukaghir, Nikolai Likhachev:

> The world is like a cupboard with two shelves, which separate the Middle World from the Lower and Upper Worlds. In certain places there are cracks in the shelves, and these are the pathways between the worlds. Each shelf contains a large number of drawers of various sizes, which are the lands of different creatures. In the Middle World one such drawer is the land of the living human beings, others are the lands of the various animal species, and others again are the lands of the animals' master-spirits. . . . In the highest part of the Upper World lives Jesus with his father, God, who rules the sky. Below them live the People of the Light [Rus. Lyudi Sveta], who are creatures from outer space that fly around in UFOs [Rus. *letaushchaya tarelka*]. Little is known about them except that they are extremely bright, like Lenin, and that they sometimes capture humans in the Middle World in order to subject them to various experiments. This is why it occasionally happens that a hunter returns from the forest with no memory of where he has been and what he has been doing. . . . At the bottom of the cupboard, in the lowest part of the Lower World, is a small drawer, which is the dwelling place of the Grandfather with the Pointed Head [Yiodeiis'ien'ulben], who is the head of the evil spirits *[abasylar]*. Above him is another and much bigger drawer, which is the Land of Shadows [Ayibii-lebie]. This is the dwelling place for everything that has died. When one kills an elk or another animal, its *ayibii* [soul] will go to this place. The same with a cup that breaks or a house that burns down; their *ayibii* will go to the Land of Shadows, where they will regain their shapes[3] and stay until they are reborn in a new cup and a new house in the Middle World. Likewise, when a human person dies, his or her *ayibii* leaves the body in which it has resided, to take up its abode in the body of a raven or some other bird and travel to the Land of Shadows. . . . This land is similar to that of the living, but upside-down. People live in houses and tents with their families, eat, and hunt, as they would normally do, but many basic things, such as day and night, winter and summer, are reversed. Moreover, people who died young become old, and everyone eats decayed meat. . . . A person's *ayibii* will dwell in the Lower World until the moment a woman among its living family members becomes pregnant. Then it will strive to return to reincarnate itself. However, its journey back is difficult, full of obstacles and dangers. It does occasionally happen that an *ayibii* is eaten by *abasy* [the Sakha word for evil spirit], in which case the *ayibii* itself will become *abasy* and hunt for other *ayibii*. It can also be trapped in

the crack of a shelf.[4] But if the *ayibii* succeeds in reaching the world of the living, it will penetrate the pregnant woman through her vagina and possess the child. The two then become one and the same person, and the child will share with the deceased a common personality. . . . The child should be given the deceased person's name, or at least his or her nickname.[5]

Nikolai Likhachev's account was my first introduction to Yukaghir principles of rebirth. The first thing that struck me was the obvious difference between his account and the well-known rebirth concepts of South Asia. For the Yukaghirs, the goal of life is not liberation from the endless cycle of rebirth, as in the Buddhist and Hindu traditions, with their emphasis on *nirvána* or *moksha,* the Indic word for "salvation" (cf. Obeyesekere 1994: xii; Wicks 2002: 72–73). Rather, Yukaghirs expect people to undergo continuous rebirth, bringing back the same character traits they manifested in previous lives. Moreover, whereas Buddhists and Hindus see reincarnation as being dependent on the ethical nature of the life lived by the deceased, I did not come across any evidence among the Yukaghirs that wrong behavior (or sins, if you like) in this life would necessarily lead to retribution in the next. One can transform into other creatures or become stuck in certain places, and thereby be prevented from returning "home," but there is no such thing as a "good" or a "bad" rebirth. Furthermore, not only humans but also animals and inanimate objects are locked into their own cycles of continuous rebirth. Indeed, as Guemple (1994: 118) has described with regard to the Inuit, and as also seems to hold true for the Yukaghirs, "the system . . . is regarded as a 'closed' cycle: no new spiritual components can enter, and none are ever lost." We are, therefore, at least in principle, dealing with a fixed pool of souls that simply go round and round in an endless cycle.

This core idea that no life can ever be lost or entirely destroyed is by no means unique to the Yukaghirs, and is in fact reported throughout the circumpolar north.[6] Frazer, for example, wrote of the Bering Strait Eskimos that they "believe that the souls of dead sea-beasts . . . remain attached to their bladders, and that by returning the bladders to the sea they can cause the souls to be reincarnated in fresh bodies and so multiply the game which the hunters pursue and kill" (1993 [1922]: 610). Recently, this belief has also been described among the Cree of the Canadian subarctic: "The nominal death of an animal was only one moment in a cycle: animals live in the bush, are killed by hunters, persist as souls after their bodies are eaten, and return again to the world through birth or spontaneous regeneration" (Brightman 1993: 288).

What is more, throughout the circumpolar region we find numerous cases of "aggressive" subsistence practices, leading to the "pointless" destruction of entire herds of game. As Krupnik writes, "Massive slaughters took place when caribou were hunted at river crossings, and also when, in summer, netting was broadcast for flightless, moulting birds. At times the community might take so much more than it could use, preserve, or transport that much of the catch simply rotted and went to waste. There is evidence of massive overhunting of birds, and animals killed by the hundreds and thousands, from throughout northern Siberia, the Canadian boreal forest, coastal Greenland, and the Alaskan interior" (1993: 231).

Krupnik goes on to argue that it would be quite wrong to see native overkilling solely as a result of Russian or Anglo-American colonization, which introduced firearms and commercial hunting, since "we now know of numerous cases in which prehistoric arctic hunters as well as post-contact traditional bands with no ties to the commercial hunting economy engendered ecological crises on a local scale" (Krupnik 1993: 234). It would be equally wrong to reduce the massive slaughters to anomalies—deviations explained by confluence of extreme circumstances (Krupnik 1993: 235). Rather, overhunting should be understood, Krupnik argues, as an immanent element in the arctic peoples' subsistence system, "a reasonable risk management technique where highly unstable game resources . . . are concerned" (1993: 236). He contrasts this overkilling strategy with the more "conservationist" and, at the same time, more elaborate spiritual ecological belief system of the boreal forest hunters of the subarctic, where the scarcity of animal resources is more stable and therefore more predictable and manageable: "The idea of 'equilibrium' is fully applicable to the relationship that the boreal forest peoples maintained with their resources and environment via rational ecological knowledge and ostensibly magical practice and rituals found within their traditional animistic framework. . . . This worldview and its components have been thoroughly described among North American Indians, but can also be traced among most native peoples of the Siberian boreal forest zone" (Krupnik 1993: 239–40).

However, such stark polarization of northern hunters into "aggressive resource users" or "ecological saints" cannot easily be maintained. In his comprehensive study of hunting among Cree Indians, Brightman (1993: 254–91) totally subverts this image of the boreal forest peoples as being "intuitive" ecologists whose spirituality fosters sustained yield management, recounting numerous instances when Cree hunters in the 1700s killed caribou (wild reindeer) and other animals in such numbers that the game population plummeted, resulting in large-scale famines. Moreover, Brightman locates the reason for this merciless hunting practice in the Cree Indians' traditional subsistence ideology rather than in their encounter with new technology and commercial hunting: "the 'environmental ethic' and sustained yield management practice were not elements of Algonquian culture in the first place. . . . Rather than 'sacrificing their ideals,' Crees and other boreal forest Indians reproduced them with utmost fidelity in the fur trade. There existed no conception of 'waste' attached to the material bodies of animals, and neither was there a conception of regional populations manageable by selective hunting" (Brightman 1993: 283).

Among the Yukaghirs, we also find examples of the type of overkill hunting practices described by Krupnik and Brightman. One day in June during my fieldwork, I was paddling down the Omulevka River with Old Spiridon and his sons. At this time of year bloodthirsty mosquitoes rise in massive clouds along the grassy riverbanks, and the elk seek to avoid them by going out into the river, where the wind blows more freely and where they can immerse their bodies. However, without the forest to hide them, the animals are largely defenseless against hunters, and within just a few hours we had killed four elk, each weighing a thousand pounds or more. To my surprise, Spiridon instructed us to take only the best bits—the hearts, tongues, noses, kidneys, and some choice pieces of meat from the thighs—and we let the almost intact carcasses drift away down the river. As we continued our river journey we killed more elk in this way, and again we were told to take only the delicacies. When we eventually reached Nelemnoye we had slain a total of seven elk, but we had left huge portions of meat behind to rot.

The question that naturally arises is why Yukaghirs, like many other groups of northern hunters, kill prey in numbers greater than they can transport and eat. Moreover, since it is these hunting peoples themselves who become the chief victims of any game shortage that results from overhunting, one must wonder why they tend not to see a relationship between the two processes. If we hope to come to terms with these questions, we cannot simply approach the hunter-prey relationship in narrowly utilitarian and functional terms, as Krupnik does, but we must take the conceptual world of the hunters themselves into account. I shall begin this task by pointing out that from the Yukaghirs' perspective their killings are not merely destructive, but also a rite of regeneration. Hunters must slaughter and consume animals so that their souls, their *ayibii,* can be released and subsequently reincarnated. The hunters' predatory activity becomes, in this manner, a life-giving activity, for without the killings the animals would fail to reproduce. Moreover, as Brightman (1993: 283) describes with regard to the Cree, and as also applies to the Yukaghirs, hunters can kill prey in great numbers and make selective rather than exhaustive use of their bodies since such behavior is not contrary to the dictates of the animal master-spirits. In fact, the more one kills, the more the herds of the animal master-spirits will enlarge and the more one will be likely to kill in the future (Brightman 1993: 288). Clearly, this echoes the Yukaghir saying that "one is obliged to take what one is given by *khoziain* [the animal master-spirits]," and if a hunter is offered much, he must take much. Failure to kill all the animals available is to put one's future hunting luck at risk.

Now, while this fits neatly into Krupnik's image of northern hunters as merciless predators blindly destroying their own ecosystems, we find yet another strain in Yukaghir thinking that points in the opposite direction. As we shall see, hunters also entertain a fear of spiritual counterpredation for indiscreet slaughter. However, to understand the principal ideas on which this compelling sanction against overkilling is based and in what way it relates to its opposite—the propensity to kill as much as possible—we need to address what is commonly reported in ethnographic studies of hunter-gatherers under the rubric of "sharing."[7]

THE PRINCIPLES OF SHARING

One of the models commonly applied to distinguish "simple" from "complex" hunter-gatherer societies is Woodburn's (1980; 1982a; 1991) distinction between "immediate-return" and "delayed-return" systems. In societies with the former, "people obtain a direct and immediate return from their labour. They go out hunting or gathering and eat the food obtained the same day or casually over the days that follow" (Woodburn 1982a: 432). Moreover, people avoid long-term commitments and obligations, the accumulation of possessions, and any substantial investment of time in the productive process (Woodburn 1980: 98). High value is attached to individual autonomy, sharing, free access to resources, and egalitarian social relations (Woodburn 1982a: 448). In delayed-return systems, by contrast, individuals hold rights to valued assets such as labor-intensive hunting technologies, processed and stored food, and other people, as in marriage bestowal (Woodburn 1991: 32). In order to hold and manage these valued assets, people depend on "a set of ordered, differentiated, jurally-defined relationships" (Woodburn

1982a: 432–33). Woodburn classifies almost all hunter-gatherer societies as delayed-return systems, and only a few groups, such as the San Bushmen of Namibia, the Hadza of Tanzania, and the Batek of Malaysia, as immediate-return systems (1991: 32–35).

Although the Yukaghirs' social organization, both past and present, has many of the characteristics that Woodburn identifies as common in delayed-return systems (e.g., intergenerational authority, committed kin-ship ties, and institutionalized leadership), it seems clear from Jochelson's descriptions and my own observations that Yukaghir society demonstrates many of Woodburn's immediate-return characteristics, such as, for example, generalized access to knowledge and hunting grounds, and the freedom to select the group of hunters with whom one wants to live and work. Because Yukaghir men are not required to hunt with any particular group, hunting groups are extremely unstable; people are constantly moving in and out of them. What is more, although particular families identify themselves and are identified by others with the rivers where they dwelled prior to their forced settlement in the 1930s, they have no more right to hunt there than anyone else. Anyone may live, hunt, and fish wherever he likes without restriction. A group's association with a particular territory and river, then, seems to provide a means of identifying oneself and others, a way of mapping out social relations spatially, rather than identifying exclusive rights to resources. What is more, the Yukaghirs' modes of sharing the products of the land and other material goods are generally typical of immediate-return systems. Jochelson informs us that when a pre-Soviet Yukaghir hunter killed a reindeer or elk, that hunter would have no ownership over the meat. Instead, it would be handed over to the clan elder's wife, who would then be in charge of its distribution (1926: 123). The hunter's family, like other clan families, would receive their share according to the number of family members. The hunter himself would receive only the head of the animal, as well as the honor of being allowed to pitch his tent in the camp first and of his wife participating in the distribution of the meat.

Although the principles of distribution are no longer as rule-bound as they were when Jochelson carried out his fieldwork, the moral necessity of sharing is still strongly stressed. Thus, the people of Nelemnoye differentiate themselves from neighboring Russians and Sakha primarily by contrasting their own enthusiasm for sharing against the individualistic greed of these outsiders, who are said to be stingy and unwilling to share. Related to this notion that sharing is virtuous is the notion that the accumulation of wealth is deeply objectionable (Woodburn 1998: 54). Rich people are, by definition, "bad people" (Rus. *plokhie lyudi*). During Soviet times the wealthy were mainly Russian skilled laborers who were drawn to Nelemnoye by high salaries and other economic inducements. The great majority of these immigrants, however, left during the economic crisis that followed the collapse of the Soviet Union. The few that have stayed have largely adapted to the local cultural values of sharing. At present, there is only one man who has become remarkably wealthier than the others. He is a Sakha from Verkhne Kolymsk who was put in power as the leader of Nelemnoye's administration by the head of the regional administration in Zyrianka. Although he is married to a local Yukaghir woman, most people despise him because of his high salary, his car, his two snowmobiles, and his unwillingness to share his wealth with the wider community. Even his wife's relatives refer to him as the "greedy Yakut" or the "*kurkul*'," which is a Russian diminutive for "Ukrainian," implying stinginess.

The Yukaghirs' aversion to the accumulation of wealth and the inequality of its distribution is also apparent in what anthropological accounts of hunter-gatherers commonly label "leveling" or "humility-enforcing" mechanisms (Barnard and Woodburn 1991: 25; Myers 1991: 56; Guenther 1999: 43). If, for instance, a hunter returns to the village with a large number of sable pelts and starts boasting about his success, people will taunt him mercilessly: "These pelts you got there must be from cats or something. They can't be from sables. Not a single silvery hair, only filth." Such insulting remarks have just one goal: to "pull down" the arrogant hunter and make him feel ashamed. Consequently, hunters are usually careful to break the news of their success in a very low-key way. Ivan Danilov, a Sakha hunter with whom I trapped sable, put it this way: "When we come back to Nelemnoye and people ask you how many sables we've taken, look disappointed and say: 'We hardly got any.' When they ask again, reply, 'Definitely not more than five or six sables, all of a very poor quality.' Remember that the correct behavior of a great hunter is modesty and understatement."

People know, of course, that when a hunter is cautious about semantics in this fashion, it often implies the direct opposite; namely, that he has caught many sables of high quality. However, the point is that the hunter, by expressing indifference or negativity toward his own accomplishments, "demonstrates . . . that his success has not gone to his head, that he has 'leveled'—or 'humiliated'—himself, maintaining through his display of humility the ethos of equality" (Guenther 1999: 43).

The situation is somewhat different with regard to success in elk, bear,

and reindeer hunting. Hunters who are good at these tasks are often pub-
licly praised for their skills. For example, when Yura, the oldest son of
Old Spiridon, and I met old people in the street, they would sometimes
compliment us by chattering their teeth and saying, "Due to your good
[hunting] luck, our teeth are chewing [we are eating well]." This difference in attitude is perhaps explained by the fact that whereas meat is for
the most part distributed among the villagers, furs are not. After being
divided equally among the hunters in the group, the furs from sable and
other fur-bearing animals are considered the private property of the individual hunter. Therefore, whereas meat cannot easily become a source
for the accumulation of wealth, furs can be, at least in theory. Sable
hunting rather than meat hunting has thus become the focus of morally
valued leveling mechanisms, such as rough insults and ridicule, which
actively seek to restrict the development of status inequalities based on
differences in wealth.

However, even the most successful sable hunter has difficulty accumulating wealth, because although he can sell or barter his furs to pro-
cure various commodities, he is morally obliged to share them with his
kinsmen. A barrel of fuel or several boxes of ammunition are thus
unlikely to last more than a day or two. Ultimately, endless demands will
result in him having to hand over the extra possessions. A person could
in theory say "no" to his relatives, but then they would start complaining
and gossiping about him. If he wants to keep his possessions to himself,
his only option is to conceal them. I witnessed numerous occasions on
which people sought to hide their possessions from others. During hunting expeditions, for example, people would frequently ask others to
share their cigarettes while keeping hidden in their pockets their own
tobacco, which they would smoke while alone in the forest. Likewise,
people in the village often hide their fuel barrels in garages or cover them
with snow. If they are kept where people can see them one relative after
another will turn up to claim his share until the fuel is gone.

We often think of sharing as deriving from generosity. Spencer, for
instance, writes about the Alaskan Eskimos, "In times of food shortage,
it was the successful hunter and his family who might go hungry, since in
his generosity he gave away whatever he had at hand" (1959: 164).
However, sharing among the Yukaghirs is, as should be clear by now,
quite different. Although they *do* emphasize the moral imperative of generosity as the principle dynamic, most sharing in fact takes place in
response to direct demands. We are therefore dealing with what Peterson
(1993) has appropriately called "demand sharing." People believe that

they are entitled to their share and do not hold back when making demands. "The whole emphasis is on donor obligation and recipient entitlement, [and] the donor has little or no choice as to whether his goods are shared" (Woodburn 1998: 49).

Moreover, people are expected to give freely without expectation of repayment, which means that recipients are under no obligation to give back—though of course they, too, must share when they obtain goods beyond their immediate needs (Barnard and Woodburn 1991: 21). Only the general obligation to share is carried forward over time; specific claims with regard to the quality or quantity of the return are not. I therefore agree with Woodburn, among others, when he argues that to treat this type of sharing as a form of reciprocity seriously distorts our understanding of what is going on (1998: 50; Bird-David 1990: 195; Ingold 1986b: 209; Rival 2002: 104). Sharing among the Yukaghirs is clearly not "direct" or "balanced" reciprocity. In their view, people are obliged to give away their possessions, not as gifts for which eventual reciprocation is expected, but unconditionally. In this sense, their notion of sharing corresponds in part to what Sahlins has called "generalised reciprocity" (1972: 193–94). However, to call sharing "reciprocity" is misleading, because mutual indebtedness is just what one does not find among people like the Yukaghirs. Gell, it seems, makes exactly this point, when he writes, " 'Generalised' and 'balanced' are *not* two alternative forms of reciprocity; balanced reciprocity is reciprocity, because 'balance' . . . is built into the notion of reciprocity as such: 'generalized' reciprocity is the absence of reciprocity, i.e., *non*-reciprocity" (Gell 1992: 152; my emphasis).

While the ethos of unconditional sharing pervades the principle of exchange as a whole among the Yukaghirs, it is above all focused on meat: "I eat, you eat. I have nothing, you have nothing. We all share out of one pot," say the Yukaghirs.[8] There are several stages of meat sharing. First, the meat is shared in the forest among the hunters who are living and working together. Shares are put in piles according to the number of hunters in the group, and everybody gets an equal share, irrespective of age and skill. Hunters say that they own the slain animal collectively, because everybody has in one way or another applied his labor and skill to the hunt. Thus, what we are dealing with here is, in principle, what Bodenhorn has called "shares," which are earned "by contributing labour, material, or intellectual technology to the hunting effort" (2000: 134).

Back in the village, the meat is shared again. Hunters are not obliged to share with everybody, but only with kinsmen of one sort or another. The kinsmen will come to the household of the hunter, usually on the day of his arrival, and simply say, "Give!" in a matter-of-fact, "demanding" way. The hunter or his wife will then give them a share of meat, whereupon they will leave. "Please" and "thank you" are not normally part of the vocabulary of sharing. As Lee puts it with regard to the San, "Since sharing is given, why say thank you?" (1991: 264). No rule prescribes that any particular part of the animal must be given to any particular category of kin or affinity. People give different parts of the meat and different amounts, this time to some relatives, next time to others, more or less generously. It is considered improper for the receiver to complain about what he or she is given—at least at the moment of the transaction. Afterward, however, people will openly express satisfaction or dissatisfaction with their share. Disputes over meat are generally indirect, resulting in ill feeling and gossip rather than in direct confrontation (see Altman and Peterson 1991: 86).

When the meat has been cooked it is shared again among those present, usually the members of the household. Meat is rarely preserved or stored by the Yukaghirs, who prefer to live on fresh meat. Very few households in Nelemnoye own ice cellars for storage. Moreover, hunters claim that to store meat brings bad luck in hunting, because it discourages the generosity of the animal spirits, which is best secured by actually needing meat to eat. This notion is also apparent in Yukaghir hunting preparations. Hunters will deliberately bring provisions for only a few days when going to the forest, for as one hunter commented, "*khoziain* won't feed people who don't need to be fed, and people don't need to be fed if they have stored food readily available." Thus, the general assumption is that the consumption of preserved meat is undesirable. Ideally, people should hunt and eat until all the meat is consumed, and then go hunting again. In effect, this means that a hunter's meat is usually distributed and consumed within one or two days.

Although a hunter, as we have seen, has little or no choice as to whether his meat is shared, he does have some influence over who gets it. As I have already pointed out, sharing relationships in Nelemnoye normally follow kinship ties; that is, a person must share meat and other goods with his or her kinsmen but is not obliged to do so with nonkin. Among Yukaghirs, kinship is reckoned bilaterally. In effect, this means that everyone in Nelemnoye has kinship or quasi-kinship ties to everybody else. The Yukaghirs themselves are quite aware of this and often say, "In one way or another, we are all related." This, however, does not mean that all kinship ties are active. The number of potential kin is much larger than one could possibly maintain if one were to satisfy the obligation of sharing that kinship entails. This gives rise to what Bodenhorn (1997) has called "optative" and "non-optative" kinship spheres. Parents, siblings, and grandparents on both the mother's and father's side fall under the latter category. Their relatedness cannot be denied without incurring social disapproval, and thus they are always entitled to their share. The optative category describes virtually everybody else, that is, "kin who are kin because they, and you, act like kin" (Bodenhorn 1997: 115) and share with one another.

The fact that a person may choose to recognize, or not, the people that are his or her kin allows considerable room for tactical maneuvering. A genealogical relationship can be conveniently "forgotten" if a person regards that relationship as unsatisfactory. The reverse, however, is also true: one might choose to regard a distant relative as a member of the family if it is seen as advantageous. The following story about Nikolai Shalugin, a Yukaghir and the first head of Nelemnoye's *obshchina* (a cooperative unit in postsocialist Siberia), serves as an example of how kin ties can suddenly be "discovered" and put into effect.

When the *sovkhoz* (state farm) of Verkhne Kolymsk disbanded in 1991 and its technology and livestock assets were divided among the newly established *obshchina* organizations, Nikolai Shalugin was elected head of Nelemnoye's *obshchina*, Teki Odulok, and put in charge of an abundance of tractors, cars, snowmobiles, and horses. The *obshchina* organization was originally intended as a village-based cooperative of hunters and fishermen, which over time would develop into a local organ of indigenous self-rule.[9] The government in Yakutsk believed that if the Yukaghirs and the other indigenous peoples of the north were given more self-determination they would feel encouraged to work harder and develop their internal economies. In Nelemnoye, however, things took a different turn. Instead of regarding the possessions of the *obshchina* as collective property, people saw them as Shalugin's private possessions, and in accordance with Yukaghir practice, they turned up and demanded that he share his goods with them. What is more, it was not only his usual group of close relatives who put forward their claims. Practically everyone in Nelemnoye maintained that they were somehow related to him and claimed that he was therefore obliged to share with them. The poor man saw no option but to comply with the many demands. First, he slaughtered most of the livestock and distributed the meat among the families in Nelemnoye. In 1991, for example, the *obshchina* owned 154 horses; by 1994 this number had fallen to 56. Yet the people still kept putting forward claims, and so he sold off the cars, tractors, and snow-mobiles, and with the money he bought fuel and meat, which he then dis-tributed among the village population. When representatives of the Sakha government turned up in Nelemnoye in 1997 and saw that the vil-lage's *obshchina*, rather than being a profitable economic enterprise, was in a state of bankruptcy, completely divested of all its former technology and resources, they accused Shalugin of corruption. However, he was never arrested because the police could find no proof that he had been using the community's assets to accumulate personal wealth. In fact, Shalugin found himself obliged to give away most of his own private belongings, such as his guns, television, and snowmobile, in order to comply with the many "sharing" demands, and had thereby become one of the poorest people in the village. Although he was forced to step down as head of the *obshchina*, he never went to jail.

This story is interesting because it clearly illustrates many of the issues discussed earlier. First, it shows that kinship networks among the Yukaghirs, rather than being finite and fixed, are highly manipulable and constantly changing. Moreover, the story reveals how individuals who possess goods for which they appear to have no immediate need are under the greatest pressure to give them up, and they must do so without expecting anything in return. Lastly, the story illustrates the fact that, although Yukaghirs acknowledge leadership, the authority of their lead-ers rests not in acquiring and holding personal wealth, but in giving it away. A leader must give away everything to preserve his popularity, and is therefore among the poorest people in the community.[10]

THE RISK OF SHARING

When entering the forest Yukaghir hunters often address the master-spir-its of the rivers and places where they hunt as "fathers" and "mothers" or "grandfathers" and "grandmothers." Similarly, they refer to them-selves in this context as the "children" or "grandchildren" of the spirits. They will, for example, say, "Grandfather, your children are hungry and poor. Feed us as you have fed us before," or, perhaps, "*Khoziain*, you are our mother, we are your children, so feed us."

It has been suggested, in the context of other hunter-gatherer groups, that this combination of praising the benevolence and generosity of the spirits while also complaining about one's own hunger and needs repre-sents "complementary idioms in an economic discourse premised on giving" (Bird-David 1992: 31). I have no doubt that this applies to the Yukaghirs as well. In fact, they believe that the animal master-spirits, in their role as nurturer, are obliged to share their abundance of game with them, in much the same way as fellow humans who possess resources beyond their immediate needs are obliged to give them up. In other words, hunters think that they are entitled to prey and that the spirit should give it to them, not in return for appropriate repayment, but unconditionally. This notion, I believe, is reflected in the fact that although hunters often praise the benevolence and generosity of the spirits before hunting, I have never heard them thank the spirits after a successful hunt. From their viewpoint the spirit is doing no more than it should when it provides them with a kill. Moreover, whenever our hunting luck failed us, and when this could not be blamed on our disregard for some ritual procedure, Spiridon would walk restlessly around the encampment, swearing at his helping spirit, the Owner of the Omulevka River: "Stingy bitch! You make me ashamed. Don't come to me again [Stay out of my dreams]. I'll leave you to rot with your meat [I'll move away to another territory]." So, in much the same way that fellow humans who are not willing to share become the subjects of much grumbling and gossiping, Spiridon would openly accuse the master-spirit of being stingy whenever it rejected our request for meat.

Although it occasionally happens that the animal master-spirits withhold their herds of animals, hunters regard these occasions as exceptional, temporary, and accidental. Bad hunting luck is usually explained as being caused by the improper behavior of humans, such as when they fail to observe the ritual procedures that secure the proper circulation of game. The response of the animal master-spirits is to hold back or hide animal prey from hunters. Such mishaps, however, do not usually last for long. As soon as the hunters have admitted their guilt and start to follow the proper rules of conduct, the principle of generosity is reestablished and the spirits are said to return to their roles as generous and caring "parents."

The Yukaghirs' relations with spirits, activated during hunting, and their analogous relations with fellow humans, activated in the sharing of meat and other goods within the village, could be interpreted as an integrated system, an all-embracing cosmic economy of sharing. A similar argument is, in fact, proposed by Bird-David (1990, 1992) in her comparative study of how hunter-gatherers and cultivators relate to their natural environments. Drawing on ethnographies of the Nayaka of southern India, the Batek of Malaysia, and the Mbuti of Zaire, she argues that these groups of hunter-gatherers all regard their forest environment as a "parent" who gives them food in abundance without expecting anything in return—what she labels the "giving environment" (1992: 28). Among the neighboring populations of cultivators, by contrast, the environment is likened to an "ancestor" that yields its bounty only reciprocally, that is, in return for favors rendered. This difference in cosmologies is, she argues, founded in the manner in which the two groups distribute their resources within their own human communities. For cultivators, such distribution is framed within a structure of reciprocal obligation; for hunter-gatherers it rests on the principle of unconditional sharing (Bird-David 1990: 194–95).

There is certainly some truth in Bird-David's account of hunter-gatherers as conceiving the natural environment as a source of inherent goodness. As we have seen, the Yukaghirs also represent their relationship to the animal master-spirits as a parent-child relationship, anchored in unconditional giving. Even so, her idea about the "giving environment" ignores the fact that the compassionate ties that exist between the two agencies also give rise to much danger, deception, and manipulation. Yukaghirs recognize in the animal master-spirits not only generosity, but also many of the negative attributes they recognize in themselves, such as sexual yearning, jealousy, and slyness. Thus, even spiritual powers that they regard as "good" are good only in a very relative and dangerously unstable sense. Below, I shall describe how a spirit that develops uncontrolled feelings of love for a particular hunter will strive to kill him to bring his *ayibii* back to its household as its spouse. Likewise, I was told that the birth of a human child at times makes an animal master-spirit profoundly jealous. The spirit's envy stems from the fact that the hunter, whom it loves, fathered the child with another woman. The spirit will set out to kill the child and take its *ayibii* and put it into an animal body. The child will then leave the circle of human rebirth and instead be reincarnated as an animal—that is, as the spirit's own offspring. To illustrate this mode of thinking, let me quote a story that was told to me by an elderly Yukaghir woman, Akulina Shalugin:

> Grisia [her husband] and I went fishing together with our friend Igor Slepsov. Igor caught a strange fish. I've never seen anything like it. It was singing with different voices. Every time it turned around on the ground, it sang with a new voice. I got scared and told Igor to put it back into the river, so he did. That winter, he had great luck in hunting. I believe he took more than fifty sables and God knows how many elk. They just came to him time and time again. The next year was the same. The animals kept coming. However, he

did not notice that, as his good luck continued, so his son's health worsened. He [the son] kept to himself and looked increasingly depressed. In the end, he went and hanged himself, and you saw for yourself how the father died shortly after, while hunting in the forest. Khoziain was in love with Igor and wanted to live with him. This is why it sent him prey in overabundance. In taking what he was given, Igor was gathering the *ayibii* of Khoziain's children [the souls of animals]. For that reason Khoziain could go and kill him and drag his *ayibii* back to its house. Therefore, I tell you, if you are too lucky and animals keep coming to you, stop hunting at once. It might be Khoziain, who wants your *ayibii*.

The image of Khoziain presented here is not that of a generous parent who nurtures its human children. Although the spirit provides the hunter with prey, it does so with the aim of taking human lives in turn. Hamayon (1990: 653–72; 1994: 79) relates this prey-predator oscillation to a principle of nature-culture reciprocity in Siberian hunting societies. According to her, the death of the human hunter and his relatives is conceptualized in these societies as the ultimate retribution for their prolonged consumption of animal flesh, which must be balanced by compensation: "humans eat the meat of game animals in the same way that animal spirits feed on human flesh and blood. This is the reason why sickness (experienced as loss of vitality) and death in the community as a whole are understood as a just payment for its successful hunting life in both the past and future" (Hamayon 1994: 79).

In my view, however, this explanation misses the mark. Yukaghirs, like other hunter-gatherers, do not model their interaction with the natural agencies on a principle of balanced reciprocity, but on a principle of sharing. As already pointed out, sharing does not involve a debtor-creditor relationship, with a definite expectation of a return. Quite the opposite, sharing implies that equality is actively promoted and inequality is actively restricted through the principle of demand sharing. People have the acknowledged right to demand that those who possess goods beyond their immediate needs give them up, and the owner of those goods must comply with the demands or risk social disapproval. With regard to the hunter-spirit relationship, this means that as long as an animal master-spirit possesses plenty of game the hunter is entitled to ask or even demand that the spirit share its animal resources with him, and the spirit for its part is morally obliged to comply with the hunter's demands. However—and this is the key point—if the wealth divide between the two agencies somehow becomes altered, their roles as donor and recipient might switch, so it is the spirit that becomes entitled to demand that the hunter share his resources. Such a reversal of roles is exactly what we see in the story cited above: the spirit provides the hunter with game in overabundance, and the latter takes all the animals "offered." As a result, he is seen as accumulating a surplus of animal souls. This in turn gives the spirit the right to demand that the hunter share with it, and it asserts its claim by striking him and his son with sickness and death so that it can then drag their *ayibii* back to its dwelling place. Note that the spirit does not kill the hunter and his offspring to balance out long-term credits. It is quite wrong to view the spirit as placing the hunter in debt, as Hamayon does, since the passing along of gifts among hunter-gatherers like the Yukaghirs does not involve any such notion of obligatory reciprocation, exact accounting, or compensation. Rather, the spirit deliberately manipulates the moral principle of sharing to put the hunter in the position of wealthy donor, which justifies it in "demanding" his soul. What is more, the spirit's predatory violence is not so much economically motivated as emotionally motivated. It sets out to trick and kill the hunter not because its wants to regain its property, but because it "loves him" and wants to "live with him."

The important point that follows from all this is that Yukaghirs, rather than regarding the animal master-spirits as inherently benevolent, regard them with a great deal of ambivalence. The spirits' shifting personas, ranging from altruistic to wicked, blend into each other, resulting in trickster figures that, despite their generally benign natures, are deceitful and should never be fully trusted. This, I believe, is exactly what an old Yukaghir was calling attention to when he repeatedly insisted that the Owner of the Earth (Lebie'-po'gil), whom Jochelson (1926: 150) places among the highest of the benevolent beings, is the same as the head of the evil spirits, the Grandfather with the Pointed Head (Yiodeiis'ien'ulben). For what we are dealing with is not a pantheon of spirits that is subdivided into beneficent and hostile powers in any rigid sense. Rather, we are dealing with what I shall characterize as a "double perspective." By this I mean to suggest that nested within the hunters' perspective of the animal master-spirits as generous parents who are obliged to feed their hungry children is a sort of counter-perspective, the spirits as predators who seek to trick and kill humans in order to satisfy their selfish love for them. Thus, although hunters address the spirits as "parents" and make an appeal for benevolence and active sharing, they never lose sight of the fact that such a sharing relationship involves much danger. For, contrary to what Bird-David (1992: 28) asserts when she talks about the "giving environment," the roles of nature as donor and

Figure 3. Wooden representation of the Grandfather with the Pointed Head (3 cm wide, 19 cm long). The spirit's ambiguous nature is emphasized by the fact that it holds a crucifix. The figure used to be placed next to infants when they were sleeping. If an evil spirit approached the child, it would recognize the child as one of its own kind and leave it alone. Drawing by Mads Salicath.

humans as recipients are neither finite nor fixed in the "cosmic economy of sharing," but might reverse, in which case hunters face the risk of being struck with illness and death.

WHEN THE HUNTER BECOMES THE PREY

This potential for the roles in the sharing relationship between human and natural agencies to reverse gives rise to much anxiety among hunters. Their anxiety stems from the fact that whenever they succeed in killing plenty of animals, they can never be certain about the intention of the animal master-spirits in providing them with good hunting luck. Are the spirits simply fulfilling their moral obligation as "parents" to share their animal resources with them, or are they about to trick them into the position of "donors," which allows for a divine predatory attack? No hunter knows for sure. Hallowell, it seems to me, makes a similar statement when he writes about the spirits through the eyes of a Canadian Ojibwa

Indian: "I cannot predict exactly how they [the spirits] will act, although most of the time their behavior meets my expectations. . . . They may be friendly and help me when I need them but, at the same time, I have to be prepared for hostile acts too. I must be cautious in my relations with other [than human] persons because appearances may be deceptive" (Hallowell 1960: 43).

In the case of Yukaghir hunters, they respond to this uncertainty by taking the exchange process with the natural agencies to a further stage, which they refer to as *pákostit'*, meaning "to play dirty tricks" in Russian, and which I shall later describe in terms of a process of sexual seduction. In short, the hunter seeks to induce in the animal master-spirits an illusion of a lustful play. As a result, the spirits come to believe that what is going on is not a premeditated kill but a "love affair" with the hunter. After killing his prey, the hunter will cover up the fact that he was the one responsible for its death by blaming others for the violent slaughter. As a result, the hunter will not appear to have taken anything from the animal master-spirits, at least not formally, and no sharing relationship was therefore ever established between the two. This in turn rules out the spirit's right to demand the hunter's *ayibii*. In other words, *pákostit* involves the hunter seeking to maximize utility at the spirits' expense while avoiding the risk of falling into the position of potential donor. In this sense, *pákostit* corresponds in part to what Sahlins (1972: 195) has called "theft," which he characterizes as "the attempt to get something for nothing," and which he argues to be "the most impersonal sort of exchange," which "ranges through various degrees of cunning, guile, stealth, and violence." Although guile is an integral part of the game of seduction, we are talking about neither an impersonal sort of exchange, nor guile as a simulacrum or lying in any strict sense. To seduce an animal and its associated spiritual beings, the hunter must emphatically project himself into their agencies, even to the point where the boundaries between them are blurred and they become of the same kind.

I shall return to a discussion of the issue of seduction and its implications for the hunter's sense of identity in chapter 5. For now, however, I shall return to Krupnik and his depiction of northern hunters as "aggressive resource users" who ascribe to an "overkill hunting strategy" (1993: 236). If what I have been arguing in relation to the Yukaghirs holds true for other groups of northern hunters as well, then it seems clear that Krupnik's assessment is not altogether correct. Although it is true that the Yukaghirs do not invariably exist in a condition of equilibrium with their game resources, and that they have no conception of "waste" attached to the material bodies of animals, there is also another side to their hunting cosmology that counterbalances the inclination to engage in indiscriminate slaughter. In fact, it would be fair to say that we find two polar tendencies in Yukaghir subsistence practices: one in the direction of overpredation, which is believed to increase the future animal population, the other in the direction of limiting one's killings to an absolute minimum, to avoid putting oneself in the precarious position of donor and risking counterpredation by the master-spirits. Hunters usually seek to find a balance between these two extremes by killing all animals offered, yet ceasing to hunt the moment their good luck exceeds what is considered "normal" hunting success. Thus, as I shall describe more fully in chapter 8, Old Spiridon, who habitually kills each and every elk he encounters, stopped hunting altogether after falling ill one day in the forest. He ascribed his illness to his helping spirit, the Owner of the Omulevka River, whom he claimed was in "love" with him and had attempted to kill him by providing him with prey in overabundance. An incident I observed while out trapping with a Sakha from Nelemnoye illustrates the same point. We succeeded in taking sable in great numbers, but when my Sakha friend sensed that our good luck was getting out of hand, he insisted that we take a break. To continue trapping, he assured me, would simply be too risky. My point is that overkilling and not killing reciprocally constitute the "side–other side" of two interdependent resource and risk management strategies. Though any hunter may by an act of will reverse the two so that one takes primacy over the other for the time being, the point to keep in mind is that the two aspects belong together as two sides of one and the same ethnographic reality. As a couple they form a more accurate depiction of northern hunting practice than either of them seen in isolation.

CHAPTER 3

Body-Soul Dialectics

Human Rebirth Beliefs

Having described Yukaghir reincarnation beliefs in relation to animals and the implications for the hunter-prey relationship, I shall now turn to discuss those beliefs in relation to humans. What Nikolai Likhachev's account in chapter 2 reveals is that each living person is seen as a kind of new embodiment of a particular dead relative. In fact, everyone in Nelemnoye would always insist that the living person *is* the dead relative of whom he or she is a reincarnation. "The two are one and the same person," they assured me. Yet some people would add, "but a person's body is also him or herself," thereby illustrating that it is an aspect of the person, his *ayibii* or soul, rather than the person *in toto* that is reincarnated. An individual's body is, in principle, himself or herself, but, as we shall see below, it can at times be "colonized" by the *ayibii*, which might divide itself into its various parts and take control. This body-soul dialectic is, it seems, also reflected in the Yukaghirs' own phrase for rebirth, *shoromo ayibii kel'iel io'nin*, which means, "a person's *ayibii* came back in this person's body."

Although for the Inuit reincarnation is not tied to gender, and a child can receive the name of either a deceased male or female (Nuttall 1994: 128; Saladin d'Anglure 1994: 82–107; Bodenhorn 1997: 119), Yukaghir ideas about rebirth tend to be dependent upon gender. Although people would not deny that a female could be reincarnated in a male's body or vice versa, I never encountered any actual examples of this, not even in

Yukaghir myths. Moreover, in the great majority of cases the reincarnated person is a member of the immediate family, that is, a parent or sibling of the child's father or mother who has passed away recently. In this respect, their ideas about human rebirth clearly reflect the fact that they reckon kinship bilaterally, and that genealogical knowledge is blurred with distance across generations. Few people know the name of their great-grandparents, and a person's namesake will usually be no more than two generations removed.

There are, however, exceptions to this rule. In one case, for example, a young mother told me that her son was the reincarnation of her great-grandfather, who had died long ago and whom she had never known personally. According to her story, when she addressed her son by his name, Igor, he replied, "My name is not Igor but Tompúla." The boy was only three years old at the time, and the young mother simply assumed that he was talking nonsense. Nevertheless, she mentioned the incident to some older relatives, who told her that Tompúla (meaning "the small river with a strong stream" in Yukaghir) used to be the nickname of her great-grandfather on her mother's side. This convinced her that what the boy had been telling her was that he was in fact the reincarnation of his great-great-grandfather and had been given the wrong name. Therefore, although the boy's Christian name is Igor, she now addresses him as Tompúla. "Since then," she assured me, "my son has become much more cheerful and much less offensive."

I was told that if a child's identity is not correctly identified and is given the wrong name, his *ayibii* will feel offended and dislike him, and it will tend to work against him rather than assist him in life. Consequently, people are highly concerned about establishing the true identity of their children. Sometimes a dying person will reveal in advance the name of the woman he or she will attempt to enter. At other times, a woman will dream about a specific deceased person during her pregnancy and she will thus know which relative's *ayibii* has entered her. At still other times, the child may announce whom the *ayibii* is, as in the story just described.

MIMETIC AGENTS AND DOUBLE PERSPECTIVES

The acquisition of a dead relative's *ayibii* and name confers a social identity on a person, who, while being him- or herself, is also regarded as the returned deceased relative (Nuttall 1994: 124). This allows for the continuity of personal relationships, a continuity that at times can be loaded with much emotional intensity, as in the case of an elderly woman, Irina Iakovlevna, and her grandson, Pavel:

> The winter night my grandson Pavel was born, I had a dream. I saw my [dead] husband standing naked in front of the oven. He was shivering all over and his skin was blue with cold. The very same night, a helicopter arrived from Zyrianka to take my daughter to the hospital. You see, major complications followed the delivery. She was unconscious when they transported her, so they completely forgot about Pavel [the infant], who was lying almost naked in the helicopter. He nearly froze to death. Already then, I suspected that he [her husband] had come back [as a reincarnation in her grandson]. . . . At that time, I worked in the kindergarten. Pavel comes up to me all the time and wants to help me with different things. During the breaks, he also wants to lie beside me in the bed. . . . When he was five years old, he said to me, "Do you remember those boots that you lost while we were hunting in the forest? I found them and put them in a tree together with our food . . ." Everything he told me was true. I was very upset and went to my daughter and asked if she had been telling him these things. But she said no, she hadn't said anything. . . . Sometimes when I hear him talking, I hear his [her husband's] voice. [She starts to cry.] Today, he [Pavel] is twelve years old. He brings me all the hares and fish that he catches. The way he hunts is also the same . . . and the way he talks . . . he [her husband] has come home to provide for me. . . . I dress him like I used to do and mend his clothes . . .

Nuttall informs us that, in traditional Inuit society, the newborn child would actually take the position within the kin group of the deceased person of whom he or she was considered a reincarnation, and would be addressed by the same kin terms as would normally be applied to the dead relative (1994: 128–29). Among the Yukaghirs, at least of the present day, we do not find such a formal slant to their reincarnation beliefs. I did not, for example, ever hear Irina address Pavel directly as her husband, nor did I hear Pavel's mother call her son her father. However, the story clearly reveals that, on an emotional level, the original bond between the deceased and the bereaved may be strongly reestablished. Irina, for example, tells us that her husband "has come home to provide" for her. Therefore, while she calls Pavel her grandson, she also sees him as her returned husband. It is this combination of *two* perspectives within *one* person that suggests that she acts towards Pavel as a mimetic agent. Later, in chapter 5, I will show how the hunter, when approaching his prey, acts as a mimetic agent; he is neither hunter nor animal in any absolute sense, but instead moves somewhere in between human and nonhuman perspectives. A somewhat similar experience of being betwixt and between two perspectives is apparent in Irina's relationship to Pavel.

When she "dress[es] him like [she] used to do" and "mend[s] his clothes," she looks upon Pavel neither from the single viewpoint of a wife nor from that of a grandmother, but she assumes both of these perspectives at once. This allows her to experience her husband's presence through her daily contact with the grandson, without at the same time reducing the boy to an exact image of her husband, which, even from the viewpoint of the Yukaghirs, would be regarded as abnormal behavior and a violation of the child's autonomy.

I did, in fact, witness one such tragic relationship between a grandfather and his grandson. A man from the village (whom I shall call Sergei) lost both of his sons within a period of a few years. One drowned, and a young relative killed the other while drunk. Sergei now considers his daughter's son (whom I shall call Vasili) to be the reincarnation of one of his dead sons. People say, however, that Sergei has not got over the death of his sons and that grief has driven him to insanity. "He has lost his senses," his wife explained to me. "He won't leave Vasili alone. . . . The boy is both nervous and afraid of his grandfather."

I attempted to set up an interview with Vasili to ask him about his sense of identity and his feelings about being named after his dead relative, but on the day of our meeting he had left the house. His mother apologized to me for her son's disappearance, but said, "Vasili doesn't believe that he is my dead brother. It is my father who has gone mad. He doesn't understand that nothing can bring back his son."

What is it, precisely, that makes people in Nelemnoye regard Sergei as mad, but not Irina Iakovlevna, who also believes her grandson to be a returned deceased relative? I have already pointed out that, although a child is considered the new embodiment of a dead relative, he is also seen as a person in his own right. He carries within him an aspect of the dead relative, his *ayibii,* but is not the deceased person in any absolute sense. This is why one cannot simply interact with the child in the same way as one did with his namesake, but instead must act toward the child as a mimetic agent. The problem with Sergei is that he relates to Vasili as if the boy were in fact his dead son. So, instead of acting toward Vasili as a mimetic agent, moving between the perspectives of grandfather and father, Sergei has surrendered, so to speak, to the *single* perspective of father. He thereby claims the unity of identity between two persons, who are considered by the Yukaghirs similar but not identical, and it is precisely this confusion of analogy with identity that makes him mad in the eyes of the community. We must bear in mind that in the world of the Yukaghirs, where the various boundaries between self and other, such as the ones between living and dead or human and animal, are permeable and easily crossed, the ability *not* to confuse analogy with identity is of paramount importance. This is probably most clearly revealed with regard to the Yukaghir hunter and his prey. As I shall describe in chapter 5, hunters consider it necessary to assume the identity of their prey in order to kill it. However, if the hunter loses sight of his own human self in this process and surrenders to the single perspective of the animal, he will undergo an irreversible metamorphosis and transform into the animal imitated. In this case, then, confusion between analogy and identity does not lead to madness as such, but instead to something just as dreadful, namely "othering" beyond recovery.

In any case, the tragic story of Sergei and his grandson Vasili reveals that although Yukaghir ideas about the reincarnation of dead relatives into newborn children can be seen as a particular cultural model for dealing with grief, a model that emphasizes the continuity rather than the finality of personal relationships, it does not always achieve the feelings of comfort intended. The relationship between the child and the bereaved is in fact a contingent process that is inherently interactive and fundamentally risky. Everything, from the development of emotional bonds between the child and the bereaved to the latter's sense of moving from grief into contentment, all depend on whether the parties involved can "bring it off," so to speak, in their daily interaction with each other. There are strong emotions at stake, and many things can go wrong. The child may feel that his autonomy is being violated and therefore reject the identity ascribed to him, or the grief of the bereaved may be so overwhelming that the child is never actually allowed to fill the void left by the death of their beloved.

It is my experience, however, that often an individual will identify strongly with the deceased relative he or she is said to be. This is the case, for instance, for Peter Spiridonov, a young hunter from my hunting group who claims to be the reincarnation of his dead uncle:

> I am my mother's brother, Peter Vasilievich, no doubt about it. A trunk from a tree crushed him and he died a few years before I was born. When I was four years old, I suddenly described to my parents the entire accident, while I continued with my play as if nothing unusual was happening. . . . Once, Peter Vasilievich's sister, Anna Vasilievna, came to our house. I believe I was six years old at the time. I said to her, "You look sad, sister, what is bothering you?" She couldn't believe her ears. . . . When I walk down the street, I occasionally hear the old men sitting on the doorsteps say to each other, "Look at the way he walks, it's just like the old Peter." . . . Two weeks ago, I had a somewhat strange experience. It was when you and Yura [his brother]

were in the forest hunting. I was sitting in Fimka's [his sister's] kitchen and she was making me tea. Suddenly, a huge pile of raw meat appeared on the table, just like that, out of nowhere. "Look, Fimka," I said. "Look at all the meat!" But she couldn't see it. Then it disappeared. But then I knew that you and Yura had killed an elk or something. You see, it was him [Peter's *ayibii*, or the soul of his mother's brother] who showed it to me.

What is interesting about Peter's account is that it reveals how the perspective of the dead person he claims to be can sometimes penetrate his own perspective, so that he starts to experience the world simultaneously from a double perspective. Thus when, as a child, he suddenly began to speak from the point of view of the deceased, he did not stop being himself, but kept playing with his toys as if nothing extraordinary were happening. Similarly, when a pile of meat mysteriously appeared in front of his eyes, he remained aware of both his sister and the environment in which he was situated. It is clear that he does not cease to be himself when he adopts the perspective of his dead relative. Rather, multiple selves and perspectives coexist within him in a kind of unresolved dialectical tension. We have seen on a more fundamental level that this is grounded in the fact that he is neither himself nor his dead relative in any absolute sense, but is somewhere in between or both at once. The implication of this, however, involves not only perceptual experience, but the very structures of embodiment as well.

BODILY AGENTS

According to the phenomenological literature, our bodies are essentially characterized by "absence" (Lender 1990: 1). That is, one's own body is rarely the thematic object of experience: we simply live through our body in the world of everydayness, in which it disappears from our awareness. As Sartre writes, "My body is for me not like any other physical object. I do not apprehend my body in the way that I apprehend objects in the world. I have a first-person experience of my body as the basis of my action" (2000 [1958]: 304). Merleau-Ponty takes a similar stance when arguing, "I am *not* in front of my body, I am in it, or rather I *am* it" (1998 [1962]: 150; my emphasis). Thus, from a phenomenological standpoint, the body is the primary self: we are not related to our bodies in a detached way. Our bodies do not constitute something that we have as a thing, but signify who we are; that is, we *exist* as bodies.

For the Yukaghirs, however, people do not experience their bodies entirely as something preobjective and fully controlled. Each hunter ascribes different parts of his body agency, agency that at times is coterminous with his own intentions but at other times can be distinct from them. In the latter case hunters might experience a sense of losing control over their bodies, as if their bodies were contradicting or working against their intentions. Let me illustrate this with an incident that took place while I was hunting for elk with Yura. We had been following a track for two hours or more when Yura lifted his hand to signal me to stop and keep silent. The tracks were dewy and the elk could be standing anywhere behind the tall willow bushes, twenty meters or so in front of us. Yura started to go on ahead on his skis in the waddling manner that hunters use when they attempt to draw an elk out into the open so it can be shot. He had moved no more than six meters when he stumbled over his skis and fell in the snow. Behind the bushes we heard the noise of an animal escaping in a wild panic. "Damn you!" Yura cried while trying to get back on his feet. "What the devil do you mean?" I cried back. "I did nothing." "Not you," he replied. "Didn't you see? For some damn reason, my legs did not approve of me getting that elk."

I wish to stress, however, that it does not require an experience such as this one for a hunter to switch into an attitude of explicit body awareness. In the phenomenological literature, bodily self-objectification is often understood to occur in those extreme situations where our absorbed bodily coping runs into trouble or is under threat, for example, during physical breakdown, pain, and disease (Lender 1990: 76; Jackson 1994). At that moment, it is argued, we no longer simply exist in our body as the unthematized ground of our being, but are confronted by it as a thinglike object of our contemplation and awareness. Our body is experienced as not belonging to us entirely, and we therefore feel estranged.

However, the Yukaghirs' conception of the "thematic" body does not imply a philosophical bias toward the negative. For them, as we shall see, the body plays an ambiguous role from the very outset as both self and other in experience, and it does not necessarily take problematic performance or dysfunction to render bodily awareness explicit. Rather, it is a type of attitude that is evoked whenever some bodily sign prompts one's attention. Hunters thus explained to me how their bodily agents tend to assist them by providing prognosticative bodily signs of either good or bad luck in the forthcoming hunt. For instance, an elderly woman said that a quiver in her lower lip is a sign of hunting luck, because it implies that she will be eating soon. When she senses an itching under her armpit, this is also a sign of luck, because it indicates where on the elk's body the bullet will strike. As another example, a young hunter explained that when his back hurts, it means that he will kill some big game, because "back pain is my back's way of telling me that I will soon have to carry a lot of meat." While a twitching eyebrow might be a sign of luck for one hunter, for another it is an itching ear. The point is that all hunters share a belief *in* their bodies, or rather parts of them, which convey facts about success in a forthcoming hunt. For each hunter, this bodily information is a critical factor in decision making. Thus, if someone receives a bodily sign indicating bad luck, he usually changes his plans. He stops pursuing prey until his body has provided him with a sign of good luck.

THE *AYIBII*

Sometimes Yukaghirs explain the agency of their body parts by saying that it is in fact their *ayibii* that inhabits a particular area of their body and tells them the outcome of a future hunt. *Ayibii* literally means "shadow" in the Yukaghir language, as in the shadow cast by a stone. Jochelson, like his contemporaries, translated it as "soul" (Jochelson 1926: 156; Bogoras 1904–9: 332–33; Hultkrantz 1953). Although the Yukaghirs themselves occasionally use the Russian word *dusha,* or "soul," interchangeably with their own word *ayibii,* the term is somewhat misleading. The notion of soul in Christian discourse is part and parcel of an ontological opposition of spirit and matter, which implies that souls are immaterial. The soul's substance is *spiritus,* "breath"— "what is most invisible in the visible, most immaterial in the material" (Valeri 2000: 24). For us, therefore, body and soul are seen as two quite distinct substances, one physical, the other entirely immaterial.[1] Among the Yukaghirs, however, souls do not have this disembodied existence but are vested with a good deal of physicality. We need only point out that the hunter occasionally sees his *ayibii* in dreams as a freely operating being, and in waking life he sees his own soul or that of his fellows in the shape of an animal.[2] Moreover, as will be described below, some hunters also carve wooden representations of their *ayibii,* which they feed with fat and blood from the animals they kill, illustrating that the *ayibii* is believed to have material needs: it eats and drinks, and can be hunted and eaten by other creatures as well.

Jochelson, in his classic monograph on the Yukaghirs, attempted to establish the number of souls a Yukaghir person is believed to possess, their function, and their location in the body. However, he faced contradictory and fragmented statements. Some people would talk about the existence of three or more souls, others about one soul that pervades the entire body. "Numerous contradictions," he writes, "have crept into the Yukaghir conception of the soul, contradictions due to the absence of logical reasoning, as well as to the fact that many of the ancient beliefs are no longer current among the modern Yukaghir" (1926: 156). His principal thesis, however, was that the Yukaghirs operate with three souls, the "head-soul," which represents the intellect; the "heart-soul," which controls motion; and a third soul, which pervades the whole body and presides over the physiological functions (Jochelson 1926: 156). The fact that the Yukaghirs have only one word for soul, *ayibii*, made Jochelson suggest that their idea of three souls was borrowed from the neighboring Sakha, who see the soul *(kut)* as being manifested in three forms, each with a special designation: *salgin-kut* (air-soul), *iiä-kut* (mother-soul), and *boyor-kut* (earth-soul) (Jochelson 1933: 103–7). He went on to suggest that the Yukaghirs originally shared the belief of the Koryak and Chukchi that people only have one soul, which can, however, divide itself into several "limb-souls" (Bogoras 1904–9: 332–33; Jochelson 1908: 100–104; Jochelson 1926: 158).

In general, Yukaghirs showed little interest in my questions about the number of souls and where in the person's body they might possibly dwell. Insofar as they attempted to answer my questions, their responses were often fragmented and self-contradictory. One man, for example, claimed that a person has only one soul, his shadow, and he explained this by saying that "everybody can see that each person has only one shadow." I then asked him what happens to one's soul after death. He immediately turned his argument on its head, replying that one soul will die with the person, the second will travel to the Land of Shadows, and the third will join God in heaven. Other people confirmed that the *ayibii* appears in three forms, but gave inconsistent reasons for this. One said this is because the world exists in three layers, while another claimed it is due to the soul's ability to reincarnate itself three times.

Still, one should not necessarily take the Yukaghirs' fragmented and sometimes highly self-contradictory statements about the *ayibii* as an indication of cultural loss or a lack of logical reasoning, as Jochelson did. For the Yukaghirs, knowing is deeply related to doing, and people's knowledge about various spiritual matters resides primarily in their activities rather than in discourse. By this I mean that spiritual issues are not so much talked about in the abstract as deeply embedded in people's everyday practices, such as hunting and dreaming. Later, in chapters 7 and 8, I

Figure 4. Nikolai Likhachev making a pair of skis.
Photo by Rane Willerslev.

shall return to discuss the issue of practical versus abstract types of knowledge. There I will show that the Yukaghir hunters' overall prosaic mindset
is, on a fundamental level, grounded in an ontology of language and
knowledge that considers linguistically conveyed information to be an
inferior way of knowing compared with lived, practical experience.

Although the large majority of Yukaghirs could be deemed prosaic,
the old man, Nikolai Likhachev, is somewhat different from the rest. He
lives on the edge of the village and prefers to keep to himself. People tend
to fear him, claiming that he possesses various shamanic powers, such as
the ability to perform black magic, although they do not regard him as a
shaman as such.[3] I succeeded in establishing a rather close friendship
with him, not least because I kept bringing him meat from my hunting
expeditions. It turned out that his father and grandfather were among the

last Yukaghir shamans, and although he failed the test to become a shaman himself, he did manage, through years of apprenticeship, to gain considerable knowledge about such matters as the nature of the *ayibii*. What is interesting about his account is that it confirms the notion of "limb-souls." He explained that people have only one *ayibii*. It lives in one's bone structure but can divide itself and move into different regions and products of the body. The heart, head, and shadow are among its favorite locations, which is why people tend to talk about three souls, the head-*ayibii*, the heart-*ayibii*, and the shadow. However, the *ayibii* can, in principle, reside in all body parts and organs.[4] Diffused throughout the body in this way, the *ayibii* becomes individualized into different agents or "persons" (Rus. *lyudi*), as he called them, each of which takes its specific character from the body part or organ it inhabits. "If you are stupid," he said, "the *ayibii* living in your head will do stupid things; if you are brave, the *ayibii* living in your heart will do brave things; and so forth." Thus, each of these animated body parts or organs is understood to be a kind of person within the person. However, as he emphasized, the *ayibii* is originally only one, and it can therefore gather itself into wholeness and act as a single person.

CONTROLLING ONE'S SOUL

Although the *ayibii* is often considered a "helper" that secures knowledge and acts to the advantage of its possessor, it does this at a price. It requests "feeding" in return for its services. This is why some hunters carry with them in the forest small wooden figures representing their *ayibii*, whose mouths and hands they smear with fat and blood from the animals they kill. If the hunter fails to perform this sacrifice, his *ayibii* might turn against him. It can work against him in everyday life, as in the case of Yura, who stumbled over his legs and failed to kill the elk, or it can begin to prey upon him or his relatives by striking them with sickness and misfortune. Moreover, some people told me that because the *ayibii* originally arrived from the Land of Shadows it has an innate desire to regain its independence and return to its home. Consequently, it may seek to lead its possessor into death by the use of trickery.

As an example, once, when I went to visit Nikolai Likhachev, he was unusually absentminded. When I asked him what was wrong, he explained that that very night a ghostlike creature had approached him in a dream. It was like a shadow in that it had no features. However, it had talked to him in a voice similar to his own, which made him think that it had been his *ayibii*. "Old man," it said, "you can barely walk and no one is taking care of you. Your relatives are waiting for you, and they have plenty of food." Nikolai Likhachev had become angry and replied, "So, you want me dead, you devil? I know what your world is like. I've been there already and I didn't like what I saw!"[5] At that moment, his dead mother had appeared. "Don't tell him lies," she had said to the *ayibii*. "Our house is cold, and we don't have much food either. He is better off here." Then the two of them had walked away.

If there is a moral to be learned from this account, it is that although the *ayibii* might be considered a "benevolent" agent, it is benevolent only in a very relative and dangerously unstable sense. A hasty glance through the massive compendium of soul conceptions among North Amerindian peoples by the Swedish scholar Hultkrantz reveals a somewhat similar notion:

> It is certain that the North American doppelgänger [soul] can be both an amiable spirit and a horrible demon. In the former case, when as among, e.g. the Ojibway, the spirit communicates warnings and information to its owner in signs and speech, we may best characterise it as a guardian spirit. In the latter case the doppelgänger is regarded with negative feelings, since it is either directly malicious or is thought to possess an ominous quality. If the doppelgänger is of the first-mentioned character, its malice may be directed against its owner, as among the Ungava Eskimo, where every person is believed to have a doppelgänger that annoys him, and that can only be placated with offerings of food, water and clothes. (1953: 357–58)

Thus, for the Amerindian peoples as for the Yukaghirs, the soul plays a double role, both as helper of and as traitor to its possessor. This is why Yukaghirs feel an urge to control it. Some hunters will attempt to do this by moving toward what could be called increased incorporation of the soul's agency into their own selves. This requires showing it the utmost respect, accepting its presence, and avoiding conflict with it. The Yukaghir hunter Vasili Shalugin, for example, told me that when the left side of his head hurts it is a sign of bad luck, whereas if the right side hurts it means the opposite. Thus, if he is following animal tracks and the left side of his head starts to hurt, he will immediately stop the chase, "because this is *our* will" (referring to his own will and that of his head-*ayibii*). Moreover, he would never address his head directly by saying, "My bad head is working." This might offend his head or head-soul. Instead he would say, "I will not follow this track because my bad *hair* is working."

An example from a Sakha man suggests a similar theory or explanation: a person has to make sacrifices to his *kut* (the Sakha's three souls) and ask them to cooperate during hunting. In the words of the young Sakha hunter, "Better not ask your *kut* for too many favors, because then they will get tired of you and not assist you, or at best ignore you, or even harm you." In both examples the hunters seem to believe that if one accepts and respects his soul and does not offend it, then one has better control over it.

There are, however, hunters who strive to "separate" their *ayibii* from their own selves by ignoring it to some degree, or even getting into conflict with it in an effort to control it. "Of course, you must listen to what your *ayibii* tells you," a hunter explained. "But then again, it might just tease you, and you cannot let it dictate everything to you." Yet another hunter explained, "I've stopped feeding it. I fed it week after week, but it didn't do me any good. Now I'm going to starve it, and then maybe it'll stop playing tricks on me." These hunters see themselves as apart from their *ayibii,* which is understood as an alien that needs to be ignored or forced into submission.

Whether the hunters are moving toward increased incorporation or increased separation, their ultimate goal is the same, namely, to live in some sort of harmony with their *ayibii.* Old people are usually held to have such feelings of agreement with their *ayibii.* Yukaghirs say that as a person's *ayibii* gets to know him over time, it will come to care for him. In a similar manner, a person will come to appreciate his *ayibii* and gradually become one with it: "It tends to stop contradicting you because it knows that you will be dying soon," an old woman explained. Thus, the malevolent traits of the *ayibii* are progressively neutralized with the passage of time. The older a person becomes, the nearer death he or she is, the more benevolent the *ayibii* becomes because the closer it is to regaining its independence and returning to its original existence in the Land of Shadows.

THE BODY AS SELF AND OTHER IN EXPERIENCE

The phenomenologist Schutz has argued that in the everyday world the self is experienced as the "author" of its activities, as the "originator of the ongoing actions and, thus, as an *undivided total Self*" (1962: 216; my emphasis). We act in the world *through* our bodies; our bodies are the subjects of our actions, through which we experience, comprehend, and act upon the world (Schutz 1962: 216). This is, of course, a particularly Western model of the individual and his body, and one that the

Yukaghirs may challenge. From their perspective, the self is experienced at least occasionally as multiple or "dividual," to use Strathern's phrase (1990: 13). We have seen how Yukaghirs undergo existential struggles for control over their bodies, which implies experiencing one's body both as "me" and "not me," as "self" and "other." One is sometimes a person whose conscious mind coexists with multiple bodily agents that have their own intentions, and sometimes a person that exists as an undivided bodily subject.

The Yukaghirs, however, are not unique in this respect. Smith (1981) has suggested that for the Maori it was generally not the self that encompassed experience, but rather experience that encompassed the self. The Maori individual was conceived as being made up of various independent organs of experience, and these organs each reacted to external stimuli independently of the self. Thus, the self was not viewed as fully controlling bodily experience, and an individual's experience was not felt to be integral to him: "It happened *in* him but not *of* him" (Smith 1981: 152).

Similarly, McCallum (1996: 362) describes how the Cashinahua of the Amazon see different parts of the body as the loci of different kinds of knowledge, and this again is linked to a notion of bodily spirits. For instance, the knowledge/spirit dwelling in a person's skin is said to tell him where to find prey. Thus, for the Cashinahua, as for the Yukaghirs, a human person is not just considered to be him or herself, but is believed to contain multiple agents or persons within.

Becker (1994) provides a different but somewhat related example from Fiji, where the body is a function not of the individual self but of the community. She describes an ongoing surveillance, monitoring, and commentary on the body shape, which includes changes due to hunger versus being well fed, and changes that begin when a woman becomes pregnant. For Fijians, not revealing a pregnancy is spiritually dangerous and can both cause destructive events and be manifest in the bodily experience of other relatives. She reports that this phenomenon was fully developed as a bodily mode of attention by one woman, who typically experienced an itch in her breast whenever a member of her family became pregnant (Becker 1994: 110).

This review of some indigenous ideas about the self and its relation to the body raises the question of how we can come to terms with the somewhat puzzling fact that the lived body can be both "subject" and "object," "self" and "other," in experience. If it is "subject," it is "*my* body," responsive only to my will. If it is "object," it is "other," disobedient of my will. An adequate account of the self and its body would have to accommodate both of these aspects within a unitary and coherent view of lived experience.

Three scholars in particular, Sartre (2000), Merleau-Ponty (1964), and Lacan (1989), have given this issue considerable thought. I will discuss their work in turn and argue that rather than Sartre, it is Merleau-Ponty and especially Lacan that allow us to overcome the problem confronting us.

In his long and dense treatise *Being and Nothingness,* Sartre distinguishes between two basic ontological categories of the body. The first is "my body-for-me," which belongs within the sphere of subjectivity (2000: 330). The second is "my body-for-others," which he claims is equivalent to "the other's body-for-me" and belongs within the sphere of objectivity (p. 304). My own body, Sartre argues, is not for me a *thing.* It is a thing from the perspective of another, and another's body is a thing from my perspective, but my own body is not presented to me as an object in the world, as something I can encounter as a third person or straightforwardly observe. Rather, my body signifies who I am. In other words, "I *am* my body" (p. 351; emphasis in the original).

However, Sartre describes yet another ontological, or perhaps quasi-ontological, category of the body, "my being-for-others," which refers to my experience of my body as objectified by the other's gaze (p. 353). He invites us to imagine him staring through a keyhole, attempting to spy on the person on the other side of the door. Suddenly he hears footsteps behind him. He is under the gaze of another and feels shame. He has internalized the point of view of the other and sees himself through the other's eyes, that is, as an object within the world. At this level, "my body is designated as alienated" (p. 353), because the other assigns it a meaning that does not correspond to how I experience myself to be, which is as a "body-subject."

Thus, for Sartre, "my body-as-subject" is ontologically distinct from "my body-as-object." Either my body is experienced as a thing among other things, or else it is that by which things are revealed to me. But it cannot be both at the same time. As he puts it, "As subject the body cannot be object and as object the body cannot be subject . . . being the subject of an experience precludes being simultaneously the object of that same experience" (p. 304).

However, as Dillon (1988: 142–45) has pointed out, Sartre's essentially dualistic account of the body is logically incoherent. First, if it were truly the case that the "body-as-subject" had no common ground, no point of intersection, with the "body-as-object," then it is difficult to see how my body could ever be the object of shame. "If I am *not* the body objectified by another's look, if I am *not* the body I see through his eyes, then I can feel no shame at the exposure of that body to objectification" (Dillon 1988: 143; emphasis in the original), since it would simply be alien to me. The experience of shame requires a "double perspective" in which I am both the object of the shame that I adopt toward myself through another's perspective on me *and* the subject, who witnesses this shaming objectification. In other words, feelings of shame must imply a mode of fundamental ambiguity in which my own body is experienced simultaneously as both "subject" and "object," "me" and "not me." Hence, it is not, as Sartre contends, that the "body-as-subject" is onto-logically distinct from the "body-as-object." It is rather the case that the *same* lived body manifests itself in *both* roles simultaneously.

This, as we shall see in a moment, is also Lacan's key argument. However, I shall begin with Merleau-Ponty, whose theoretical criticism of Sartre brings us directly to Lacan's work. The problem of alienation through the gaze of the other is not a problem for the very young child, Merleau-Ponty argues. Traditional accounts of the subject, such as that offered by Sartre, presuppose that conscious life begins in a sphere of "ownness," characterized as a nascent solipsism or self-centeredness. But, says Merleau-Ponty, the earliest stage of childhood is in fact marked by an undifferentiated anonymous collectivity in which the child has no sense of differentiation from others. One of the phenomena he cites in his description of this original state of syncretism is the "contagion of cries" among babies (Merleau-Ponty 1964: 124). If one infant in a nursery begins to cry, the crying spreads to the other infants, and within seconds they are all crying. This is because an infant does not distinguish between its own body and those of others, between sensations of internal and external origin. In terms of the gaze, then, the child can neither feel estranged from itself nor be captured by another's look because it has no sense of self-differentiation or alterity. The question, then, is how the child transcends this aboriginal state of syncretism and learns to distin-guish its experiences of itself from its experiences of others. In his various writings on this issue, Merleau-Ponty posits different explanations for the birth of the possibility of self. He sometimes argues that it is an immanent aspect that is already given within our body: when one hand touches the other (what is generally referred to as "double sensation"), our body articulates a sort of self-reflection and we come to experience ourselves ambiguously as both subject and object, self and other

(Merleau-Ponty 1998 [1962]: 93). In his most sustained and detailed consideration of the issue, however, he posits Lacan's "mirror stage" as the point at which the child is launched into the world of self-awareness and also of alienation (Merleau-Ponty 1964: 136).

In Lacan's account, the mirror stage is the first step in the open-ended process of self-individuation, and marks the child's entry into what he calls the "imaginary order," that is, the order of images, reflections, and doubles. This stage also lays the foundation for symbolic and linguistic identity. The mirror stage takes place between six and eighteen months and begins with the child's recognition of its own body image in a mirror. The reflected image provides the child with a promise or anticipation of self-mastery and bodily unity, which is in conflict with the child's actual experience of its body as a discrete assemblage of parts, exhibiting no regulated organization or internal cohesion. As Grosz writes, "[The child's] body is an uncoordinated *aggregate,* a series of parts, zones, organs, sensations, needs, and impulses rather than an integrated totality. Each part strives for its own satisfaction, with no concern for the body as a whole. . . . Sensory/perceptual impingements, which may animate certain organs and body parts, cannot be attributed to a continuous, homogenous subjectivity" (1990: 33–34; emphasis in the original).

In its desire to become "complete," the child attaches itself to the reflected image of a total body-subject, as seen in the mirror. As a result, the ideal unified image of selfhood, or *imago,* is formed (Lacan 1989 [1966]: 2–3). The child now becomes enmeshed in a state of confused recognition/*mis*recognition: it internalizes an image of itself that is both "accurate" (since it is an inverted reflection of the child's actual body) and "delusory" (since the child is not really as integrated as its image in the mirror suggests). The result is a radically "split" subject, divided between its actual experience of its "body-in-bits-and-pieces" and its organized and integrated body image that is manifestly different from itself, though it also clearly resembles it in some respects.

It seems to me that Lacan's account of the "mirror stage," although it cannot be applied directly, offers a potentially appropriate framework for coming to terms with the Yukighirs' ideas about a body-soul dialectic. Let me begin by drawing attention to some of the important similarities between the two accounts. In both cases we are basically dealing with a dual relationship with a conflict at its core. In other words, for the Yukaghirs as for Lacan, the subject, to become a subject at all, must internalize otherness as a condition of its possibility. For the Yukaghirs, this other with whom the subject must identify does not take the form of a figure in a mirror but is instead the *ayibii* (shadow) of a deceased relative.[6] The crucial point of analogy, however, is that according to both accounts it takes *two* to make *one:* the subject recognizes itself as such only at the moment it "loses" itself in/as another. This is because it is by identifying and incorporating the image of another, which in turn becomes the image of itself, that the subject begins to represent itself to itself as a separate being. There is a paradox here in that the subject must experience self-objectification or self-alienation in order to gain a sense of itself as self. As Dillon puts it, "It is the other who alienates me from myself and thereby introduces me to myself. The other is the locus of the external perspective upon myself" (1988: 125).

For both the Yukaghirs and Lacan, the result is a subject that takes itself as its own object and is never quite identical with itself. In other words, the relation of the subject to its *imago* or *ayibii* comes to reside in that "double-negative field," which I have characterized as "not me, *not* not-me." Indeed, it is this dialectic or contradiction that causes the subject to manifest a variety of conflicting attitudes toward its specular counterpart, ranging from fascination and playful interaction to rejection and aggression. The first attitude is grounded in the anticipation of self-mastery and control, which the *imago* promises the subject. The latter is the result of the frustration that springs from the fact that such self-mastery is just an illusion, based on a "false" recognition of another as the same. As Grosz writes, "[The subject] invests the specular image of itself or another with all the hostility directed towards its *own lack of satisfaction,* the very motivation for internalising the image in the first place. The *imago* or internalised image becomes an intra-psychic object of aggression" (1990: 41; my emphasis). Moreover, Boothby states, "[It is] in the confusion of self and other in the imaginary [that] establishes the fundamental structure of *desire* as the *desire to become the other*" (1991: 42; my emphasis).

Human desire thus springs from experiences of lack, initially caused by the incorporation of otherness into the self. The subject strives continually to fill this lack either by seeking to advance the integration of its *imago* into its own self or by aggressively rejecting it. We see an obvious analogy with the Yukaghirs, who, as I have described, attempt to control their *ayibii* by moving back and forth between "incorporation" and "separation" of its agency. The tragic irony of this, however, is the fact that the ultimate drive of all desire is to "kill itself" so as to put an end to the intrapsychic battle between the "real me" and the "imagined me." Freud (1961: 30) refers to this as the "death drive," which is "an urge inherent in organic life to restore an earlier state of things" and reduce all tensions to an absolute "zero": "[There] must be an *old* state of things, an initial state from which the living entity has one time or other departed and to which it is striving to return by the circuitous paths along which its development leads. . . . *The aim of all life is death,* and looking backwards . . . *inanimate things existed before living ones*" (Freud 1961: 32; emphasis in the original).

From this perspective, the death drive aims toward the transcendence of tension and discontent, and toward the return of the living subject to the inorganic form from which it developed. We find a striking parallel in Yukaghir notions of the *ayibii* as a "trickster" that seeks to deceive its possessor into death in order to return to its original state of being in the Land of Shadows. In both cases, the specular counterpart of the self plays a double part as both "helper" and "traitor" of the subject: while it is what makes possible the formation of the subject, it is also that which threatens it with dissolution.

Although there are remarkable similarities between the Yukaghir and Lacanian ideas about the construction of the subject and of subjectivity, the Yukaghir material can hardly be said to prove Lacan's ideas. The two conceptions can at best be considered mutually enlightening discourses that provide insight into each other. Part of the difficulty in applying Lacan's theory directly to the Yukaghirs is that, for Lacan, the imaginary is basically seen as a stage in the subject's maturation process, one that needs to fizzle out and be replaced by the next and final stage of differentiation, the "symbolic order of language." In gaining access to language, the child comes to grasp Saussure's point that identities come about only as a result of difference—that one thing or subject is what it is *only* by excluding another. Thus, what the acquisition of language does, in effect, is to bring the child out of the dyadically enclosed situation in which it is held in thrall by its specular double. The child's identity no longer depends on an alienating narcissistic identification with imaginary counterparts, but comes to be constituted by its relations of *difference* to things and people around it. A subject who remains fixed in the imaginary state of affairs would be incapable of situating itself and others in their respective places and, as Lemaire states, "be reduced to the level of animal life; he would not, that is to say, have at his disposal the common symbolic ground through which any human 'relationship' passes. This is what happened with the psychotic" (1996: 78).

Likewise, Grosz writes, "The imaginary is the order of identification with images. It is the order of dual, narcissistic relations with others, of libidinal pleasure unregulated by law, and indistinguishably intra- and inter-psychical aggression. In psychoses of 'cenesthesia' (where the subject hears voices in his head or bodily parts), we have the obliteration of a tenuous boundary between self and other. If the subject hears another's voice from within his or her own body, this is because the self and other remain confused" (1990: 43). The question, then, is what we are to make of the Yukaghirs, who, as we have seen, not only regard their body parts as persons within the person, but more generally conceive the world as a hall of mirrors in which everything reflects all the others into infinity. Does this mean that the Yukaghirs are somehow trapped within the order of imaginary identifications, dominated by confused identifications of self with other? Alternatively, could it be that they are victims of some sort of collective psychosis? I believe that neither is the case, and that something very different is at issue.

First, it must be pointed out that the Yukaghirs stress, as much as does Lacan, the importance of language for the development and growth of the individual subject. For example, they argue that a child does not become fully "alive" before it learns to speak. Prior to acquiring language, "the child is mostly its shadow," which means that the child is its *ayibii*, or deceased relative, more than it is itself. In other words, the Yukaghirs seem to agree with Lacan that without language the relation of the subject to its specular counterpart must be enclosed and circular, making any relations with a "third"—that is, social relations—impossible. They can therefore hardly be seen as trapped within the imaginary order of things.

Even so, Yukaghirs put enormous emphasis on firsthand interaction with the world, especially the world of the forest. This is not to say that language is insignificant. As a matter of fact, I will show in chapter 8 how the very sound of words is understood by the Yukaghirs to be full of transformative power, and how the act of telling stories is seen to be more important than the narratives themselves. All the same, storytelling is never sufficient as a source of knowledge. The greatest validity is given to firsthand, experiential knowledge attained in waking life or in dreams. To be sure, only what the subject himself has experienced is considered knowledge as such. In effect, this means that "knowing" for the Yukaghirs is largely a matter of overcoming the boundary between self and world, initially created by language. We see this reflected in the fact that they refrain from using explicit instruction when teaching children, who are instead encouraged to discover meanings in the world on their own (I will return to this in chapter 8). Likewise, in the next chapter I shall describe how hunters deliberately seek to suspend their separation from prey by refraining from talking in human language when hunting. There is a real sense, then, in which Yukaghirs, at least in certain contexts, seek to transcend the symbolic order of language, whose principle of negation is to divide and differentiate all identities, and (re)enter the realm of the "imaginary." I find it likely that this is what we see reflected in Yukaghir people's cosmological obsession with symmetry and in their numerous ideas about mirror reversals, look-alikes, doppelgängers, shadows, and so forth—all of which emphasize the essential similitude between self and the world.

This, however, should not be understood in romantic terms as an attempt by the Yukaghirs to return to "nature" or to an earlier state of being in which all differences or divisions between self and the world are overcome. In fact, they are highly careful *not* to deliver themselves up to their surroundings in any absolute sense. Indeed, I shall describe later how the hunter's "double perspective" represents such a defense mechanism against the dissolution of the self. Rather, what I am suggesting is that the mimetic cosmos of the Yukaghirs, in which all the various dimensions of reality are conceived as endless replicas or reflections of the others, might in fact be an outcome of the Yukaghirs' deliberate attempt to penetrate the hither side of words and concepts so as to gain direct, perceptual access to the world.

THE SELF AS RELATIONAL

My point is not that we should distinguish between two different notions of the person, a Western one and a Yukaghir one. The anthropological literature is crammed with typologies of this kind that crudely contrast the firm self-other boundary of the Western person with the fluid self-other boundary of the non-Western one.[7] In my view, however, such bipolar types of personhood, even if conceived as ideal types, are widely overdrawn, and I shall illustrate this by returning to Lacan and the question about the human body as both subject and object in experience. For Lacan, the child's experiences of its body-in-bits-and-pieces result from the fact that the different parts of its body mature at different rates, and, like the mirror stage itself, this fragmented and fragmentary experience of the body must come to an end and be replaced by a more coherent body image. Still, we know from our own experiences that, although we habitually experience our bodies as "subjects," that is, as something we live through but do not explicitly take notice of, it occasionally happens that our bodies surprise us, disappoint us, and defy our attempts to control and master them. Jackson (1994), in an article analyzing the subject-object problem in the experience of chronic pain sufferers whose bodies are otherwise intact, describes how they tend to identify with their selves apart from their painful bodies, which are experienced as "alien, an intruder, an invader" (Jackson 1994: 209). Lender further elaborates on this point, writing, "In pain, the body or a certain part of the body emerges as an *alien presence*. The sensory insistence of pain draws the corporal out of self-concealment, rendering it thematic. No event more radically and inescapably reminds us of our bodily presence" (1990: 76; emphasis in the original).

He goes on to suggest that the reason why Western philosophy has tended to devalue the body—through either neglect, criticism, or outright condemnation—is largely rooted in the fact that our bodies come to thematic attention especially when our health is in some way disturbed (1990: 127). Although this might be true, it is worth stressing that we do not need to draw on the experience of medical conditions to find examples of how one's body can be experienced as somehow distinct from oneself. In fact, instances in which the body refuses to do as it is bidden by the self are not hard to find: Dillon lists "the inability to swing a golf club or tennis racquet in accordance with a form one understands perfectly well, the inability to stop oneself from flinching when shooting skeet or trap, the sheer impossibility of not scratching when one itches" (1974: 145). In all these instances we might regard our bodies as responsive to laws that we have neither drafted nor ratified. As such, our bodies invite objectification and reification. They are experienced not simply as a part of us, but also as other. A similar experience can be described by the novice who is learning a new skill. As I shall discuss in chapter 8 in relation to finding one's way when first confronted with an unfamiliar landscape, one needs to concentrate explicitly on one's bodily performance in order to navigate, though this will later become tacit knowledge. There is, in other words, an unease with novel situations that provokes bodily objectification or self-awareness. Furthermore, as Smith (1981) reminds us, insofar as we refer in everyday conversation to "faint hearts" and "fluttering stomachs," and we commonly use distancing expressions in relation to feelings such as love and anger, we demonstrate that the "undivided total self" is not altogether supreme in our own indigenous psychology. When, for example, I say, "My nerves are playing me up," am I not implying that I feel myself to be the victim of a bodily agency outside my control? Indeed, many common phrases that we use concerning organs and body parts do suggest a model of experience not so far distant from that of the Yukaghirs. Thus, it cannot be the case that it is only non-Westerners such as the Yukaghirs who feel otherness as included within the boundaries of the self. Rather, this condition seems to be a distinguishing feature of what it means to exist as an embodied person.

What this points to, I believe, is that it is perhaps a mistake to think of the mirror stage as a developmental one. As I have already pointed out, the main difficulty in applying Lacan's approach to the Yukaghirs lies precisely in his notion of the "stage," which comes dangerously close to correlating "traditional" hunting peoples with the life-stage of Western children. However, in light of many empirical examples of how our own bodily fragmentation is never fully overcome and how the boundary between self and other remains somewhat fluid and indistinct, it seems to me that what Lacan's theory is really describing is the nature of selfhood and embodiment, not a moment in real time. What he provides is a relational framework in which intrinsic or essentialist identities are indeed impossible to maintain. For Lacan, as for the Yukaghirs, the self cannot be understood as a bounded and unitary entity because it is developed and constituted only in and through a rivalry with otherness—a rivalry that in fact is never reconciled but continues to trouble us through our lives. We have thus seen that although we might habitually experience our own body as the most private of all of our possessions, in fact the body and the way each of us lives in it has about it a germ of otherness, which might be especially strongly felt in extreme situations, such as at times of illness or when our absorbed bodily coping runs into trouble, but which nonetheless is constitutive of our embodiment rather than incidental to it. Our body, therefore, is not wholly and utterly our own, and we will never totally dominate or subjugate it to our own ends, just as we will never be able entirely to shake off the dominant role that others play in its constitution. Another way of saying this is that our body is not a thing-in-itself but an effect of our relations with others. The social world of the Yukaghirs is, as we shall see, permeated by phenomena that seem to have this characteristic, that is, things that are identifiable only in and through the relationships into which they enter. The idea with which we now have to come to grips is that these relationships include not only human and humanlike entities, as with the person and his or her soul, but also relations with nonhuman entities, such as prey animals and spirits. It is these human-nonhuman relations to which we shall now attend.

CHAPTER 4

Ideas of Species and Personhood

THE CATEGORY OF PERSON

In the world of the Yukaghirs, as we have seen, everything—human, animal, and inanimate object—is said to have an *ayibii*, or what we would call a soul or life essence. For the Yukaghirs, the whole world is thus animated by living souls in the sense of Tylorian animism. Although everything is understood to be alive, people do nevertheless differentiate between conscious and unconscious beings. On a conceptual level this distinction corresponds, at least roughly, to our categories of the animate and inanimate. An elderly Yukaghir hunter, Vasili Shalugin, told me that animals, trees, and rivers are "people like us" (Rus. *lyudi kak my*)[1] because they move, grow, and breathe, but they are distinct from inanimate objects such as stones, skis, and food products, which, he claimed, are alive but immovable.[2] He continued by saying that things that are static are not people because they have only one soul, the shadow-*ayibii*, whereas things that are active are considered to be people because they have two more souls in addition to their shadows: the heart-*ayibii*, which makes them "move" and "grow," and the head-*ayibii*, which makes them "breathe."[3] He ended by saying, "Only things that can move come to us [in dreams] and give us presents," implying that hunters only engage in social relationships of sharing with animate entities that they consider to be persons.

It is important to realize, however, that Shalugin's distinction between things that are "alive" and those that are both "alive" and also "persons" is far from rigid. Although the category of person recognized by hunters is by no means limited to humans (it includes various animate beings), there are nevertheless certain points at which this continuum of personhood breaks down (Descola 1996: 324). First, the status of person is not ascribed equally to all animate beings. Hunters generally seem to reserve this classification for the principal species of prey, including the elk and reindeer, as well as for the predatory mammals, including the bear, wolf, wolverine, and fox. Certain species of birds, most notably the raven, may also be thought of as persons. Other kinds of animate beings, including insects, fish, and plants, are hardly ever spoken of as conscious beings with powers of language and intentionality, and are in general seen to lead a mechanical, inconsequential existence. Therefore "nature," as we understand it, may indeed exist for the Yukaghirs, but instead of being perceived as a unified realm, it is a randomly occurring series of ruptures to be encountered here and there within an otherwise highly personified world (Pedersen 2001: 416).

Moreover, although some animals are considered to be persons, there is nevertheless a difference between the ways in which human and animal personhood are conceived. As Ingold has pointed out, whereas northern hunters tend to refer to humans by their proper name, conferring upon them a unique identity, the animal is regarded more as a type of its species than as an individual, and *"it is the type rather than its manifestations that is personified"* (1986a: 247; emphasis in the original). We see this revealed in the Yukaghir mythology, in which animals tend to bear the name of their species, sometimes with the suffix "man" or "woman," such as "bearman," "hare-man," and "fox-woman," in contrast to mythical human characters, who tend to have individual names. Ingold has suggested that this indicates that northern hunting peoples do not regard the animals themselves but only their higher-ranked spiritual owners as persons (1986a: 247). His argument, however, does not hold for the Yukaghirs. Although hunters do not usually distinguish between an animal and its associated spiritual being, the hunters I spoke to always insisted that animals do not simply derive their personhood from their master-spirits, but that both are persons in their own right. In his classic study of the Yukaghirs, Jochelson also seems to have observed this. He writes, "In the opinion of the Yukaghir, a lucky hunt depends on the good-will of the animal's guardian-spirit but also on that of the animal itself. Thus they say: 'tolo'w xanice e'rietum el kude'deti'—that is: 'if the reindeer does not like the hunter, he will not be able to kill it'" (1926: 146).

It is therefore not simply that an animal's personhood is an extension of its master-spirit's personhood. Rather, animals are themselves persons. I suggest in the next chapter that this particular Yukaghir conception of the animal's personhood—as a type for its species rather than as an individual attribute—derives in large part from the particular manner in which hunters tend to engage with their prey through mimetic practice.

It is important to point out that with the exception of the category of human, the status of an entity as a person is neither finite nor fixed. In the everyday life of hunters entities move in and out of personhood depending on the circumstances. This is true even of the large mammals, which next to humans are considered animate beings par excellence. I once unintentionally gave offense when, during an interview in the village, I asked Old Spiridon if the elk, bear, and reindeer were persons. At first he reflected a long while as if he did not really understand my question, then he looked extremely insulted and replied, "What do you take me for, a child?" In another situation, however, when I was out hunting with him, we came across a fresh elk track. I pointed at it and said, "Look. It won't take us long to run down the animal and kill it." He hit me hard with the staff of his ski pole: "Don't say such things," he said in a grave voice. "They [the elk] talk with one another. If one of them has heard what you said, it will tell the rest and they will all move away."

At the end of the next chapter I shall return to the puzzling question of why it is that hunters see animals as conscious beings in some situations and not in others. For now, however, I shall describe Yukaghir conceptions of animals as persons in relation to those species that are most significant to their economy and spiritual beliefs, then go on to consider the more fundamental principles on which their ideas about personhood are based.[4]

Yukaghir hunters see certain animals, including the bear, reindeer, and elk, as very similar to themselves in terms of their moral values and rules of conduct.[5] The last animal, in particular, is understood to be a highly sociable and moral creature. Myths describe the elk as always tidy and eager to assist its kin. However, these character traits should be seen not simply as a manifestation of mythical thinking, but also as a reflection of empirical knowledge about the behavioral characteristics of the animal. A hunter explained to me, for example, that unlike foxes and other predators such as sables and wolverines, who are attracted to dirty and smelly spots and whose dens have a terrible stench, elk find it impossible to live in such places. If the water is dirty or the air smells because of an abandoned oil barrel, the elk will move away. He also said that when an elk is being followed by a predator and is exhausted, it will often run to a larger group of fellow elk, which will help it to escape by spreading out in all directions. The predator will then have difficulty detecting which track belongs to the worn-out elk. Similarly, when the snow is deep, elk take turns making the path and will not let the weak ones fall behind. He ended by saying that every elk has a character of its own: "One finds nervous and self-confident ones as well as stupid and clever ones. But they always seem to care a great deal about each other." These ideals are conceptualized in terms of gender. Thus, elk are generally conceived as women, who "give themselves up" to male hunters out of sexual desire for them. As I shall show later, hunters' terminology is replete with symbolic parallels between elk hunting and sexual seduction.

The dog stands clearly apart from other nonhuman persons.[6] It is the Yukaghirs' only domesticated animal and thus occupies a strange position between the human and nonhuman realms. In some respects, the dog is considered closer to human beings than any other nonhuman creature, which is why hunters sometimes refer to their dogs as their "children." Dogs warn and protect their human masters in dangerous situations. In the spring, for example, they will bark and alert people if a bear approaches the camp looking for food. Moreover, hunters are financially dependent on their dogs, not only for hunting, but also for transportation. Although snowmobiles are by far the most important means of transport today, some dog teams are still in use. In fact, the high cost of buying, maintaining, and fueling a snowmobile combined with the widespread lack of cash among hunters after the collapse of the Soviet Union has inspired a revival of dog teams over the past decade. Although the dog is appreciated for its loyal work and helpfulness in dangerous situations, the animal is also seen as "dirty" (Rus. *griaznyi*). Its presence can easily offend prey animals that are purer, and it is considered taboo to feed dogs the vital organs (heart and intestines) of an elk, reindeer, or bear. Hunters ascribe the dog's impurity to its delight in sexual promiscuity, its taste for eating excrement, and its unpleasantly strong body odor, which they contrast with the exemplary behavior and pleasantly bland body odor of the elk.

Predatory animals such as the wolf, sable, fox, and wolverine are also seen as "dirty," but for different reasons. Hunters ascribe the impurity of these animals to their uncontrolled lust to kill and their disrespectful treatment of the carcasses of slain prey. As one hunter said of wolves, "They are shameless in the way they kill and treat the elk's body. Insofar as they share the meat at all, the strongest of them will eat first and take all the best parts for himself." However, it is the wolverine that is seen as the embodiment of all that is antisocial. It is the greediest and stingiest of all the nonhuman persons, living on prey stolen from others. When it finds a dead animal, it urinates all over the carcass to make sure no other predator will touch it. I was instructed to kill the animal whenever I came across it, "because the wolverine is an anarchist and only thinks about its own well-being," as one hunter put it.

For Yukaghirs, however, the important idea is that of difference, not of hierarchy, and there is no status hierarchy as such. I realized this when a wolverine once dragged away the carcass of an elk that I had killed. When I arrived at the location of the kill with Spiridon to carry home the meat, absolutely nothing was left of the dead animal. Instead, we encountered the unmistakable stench of a wolverine's urine. "What a damn thief," I complained. Spiridon replied, "Well, this is not how the wolverine itself sees it. It sees the meat that it finds as a gift from Khoziain [the spirit-master], in much the same way that the meat we eat is a gift. Everybody needs to eat, and Khoziain feeds all his children, as well as the wolverine. Therefore, the wolverine does not see what it does as theft. To the contrary, in the wolverine's mind, we are the ones doing wrong when we try to kill it for stealing."

Spiridon pointed to the fact that in the world of Yukaghirs, "good" and "bad" behaviors are not absolute but depend upon the perspective one adopts. I shall later discuss this notion in terms of what has been called "perspectivism" (Viveiros de Castro 1998). What is important to realize at this point is that whereas hunters may generally see wolverines as their enemies and will kill them whenever they get a chance, the animal does not represent an "evil" species in contrast to other species that are inherently "good." Rather, every species is seen to behave according to its own particular social and moral code. The wolverine, therefore, only follows the custom of its kind and does not necessarily have evil intentions when it steals from hunters.

The category of person includes not only "natural" creatures, but also beings that we would label "supernatural," such as the spirit-guides of animals, cannibal spirits that eat human souls (*ku'kul* in Yukaghir, but people tend to use the word *abasylar*, borrowed from Sakha), and many others. These beings cannot usually be perceived with the waking eye, but may appear only as a smell, sound, or feeling. The Yukaghirs, then, do not see the supernatural as a level of reality separate from nature. From their point of view, mystical beings are inhabitants of the same physical world as humans and animals, and they are experienced, at least in certain situations, as being just as real.

MORAL ANXIETIES ABOUT KILLING AND EATING ANIMALS

For the Yukaghirs, killing game and eating its flesh is the very essence of life. Although small-scale greenhouse gardening was introduced in the 1930s, it is mostly the Russians in Nelemnoye who grow potatoes, tomatoes, and cucumbers during the short summer. Many Yukaghirs, particularly people of the older generation, simply refuse to eat vegetables, claiming that they taste like "wood." Instead, their passion is for meat. Red, fatty meat in particular is esteemed above all other foods, and most consider that a meal without any such meat is not a proper meal at all. Meat is also the most charged object of exchange. As I have already described, households share meat as a key expression of ties of kinship, and men use it as a gift to secure sexual favors from lovers or exchange it for fuel in the regional center of Zyrianka.

However, although meat is highly esteemed, killing and eating animals is inherently problematic. This is due in large part to the fact that the animals that are most desirable as food—elk, reindeer, and bear—are the ones understood to be most like humans in their moral values and rules of conduct. As one young hunter once expressed it, "When killing an elk or a bear, I sometimes feel that I've killed someone human. But one must banish such thoughts or one would go mad from shame." The moral dilemma that stems from killing these animals is also observable in all the various phases of the hunting process. I will show later how a hunter may develop dangerous feelings of love for his prey and thus fail to kill it. Moreover, in the ritual following the kill, hunters will attempt to cover up the fact that they were the ones responsible for the animal's death. And when the meat is distributed in the village, people may refuse to take their share if they sense that the animal has been killed in a morally improper way, such as by the use of a shaman's magic. In fact, I encountered people who refused to eat bear altogether on the grounds that bears resemble human beings too closely, and to eat them would therefore be to engage in a form of cannibalism.

Unlike some Amazonian peoples, whose shamans can, by means of magic, transform inherently problematic meat into less problematic foodstuffs (see Hugh-Jones 1996; Descola 1996: 91–92; Fausto forthcoming), the Yukaghirs have not found an absolute solution to the moral dilemma posed by killing and eating prey. Rather, what makes animals edible from their viewpoint is the fact that, although they are seen to have their own minds and thoughts, just like humans, they are at the same time conceived of as "other." Moreover, Yukaghir ideas about the continuous rebirth of the souls of killed animals might help to ease their feelings of guilt. Still, one should not lose sight of the fact that the hunter at times experiences real feelings of moral anxiety when killing his prey. What is more, although Yukaghirs usually enjoy eating meat, and there is no visible sign that they experience guilt or conflict when eating it, the problem of cannibalism is nonetheless a moral paradox at the very center of their hunting cosmology. Thus, as we shall see, Yukaghirs say that humans are cannibals from the viewpoint of their prey in much the same way as *abasylar* are cannibals from the viewpoint of humans.[7]

BODY AND SMELL

For Yukaghirs, personhood involves not only mental traits but also physiological ones. Body and odor are part of the Yukaghirs' notion of personhood and are important in determining what kind of species they are dealing with. The principal distinction with regard to odor is between *ile'ye* and *pe'yel*. The latter, which means decay, sickness, and death, is attributed to various bad things. For example, it is said that the spirit of a certain sickness discloses its presence by its foul odor, even though it cannot always be seen. "You always smell when *abasylar* seek prey," an elderly woman explained. "They have an unmistakable stench." When a person dies, his or her corpse is believed to pollute close relatives with *pe'yel*. For male relatives, this means that they are unlikely to be successful in making kills until a year has passed, because they are said to carry with them the smell of death, which frightens prey animals. *Ile'ye,* in contrast, means sweet, pleasant, and delightful and is used especially to describe the smell of delicious food and the odor of small children and women. Affection for women and children is generally expressed by sniffing rather than by kissing. People sniff the nape of the neck and under the chin, asserting that the odor is very pleasant. In fact, hunters often told me that a woman's sex appeal is not so much a matter of her looks as of her odor, which should be that of "berry flowers" or "mountain grass."

In former times, smell was used as an important marker of a person's ethnic affiliation. Jochelson describes how the Yukaghirs would recognize the Evens by their smell of squirrel and decayed reindeer meat, whereas the Sakha could be recognized by their smell of decayed fish liver and cow dung (1926: 23). "But at present," an elderly woman asserted to me, "all people smell more or less the same, because they intermarry and eat the same kind of food." Still, I was often surprised by the strong aversion that people, especially the Sakha, expressed toward the smell of Russians. For example, I was once sitting at the dinner table with a Sakha woman from Nelemnoye whose son had married a Russian girl. When the son passed his small child to his mother, she refused to hold it on the grounds that "it smells of Russian."

The smell of nonhuman persons is indicated by a different word in Yukaghir, *yo'rola*, which means, "to do with the nose." This word is applied particularly to mammals that have strong aromas: the fox, the wolverine, the elk, the reindeer bull (especially during the mating season), and the polecat, the last having the strongest smell of all. More than once I witnessed hunters detect elk or bear hiding in the dense taiga forest simply by smelling them in the air. Similarly, the droppings of prey animals will be smelled for indications of their likely whereabouts. I observed that many hunters are skilled at this and can, based on the consistency and smell of an animal's droppings, make an accurate assessment of its sex, age, and state of health. Hunters also say that the spirit-master of each locality marks its territory with odor trails in much the same way as an animal marks its territory by establishing odor trails and scent posts. In fact, one hunter told me that he would know if he had passed from one spirit's territory to that of another spirit simply by smelling the air.

However, it is important to stress that the significance that Yukaghir hunters assign to smell does not mean that the visual is not important. When hunters mimic elk by taking on its smell and imitating its bodily movements, their goal is to make the animal visible, to bring it into the open so that it can be shot. Even cultures that are reported to denigrate and suppress vision, like the Umeda of the forests of New Guinea (Gell 1996: 233–54) and the Suya of the Amazon (Classen 1993: 8–9), clearly must depend on their eyesight in their subsistence activities, especially when shooting at game. In fact, I find the tendency to typecast some nonliterate societies as "antivisual" somewhat dubious. My own experience among Yukaghir hunters echoes that of Smith (1998: 412), who writes of the Chipewyan hunters (Dene people), "Bush sensibility emphasises paying attention to as many of the senses as one can, and, even more cogently, to all the senses as they interact to produce a unique level of awareness." What this statement clearly indicates is the fact that for hunting peoples the practicalities of survival in the forest simply work against considering the senses as altogether separate, and against the construction of a well-defined sense hierarchy. When out hunting, all of one's senses must be operational, and their inputs tend to intermingle so that the contribution of each becomes largely indistinguishable in the total configuration of perception.

To give an example: A hunter's head is the common site of his senses of sight, hearing, and smell. Consequently, the action of turning his head in order to listen for game inevitably also means turning his eyes and nose in the same direction, so that they become oriented toward the same source. Thus, rather than perceiving prey through his separate channels of perception—seeing it with his eyes, hearing it with his ears, and smelling it with his nose—all of these different sense registers overlap in their functions and are subsumed under the total system of his bodily orientation (Merleau-Ponty 1998: 317–18; Ingold 2000: 262). Langer (1989: 49) provides a similar example when she writes, "If my gaze is attracted by a vase on my desk, for example, the way in which my eyes move in examining it already indicates the manner in which my fingers can explore it." What she points to is the fact that we do not necessarily see objects any more than we feel them; we might, so to speak, feel an object with our eyes and see it with our hands. Thus, in our actual experience, the different registers of sensation are brought together into that synergic system that is the phenomenal body itself, and any attempt to distinguish them intellectually therefore becomes largely a meaningless exercise.

Although there is no term in the Yukaghir language that can be equated with "mind" as opposed to "body," hunters are clear that people "think." When I asked Vasili Shalugin what it is that gives people the capacity for reasoning, he answered that thinking was a function of one's head-*ayibii*, and he confirmed that both human and nonhuman persons possess this capability. However, he also insisted that different kinds of persons think in different ways: "Naturally, humans, elk, and bears think differently. They are distinctive kinds of people," he argued. So, while there is an explicit link between the *ayibii* and the capacity to think, which is formally identical for human and nonhuman persons alike, different species are nevertheless said to think differently. The source of this difference, it seems to me, is the specificity of bodies. While the *ayibii* provides the ability to reason, the body provides the fundamental mediation point between thought and the world. In other words, nonhuman persons think differently from human persons and from other nonhuman persons of different species not because of their *ayibii* or soul, which simply gives them a similar capacity for reasoning. They do so because each species has its own corporeal nature that provides it with a particular bodily presence and orientation in relation to the world—a certain "bodily awareness," to use the words of Merleau-Ponty (1998: 317–18).

Moreover, as a result of their distinctive bodies, each species is said to perceive the world in its own way, which, however, is not altogether different from that of humans. Vasili Shalugin explained this point to me by comparing the predatory activity of humans with that of *abasylar*: "Our hunters go hunting for elk and so do *abasylar*. However, to them our *ayibii* is the elk. When they look upon a woman's *ayibii*, they see a cow, when they look upon a male's *ayibii*, they see a bull, and when they look upon a child's *ayibii*, all they see is a little elk. The same is true of fat, skinny, old, and young people. *Abasylar* will see them as elk of different sizes and ages. Thus, *abasylar* are hunters just like us, but what they see as elk differs."

When an *abasy* succeeds in killing and eating a human's *ayibii*, the person in question falls ill and dies. Nevertheless, Shalugin was at some pains to explain to me that in their own communities, *abasylar* are really good folk. They live in ways very similar to humans. They have camps, travel around on dog sledges, marry one another, and have children. *Abasylar* are not really evil creatures, and they behave badly only from the viewpoint of human beings, whose *ayibii* they kill and eat. Humans are also *abasylar* in the eyes of their animal prey. I realized this when I asked Nikolai Likhachev if the prey animals were afraid of human hunters: "Of course they are," he replied. "We eat their bodies, so to them we are devils." And, he added, "this is why they send us illnesses and other misfortunes, to punish us for killing and eating them."

Below I shall return to a more detailed discussion of the dynamics of the relationship between predator and prey. What is important to realize at this point is that while the *ayibii*, for the Yukaghirs, unites various entities and makes it possible to talk about them as potential persons, those entities' uniqueness as *other kinds of persons* is grounded in the specificity of their bodies. That is, the physicality of bodies, with their particular shapes, movements, and smells, is precisely the location from which the different species-bounded identities emerge. A hunter recognizes himself, and is recognized by others, to be a human person who thinks according to the social and moral criteria of humankind exactly because his body is that of a human being and not of a reindeer, *abasy*, or any other nonhuman person. Therefore, whereas within the community of humans it is a person's *ayibii* rather than his body that confers a particular social identity on him, with regard to interspecies relations it is the other way around. Here it is the body that defines the kind of person you are. We might say that a person's species identity is ascribed to, or grafted onto, the body; who you are and how you perceive and construct the world depend upon the kind of body you have.

HUMANITY AS A CONDITION

Neither Jochelson nor I could find any all-explanatory and widely accepted creation myth that might reveal the basic relationship between human and nonhuman persons. Despite the influence of Christianity, the Yukaghirs have apparently not adopted the biblical creation tale; it is as if the appearance of humans does not interest them. However, in response to my continuous questions about how humans came into being, an elderly woman, Akulina Shalugina, told me a short myth:

> In ancient times there lived very small people and the climate was very hot. They did not have a name for themselves, but we call them *irkinyodutyuval mril nasy sarno*, which means "so small that a squirrel fur can dress one person." They were naked, ate raw meat, and did not know how to make fire. It started to get cold and the small people killed squirrels and dressed in their fur, but they were terribly cold. Then Jesus came flying from the sky with a torch in his hand.[8] He gave it to the small people, who thus came to have fire. The smoke from their fires made them grow bigger and bigger and they became humans.

It seems to be a truism that fire is the prototypical means of converting natural substance into cultural use. Cookery is the most obvious example. However, for the Yukaghirs fire also transforms people, who through exposure to the campfire's smoke can change from one species of person to another. Let me explain this. For the Yukaghirs, a good hunter must be skilled in conquering his human smell. This speaks of their general theory that hunting is anchored in a skilled "dehumanization," the reshaping of the qualities of one's human body into those of the prey. Thus, hunters will go to the *banya* (sauna) the evening before leaving for the forest. Instead of using soap, they will wipe themselves with dry whisks from birch trees. They say that the elk recognizes the attractive smell of birch leaves and does not flee, but comes closer to the hunter. Moreover, small children, who are said to have a particularly strong human odor, should be kept at a distance from hunters. At home, as already described, affection for children is expressed by sniffing. Parents apply their noses to the napes of their children's necks and inhale the odor. When a hunter sets off for the forest, however, he rarely embraces his offspring in order to avoid contamination with their odor. Another principal precondition for hunting success is sexual abstinence. For at least one day before undertaking a hunting trip, the hunter should abstain from sex altogether. This is partly because his sexual attention should be directed toward the prey animal and its associated spiritual being, as will be described below, but also because sexual intercourse leaves an unmistakable human stench on his body. Hunters assured me that only those who do not smell of human fluids can attract prey.

When hunting, then, Yukaghirs cease to be extraneous bodies, alien to the forest world and to the animals they hunt. For them, the very nature of hunting requires that the hunter identify with his prey and attempt to ascertain its mode of perception and action by imitating its bodily movements and smell. The campsite, by contrast, is characterized by the presence of human odors, especially the smell of wood smoke. In fact, hunters argue that smoke, either from tobacco or the campfire, is the only means by which their animal odors can be neutralized. What is more, the border between the forest and the camp is not defined by any physical mark but as the location where the smoke from the campfire can no longer be detected. Wood smoke is thus a signifier of human presence, and there is a real sense in which it serves to humanize hunters, to purge otherness from their selves when returning from hunting. Wood smoke and humanity are, to the Yukaghirs, synonyms.

What is interesting, however, is that the state of humanity is ascribed not only to human beings but to all species of persons. Animals and other nonhumans are said to live lives analogous to those of humans. When they roam the forest or swim in the rivers they appear as fish, prey, and invisible spirits. However, when they enter their own lands, which are located somewhere in the forest or deep in rivers and lakes, they are said to take on human shapes and live in households similar to those of humans. The households of nonhumans, just like those of humans, are centered on the fireplace, whose smoke "humanizes" them when they return from the forest. However, the transformation is never complete. Even when in their transformed state, animals and other nonhumans are said to retain some of their former physical, mental, and social characteristics, which identify them as beings of a special class acting in a human way. In a story cited in the next chapter, a hunter encounters "reindeer people" that have human shapes and live in tents but grunt instead of using human language and eat moss instead of meat. Similarly, "fox people" are said to retain their strong smell and sly character and live in dirty households. "Elk people" are generally friendly and caring and keep tidy households.

One might observe that a consequence of this sort of movement in and out of human form is that animals reveal themselves as persons only when in their own lands, removed from their encounters with human hunters. In the bush they assume animal form and lose their cultural attributes, by which process they can be killed and consumed in a matter-of-fact fashion and without any fear of engaging in cannibalism. In fact, this is the line of interpretation suggested by Tanner (1979) with regard to the Cree, who share with the Yukaghirs the notion that prey animals take on animal or human appearance, depending on whether they are roaming the forest or are back in their own households. Tanner asserts that, for the Cree, "game animals participate simultaneously in two levels of reality, one natural and the other cultural" (1979: 137). On the natural level, they are encountered simply as material entities to be killed and consumed. On the cultural level, by contrast, they are "*re-interpreted*" as anthropomorphic beings participating in a domain "modelled on conventional Cree patterns of social and cultural organisation" (p. 137).

However, as already pointed out by authors such as Ingold (2000: 48–52) and Brightman (1993: 176–77), there exist major difficulties with this idea of two incarnations of prey animals, one "spiritual/cultural" and the other "technical/natural." First, the status of prey as persons among Yukaghirs is not only to be expressed in what anthropologists like to call symbolic activities, such as the narration of stories that precedes and follows the actual hunt. Practically all actions by the hunters while they are living in the forest refer to the prey's status as a person. The personhood of the animal hunted is not simply "added on" in discourse, then, but pervades the practical conduct of the hunt itself. The fact that Yukaghirs often ascribe a successful kill to the animal's affection for the hunter confirms this point, since such a notion "presupposes a reciprocally reactive 'other'" (Brightman 1993: 177) and not simply a creature acting in accordance with a "wired-in" behavioral program. Thus, the animals hunted are not reduced to mere objects, and hunters see them as more than mindless meat.

Moreover, Yukaghirs not only conceptualize animals in their own image, but they also conceptualize themselves in the image of their prey when hunting. As already mentioned, this involves imitating the movements and smells of the animals hunted. Likewise, it involves discouraging human talk. Hunters often go alone when checking their traplines, but when they are moving in groups to hunt elk or bear, for instance, very often not a word is spoken. If any sound is made, it will be a sound imitating the animal that they hope to attract. However, imitating an animal's voice or bodily form is not viewed by hunters as becoming "natural" as opposed to "cultural." There is no word corresponding to our term "nature" in the Yukaghir language, nor is there any equivalent of

Figure 5. Old Spiridon communicating with the
other hunters by imitating animal sounds. Photo by
Rane Willerslev.

"culture" as a uniquely human attribute. When transforming himself
into the image of his prey, as we shall see in the next chapter, the hunter
is attempting to seduce an animal into "giving itself up" by creating a
performance that somehow resonates with the animal's mood, senses,
and sensibilities. Taking on the animal's identity, therefore, is seen not as
a process of "desubjectification," but rather a process of "othering."
Hunters use their own bodily experiences, or what Nagel has called "the
subjective character of experience" (1997: 166), to vicariously understand an animal experience.

    For the Yukaghirs, as we have seen, personhood is not the manifest
form of humankind; rather, humans are one of many outward forms of
persons. Thus when Yukaghirs claim that elk or reindeer take on a
human appearance when returning to their own households, "far from
drawing a figurative parallel across two fundamentally separate

domains [culture and nature], they are rather pointing to the real unity that underwrites [the human-nonhuman] differentiation" (Ingold 2000: 50). This unity, I suggest, is "humanity as a condition" (Descola 1986: 120). Animals and other nonhuman persons, whatever they may look like to humans, are believed to experience *themselves* as participating in behaviors similar or identical to that of the Yukaghirs. This is what Viveiros de Castro (1998) in a highly innovative article calls "perspectivism," namely, the conception "according to which the world is inhabited by different kinds of persons, human and non-human, which perceive reality from distinct points of view" (1998: 469). These are not alternative points of view of the same world, but rather result from a carrying-over of the same point of view into alternative realities. Thus, every species kind in its own respective sphere will perceive the world in the same way as humans. But *what* each one sees will be different, depending on the kind of body it has: "Humans see humans as humans, animals as animals and spirits (if they see them) as spirits; however animals (predators) and spirits see humans as animals (see prey) to the same extent that animals (as prey) see humans as spirits or as animals (predators). By the same token, animals and spirits see themselves as humans: they perceive themselves as (or become) anthropomorphic beings when they are in their own houses or villages and they experience their own habits and characteristics in the form of culture" (Viveiros de Castro 1998: 470).

I believe that Viveiros de Castro's outline of perspectivism resonates with Yukaghir conceptions. We have seen examples of how beings of two different species may have completely different perceptual experiences of the same object. While *abasylar* see a human *ayıbu* as an elk, human beings see it as their soul or life essence. Humans for their part see the elk as prey, which in turn sees humans as *abasylar*. Thus, both spirits and humans see prey and both go hunting for it, but what they perceive as prey differs. In addition, who is considered an evil spirit depends on whose body perspective one adopts.

Moreover, the perspective that a particular species has of another species may be fundamentally different from the way it perceives its own manners and practices. Thus, whereas hunters see the wolverine as greedy, gluttonous, and immoral, from the wolverine's perspective it is the other way around. As Spiridon pointed out, the wolverine regards itself as a moral being, whereas it sees the human hunters as subscribing to immoral rules of conduct when they strive to kill it. Furthermore, the various species of persons each perceive themselves in more or less identical terms as human subjects who keep houses, possess fire, utilize speech, and order their lives vis-à-vis moral codes.

In the light of these observations, it is perhaps not so strange that the Yukaghirs lack an overall creation myth explaining the origin of humanity. After all, humanity is the form in which every species person experiences its own nature (Viveiros de Castro 1998: 477). The differences between the various kinds of species persons lie primarily in their distinctive external features or bodies, which are the loci of their particular perspectives. It seems no coincidence, then, that the countless Yukaghir myths about animal origins are concerned with exactly this—how different kinds of animals got their bodily appearances (see Jochelson 1926: 241–98; 1900; Zukova, Nikolaeva, and Dëmina 1989; Spiridonov 1996 [1930]: 46–57).

What is slightly more puzzling, however, is the fact that animals, even when in their own lands, are said not to be altogether identical to humans but to retain some of their former animal features. If, indeed, every species of persons sees itself anatomically and culturally as humans see themselves, how then can we account for the paradox that animals, even from their own "infrahuman" perspective, see themselves to possess also the physical and behavioral traits of animals? To come to grips with this, we need to return to the issue of the body and its relation to the dynamics of identity and otherness.

CHAPTER 5

Animals as Persons

HUMAN-ANIMAL TRANSFORMATIONS

Although Yukaghirs are quite clear in their minds about which body belongs to any given person, they do regard it as possible for someone to take on the body of a being from another species. In principle, one can take on the body of any natural entity that is ascribed the status of person. An old man thus told me that he had once seen a person turn himself into a larch tree in order to hide from the Spirit of Smallpox. In general, however, humans are most likely to transform themselves into one of the great predators, such as the bear and wolf, or the principal species of prey, such as the elk and reindeer. The process of bodily transformation implies changes in the person, which must inevitably entail the assumption of an altogether alien perspective comprising a radically unfamiliar linguistic, social, and moral code. Taking on the body of another species can, therefore, only be done for short periods of time and it does pose risks. It is possible that temporarily inhabiting the body of an alien species can result in the loss of one's own original species identity. When this happens, a true metamorphosis occurs: the transformed individual becomes an "other" and his or her memories of past experiences are lost. Nikolai Likhachev powerfully evoked an instance in which he was gradually alienated from humankind:[1]

> It was during the war. In those days we mostly hunted reindeer, because there were very few elk. I had been following a herd of reindeer, a hundred head or more, for a long time, about six hours, I believe. I was at the

Popova River. That night I made a fire and drank tea but could not sleep. I had nothing to eat and was hungry and cold. At dawn, I put on my skis and continued following the herd. As I searched the track, I had a strange feeling I was being watched. I looked up and saw an old man about twenty meters ahead of me. He was dressed in the old fashion. He smiled at me. I asked him who he was, but he did not answer me. Instead, he gestured with his hand, showing me that I should follow him. I thought he had a cabin close by and some food, so I did so. I was really hungry. All the time he did not speak. I noticed his footprints were those of a reindeer. "Strange," I thought, because the man was wearing *kamus* [skin-covered skis]. But then I thought I was just hallucinating because I was tired and hungry. We walked up a hill and behind it was a huge camp, with thirty or more tents. We walked into the camp. There were people of all ages, children playing, old men sitting smoking, and women cooking. The old man took me to his tent. He spoke to his wife by grunting just like a reindeer, and she grunted back. I did not understand. "Who are these people?" I thought. The woman served me food, and I saw it was not meat but lichen. I ate it because I was so hungry, and it was not too bad. As time passed and we sat there in the tent, I started forgetting things. I thought, for instance, about my wife, who was waiting for me back home, but I realized I had forgotten her name. Then we went to sleep. I dreamt that I was surrounded by reindeer. Someone said to me, "You do not belong here. Go away." I do not know who spoke. I woke up and thought I had to get away. I sneaked out of the tent and started walking home. In the village, people were very surprised to see me. They said they thought I had died. "What do you mean?" I asked them, "I have only been away for a week." "No," they said. "We have not seen you for more than a month." . . . It seems that the people I met were reindeer, and I should have killed them, but at the time I did not know. Maybe it was all a dream. But then why should I have been away for such a long time?

Here we see how the hunter experienced prey animals, in this case reindeer, as human beings, which is how reindeer and other nonhuman persons are said to see themselves. Similarly, the reindeer saw the hunter not as a predator or cannibalistic spirit, but as one of their own kind. "In normal conditions, [Yukaghirs] do not see animals as people, and *vice versa*, because [their] respective bodies (and the perspectives that they allow) are different" (Viveiros de Castro 1998: 478). Perhaps what underlies the story is the fact that when approaching reindeer or elk, hunters attempt to deceive an animal by taking on its bodily appearance, movement, and smell. However, here the hunter himself was tricked, so that he started to see the world from the perspective of his prey. As a result, he was on the verge of undergoing an actual metamorphosis.

I recorded another experience of transformation while hunting sable together with a young Sakha man from Nelemnoye named Ivan Danilov.

The two of us lived alone in the forest for about two months while waiting for Spiridon and his hunters to join us. Neither of us was an experienced hunter. Ivan used to work as an electrician in the village, but he had turned to hunting by the time I arrived in Nelemnoye because he had received no payment for several years. We worked very hard setting traps and were surprisingly fortunate in taking sables. In time, we became increasingly obsessed with accumulating furs. We took hardly any time to rest, eat, or collect firewood, but left our one-room cabin before dawn to set traps and did not return until after dark. We always fell asleep in a cold cabin, exhausted and hungry. Then one evening, when we were lying side by side on our plank bed, Ivan said, "Can't you feel it?" "Feel what?" I asked. "How we are turning into greedy predators, just like wolves. We have this need to kill more and more. Even if we had two hundred sables we wouldn't feel satisfied, would we? Just like the devil, you see." He paused for a while. Then he added, "I suggest we calm down [Rus. *uspokoit'sia*] and stop hunting for a week or so."

Unlike hunting elk and reindeer, which involves imitating these animals by moving, smelling, and sounding like them, trapping does not require bodily transformation. Instead, "skillful trappers" (Rus. *soboliatniki*) talk about the need to "think like a sable." As the hunter Taishin Arkadi explained to me, "To become a *soboliatnik*, you shouldn't just follow your traplines blindly. You need to be curious, like the sable. If you see that it's been up to something, you must go there and find out— see what it has been eating, touching its leftovers, and so on. . . . The character of the sable is curiosity, pure curiosity. To place your traps well, you must be curious like the sable. You need to think like this: 'What would attract my curiosity as a sable?' This is how you need to think."

Trapping, in other words, involves a kind of mental projection by which the hunter seeks to place himself imaginatively within the character of the animal, matching that which is unique about it. If he can do so, he is more likely to be successful in constructing and placing his traps in ways that will resonate with the animal's behavior, senses, and sensibilities.[2] However, trapping involves not only the ability to internalize an animal's viewpoint, but also the equally important ability to avoid the loss of one's sense of human personhood in the process. Hunters claim that sable and other predators such as the wolf, wolverine, and fox have an irresistible greed and bloodlust. If given the chance, they will kill any form of prey they encounter, without observing the ritual procedures that facilitate its rebirth. Hunters therefore call these predators *griaznyi,*

Figure 6. My Sakha friend Ivan with trapped sable.
Photo by Rane Willerslev.

which means "dirty" or "sinful." They also say that predators are "children of the devil" *(chërtevy deti)*. Similarly, a human person who kills recklessly and ignores the rituals intended to secure the proper circulation of game is called "a son of the devil" *(chërtov syn)*. The devil is said to be careless. He has no sense of either past or future but lives only in the present, and he is therefore incapable of feeling any sense of responsibility for his actions.[3] This was what Ivan was referring to when he was overcome with anxiety, claimed that we were becoming like the devil, and said we should seek to calm ourselves in the cabin for a while before going out to hunt again.

I did not encounter any other firsthand experiences of such transformations, but the notion of different species taking on each other's appearance and perspective is found in many Yukaghir myths. One finds a whole series of stories in which members of the giant cannibal tribe Cou'liye (Mystical Old People) turn themselves into nice-looking lads to seduce Yukaghir women and eat them.[4] These cannibalistic nonhumans call their intended human victims their "elk" or "reindeer" (Jochelson 1900: 31; 1926: 302–3; Spiridonov 1996 [1930]), so they address and experience human beings as animal prey, just as the human hunter does his prey. However, we also find stories in which the giant cannibals abandon their own communities to live among their new host species. Jochelson (1926) recorded one such story, in which a giant cannibal boy marries a Yukaghir girl and lives with her human kinsmen. However, the transformed cannibal cannot entirely forget about his desire for human flesh, and once, while lying in bed with his wife, he touches her breasts and says, "My late father used to feed me with such things" (1926: 304). The wife becomes worried and tells the rest of the camp about the episode. The people agree that the former cannibal is not entirely transformed and so they kill him. However, since they have in fact killed one of their own, that is, a relative, they have committed a grave sin. As a result, the Sun deity punishes them by taking away their fire, and they all freeze to death.[5]

The implications of transformation are also strikingly revealed in another story recorded by Jochelson (1900: 24–25). It concerns two girls who set out to take revenge on an old man called Lower Jaw, who had killed their parents. Simply by moving on their hands and knees like wolves the girls turned into these predators. After they had killed the old man and his son, they ate the flesh of their victims. Cannibalism is normally seen by Yukaghirs as a terrible sin that leads to punishment from either God or the Sun deity (Jochelson 1926: 304). In this case, however, it was apparently acceptable, on the grounds that the girls were in a transformed state of being and thus subscribed to the moral code of wolves rather than that of humans. The story ends with the girls taking on their human shapes and living ordinary human lives again.

However, there are also stories in which humans undergo a complete metamorphosis, never to return to their ordinary human forms. A Yukaghir woman, Akulina Shalugina, told me one such story about a mother who found it too difficult to raise her two naughty children. She clothed them in goose feathers and took them to a female goose, with the hope that the bird would have more success in making her children obedient. When after some time she returned to reclaim her children, they became afraid. They regarded her as a human predator and escaped. When autumn came, the children left with their fellow geese for the south, only to return the following spring. Akulina ended her story by saying that the poor mother remained alien to her children and could observe them only from a distance.

"NOT ANIMAL–NOT *NOT* ANIMAL"

I suggest that these and similar stories support my earlier point about the way in which so-called "perspectival" notions form an essential part of Yukaghir animism. In his article on Amerindian perspectivism, Viveiros de Castro argues that it is an ontology that converts Western ideas about "uni-naturalism" and "multi-culturalism" into very non-Western ones of "uni-culturalism" and "multi-naturalism" (1998: 470). While Western ontology is founded on a belief in "the unity of nature and the plurality of cultures," perspectivism is founded on a "spiritual unity and a corporeal diversity" (1998: 470): "The ability to adopt a point of view is undoubtedly a power of the soul . . . but the differences between viewpoints . . . [are] given in the specificity of bodies. . . . Animals see in the *same* way as we do *different* things because their bodies are different from ours" (1998: 478; emphasis in the original). Thus, he claims, species persons, human as well as nonhuman, can travel to and from bodies but remain essentially the same. This is precisely because the "point of view" that one adopts is a function of the particular body in which one has taken up residence and not of a particular life essence or soul, which is understood to be the same for human and nonhuman persons alike (1998: 478).

Although Viveiros de Castro succeeds in conceptually identifying perspectivism as a particular type of ontological way of being-in-the-world, it remains an abstract model, detached from the real experiences of people in a lifeworld.[6] This is not to deny that people may think abstractly, but even the most abstract domain, our imagination, has its basis in our bodily being-in-the-world—that is, the world in which we exist and act before we begin to theorize about it in order to explain our experience and the forms it takes. What I am arguing, in other words, is that we need to go beyond our anthropological preference for abstract representations to their roots in the concreteness of everyday perceptual experience. This is certainly true with regard to Yukaghir hunters, for whom, as I shall describe in chapter 8, an understanding of the world is *not* grounded in abstract contemplation, but emerges from concrete contexts of practical engagement. They have a clear preference for the concrete and experiential (doing) over the abstract and theoretical (saying).

Hence, their perspectivist representations, as we find them expressed in myths and other types of discourse, are not just intellectual constructs but are in a significant sense *practical,* inseparably bound up with the hunting activity in which they are engaged. The challenge, it seems to me, is therefore to bring perspectivism "down to earth," as it were, and situate it in its primary context of hunters' actual perceptual engagement with prey. Taking this condition of engagement as a point of departure, I believe that we can find a way to place Yukaghir conceptions of such matters as human-animal transformations in the lived-in world of experience instead of simply attributing them to some overarching cosmological principle.

An appropriate point at which to begin an investigation of this topic is the important element of risk involved when traveling between one's own body and an alien one. Transformation is not something that can be done easily, and it involves an experience of deeply felt anxiety of self-alienation, or what I referred to earlier as losing one's sense of human personhood. Thus, an element of self-awareness or reflexivity is crucial for protecting oneself against being carried away by an alien body. In the story above, we saw how the reindeer-man made tracks in the shape of reindeer hooves despite his human appearance. Similarly, the fox-woman is said to retain her strong smell, and the bear-man can be recognized by his jog-trot way of moving (cf. Riordan 1989: 196–201; Bogoras 1904–9: 284). It is imperative for humans and animals, when changing bodies, to retain some of their former physical qualities, which identify them as beings of a special class who act in a manner similar to, but not altogether identical with, their host species. People who have taken on the body of a species other than their own, therefore, do not simply become copies of the host species. At least, they are not what we could call faithful copies, whereby body parts correspond directly to other body parts. Instead, they are imperfect copies of the host species. It follows from this that what the Yukaghirs strive for is not to adopt the point of view of a nonhuman person in an absolute sense, because this would mean actually becoming the animal, and, as we have seen, this should be avoided at all costs. Rather, Yukaghirs attempt to assume an animal's point of view by intentionally acting as an imperfect copy. All performances in alien kinds of bodies, therefore, share a kind of double negation: the person is not the species he is imitating, but he is also not *not* that species (cf. Schechner 1985). Taking on an alien body, therefore, does not imply making one person into another in any absolute sense. Rather, it permits a person to act in between identities. It gives him a new potential for action, as he is freed from the bodily limits of both his own species and those of the species imitated.

This makes sense when we realize that Yukaghirs do not take on the bodies of animals just to represent them, but to attempt to manipulate the world around them. Often they aim to trick prey by means of its own image—what in Frazer's terms is known as "sympathetic magic," whereby "the magician infers that he can produce any effect he desires merely by imitating it" (Frazer 1993 [1922]: 11). However, what Frazer never explains is why a resemblance between the copy and the original should grant the representation power over the represented. He describes sympathetic magic as a mistaken form of causal thinking, similar to a scientific theory, but grounded in error. He simply evades the question of why sympathetic magic persists if the expected results do not materialize, and he attributes its persistence merely to wrongheadedness and conservatism on the part of the "savages" (Tambiah 1990: 46).

In his book about the "mimetic faculty," Taussig (1993) argues that the basis of sympathetic magic is not a tragic misunderstanding of the nature of physical causality, but is instead founded on a particular way of perceiving things, objects, and people outside ourselves. To mimic something is to be sensuously filled with that which is imitated, yielding to it, mirroring it—and hence imitating it bodily. It is, he claims, a particularly powerful way of understanding, representing, and controlling the surrounding world: "The wonder of mimesis lies in the copy drawing on the character and the power of the original, to the point whereby the representation may even assume that character and that power" (1993: xiii).

What I find particularly valuable in Taussig's account is his insightful observation that mimesis collapses such dichotomies as self versus other, nature versus culture, and essentialism versus constructionism (1993: 252). "It plays the trick of dancing between the very same and the very different" (p. 129), "between the real and the really made-up" (p. xvii). The important point for my argument, which can be inferred from this, is that the manipulating power that is present in hunters' imitation of prey rests in their dual capacity to incorporate its "otherness" while in some profound sense remaining the same. Let me illustrate this point. When a hunter mimics the elk to bring it into the open so that he can shoot at it, he acts simultaneously within two motivational spaces, which could be called "the space of predatory mastery" and "the space of animal imitation." The first has to do with the hunter's intention of killing the animal, the second with his need to take on its identity in order to fulfill that intention. The hunter, we might say, acts with a dual nature: he is both hunter and animal. To act in between these two identities is a highly complex task. If he lets his intentions as a hunter show through his actions, the prey animal will either run or attack him.[7] If, on the other hand, he allows his intentions to merge with his bodily movements (which are that of an elk), he will surrender to the perspective of prey and turn into it. The hunter therefore needs to be aware not only of the prey animal, but also of himself being aware of the prey, in order to make sure that his perspective is neither that of a hunter nor that of the animal, but instead somewhere in between or both at once. In other words, the success of the hunter depends upon his ability to keep up a double perspective, or act as a mimetic agent.

MIRRORING OF PERSPECTIVES

Under normal conditions, a person's body is not perceived by that person as an object in the world, a thing that he or she can encounter or straightforwardly observe. Rather, it is an object only from the perspective of another, in the same way as another's body is an object from the perspective of the ego. At least this is the argument of Sartre (2000 [1958]: 304), who, as we have seen, holds that the body as "subject" is ontologically disjunct from the body as "object." In other words, either I am an object for a subject, or that subject is an object for me, but both cannot be true at once. However, I wish to argue that, in the situation of the hunter mimicking his prey, this conceptual distinction between subject, "the body I am," and object, "the animal's body," dissolves, and that the hunter comes to experience his own body as well as the body of the animal ambiguously as both subject and object, self and other.

As we observed with Spiridon in chapter 1, when a hunter is approaching an elk he wears wooden skis covered on their undersides with the smooth skin from the leg of an elk so as to imitate the sound of the animal when moving in the snow (see figure 7). In addition, he will move his body like an elk, shifting from side to side in a waddling manner. During my fieldwork I saw this imitation-based hunting technique practiced several times, and in fact I learned to practice it myself with some success. Provided that the hunter's mimetic performance is convincing and vivid, the elk will leave its hiding place between the trees and bushes and begin to walk toward the hunter, apparently taking him for one of its own kind.[8] The two parties will thus approach one another, each imitating the actions of the other. The question is, what goes on in the head of the hunter during this act of mimicry? It is difficult to say, as

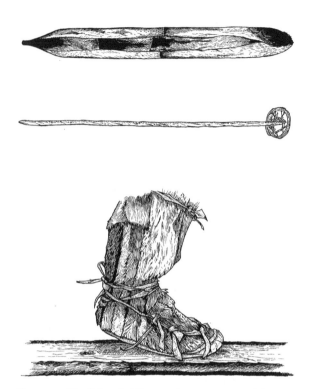

Figure 7. Traditional skiing equipment: top, a ski
(23 cm wide, 2 m long); middle, a ski pole; bottom, a
hunter's ski, covered on the underside with the smooth
leg skin from an elk in order to imitate the sound of the
animal when moving over snow. Drawings by Marie
Carsten Pedersen.

direct questioning about such matters often proved fruitless. One hunter,
for example, replied, "This is your matter, not mine. We bring you out
here so that you can find out for yourself what it is like." However,
other hunters would argue that the encounter with the elk is like meeting
a loved one or an honored friend. What this suggests, I believe, is that
this key moment during the hunt can be considered as providing, in some
fundamental fashion, the experiential ground for the hunters' perspectival representations. For what takes place, it seems to me, is in fact a
reciprocal mirroring of perspectives.[9] While the elk sees its body through
the hunter's act of mimicry—that is, it sees its own species kind—the
hunter sees the reflected image of his own body through the acts of the
elk, mimicking his acts of mimicry. In other words, the hunter does not
just see the elk walking toward him, but he also sees himself from the

"outside," as if he himself were the elk—that is, he adopts toward himself the kind of perspective that the other (as subject) has of him (as object). By this I do not mean that a metamorphosis occurs. This would require that the hunter surrender to the single perspective of the (subject) elk, and that is the inherent danger of the game, against which one must be eternally on guard. Rather, the hunter's double perspective suggests a kind of optical oscillation in which "he as subject seeing the elk as object" and "he seeing himself as object being seen by the elk as subject" shift back and forth with such rapidity that the interspecies boundary is affected and some degree of "union" is experienced.[10]

My point is that, as a result of experiencing this duality of looking at and being looked at, of objectifying and being objectified, the hunter will experience the animal as a person with a point of view that is similar to, but not altogether identical with, his own; that is, the animal comes to reside in a paradox of "like-me-but-not-me." Let me clarify this point. We have seen that during the act of mimicry the hunter's human perspective—that is, his awareness as a self-conscious subject that has his own subjective point of view on the world—transcends itself and becomes projected outward onto the elk, which is therefore experienced as taking on his human perspective. At the same time, the hunter himself undergoes an experience of dehumanization: through observing the elk's acts, which mirror his own mimetic performance, he comes to see himself from the outside as an object, from the viewpoint of the other as subject. Accordingly, the hunter's human identity comes to reside in his mimetic double rather than in himself. He can find himself mainly in the elk, which therefore comes to hold the "secret" of what he really is. Paradoxically, then, the hunter cannot easily deny the elk's personhood, because this would in effect mean rejecting his own personhood. Were he, in other words, to think that the elk were just a pure object-in-the-world without powers of intention, consciousness, and emotionality, then he would also deny himself these qualities and would in a sense be left "selfless." The hunter's psychological security, his self-awareness as a person, thus depends on the animal as a person.

Still, the hunter's experienced "humanization" of elk is not complete. The elk's body is perceived from the outside, meaning that it is external and thus somewhat alien to the hunter. The hunter knows, or rather needs to know, that the elk and he are not exactly the same. If this were not the case, he would literally have surrendered to the single perspective of the (subject) elk and have transformed into it. Therefore, the elk is perceived as similar to, but not altogether identical with, the hunter himself.

In other words, what we are dealing with is a strange fusion or synthesis of me and not me into *not* not-me: I am not the elk, but I am also not *not* the elk. Likewise, the elk is not human and yet it is also not *not* human. This fundamental ambiguity of being like yet also being different from the other is, I believe, exactly what we find expressed in Yukaghir narratives in which animals and humans, while taking on each other's bodies, act in a manner similar to, but not altogether identical with, the species impersonated. Moreover, what the hunter encounters in the context of mimicry is not an animal as a unique individual self, but rather an animal as a prototype of a person. That is, the animal is experienced not as a self-sufficient person, but rather as a mirror, vehicle, or channel of personhood. This, I suggest, is why in Yukaghir myths, time and time again, a specific hunter bearing a proper name that is all his own encounters an animal bearing the prototypical name of its species with the somewhat generic suffix "man" or "woman."

METAMORPHOSIS, LOVE, AND SEDUCTION

It is important to note, however, that Yukaghirs do not conceive of the hunter's imitation of the elk as a purely technical manipulation of the environment, but instead tend to see it as the climax of a long process of sexual seduction. This process is set in motion several days before the hunt itself when the hunter attempts to "conquer" his human smell by going to the *banya* (sauna). At this point he also abandons ordinary speech in favor of a special linguistic code that skillfully gets rid of the reality of being a human predator. Thus, allegorical expressions or special terms are employed for animals, which cannot be addressed by their real names. The elk, for instance, is generally referred to as "the big one" (Rus. *bol'shoi*), whereas the bear is called "the barefooted one" (Rus. *bosikom*). The expressions used to announce a hunting trip are also vague and full of double meanings or wordplay. I rarely if ever heard people say, "Let's go hunting for elk." Instead, they would say something like, "Let's take a look at the big one," "I'm going into the forest," or "I'm going for a walk." Likewise, when a hunter comes across an animal's track, he can pass this information along only in coded form. Once, for example, a hunter returned to the encampment and told us that he had seen the footprints of a Russian in *valenki* (felt boots), and that he believed that his cabin was not far away. Our hunting leader replied, "We'll pay him a visit tomorrow." To my surprise, it turned out that what they had actually been talking about was not a Russian but a bear, which had its den nearby. Furthermore, hunters tend not to use the word "kill" (Rus. *ubit'*) in their conversations. Instead, they make a downward movement with their hand, thereby indicating that an animal has fallen to the ground. It is also considered ill advised to sharpen one's knife or clean one's gun on the day of the hunt, as this would expose one's violent intentions and thus cause the seduction to fail.

Moreover, the evening before setting out in search of prey, hunters will sacrifice exotic trade goods to the fire. This "feeding the fire" is seen as an essential part of the process of seduction. Hunters told me that the goods they throw into the fire, especially vodka and tobacco, help to draw the master-spirit into a lustful mood. Moreover, they explained that the alcohol dims the spirit's senses, so that it fails to recognize the true identity of the hunter's *ayibii,* which during his nightly dreams travels to the spirit's house in disguise as an animal. The spirit, which is "blinded" by drunkenness and sexual desire, will perceive the intruder as a harmless lover and a member of the family and the two will jump into bed. The feelings of sexual lust that his *ayibii* evokes in the master-spirit during their nightly intercourse are somehow extended to the spirit's physical counterpart, the animal prey. Thus, when the hunter locates an elk the next morning and starts imitating it, the animal will run toward him in the expectation of experiencing a climax of sexual excitement, and he can shoot it dead. Thus, what we are dealing with is in principle two analogous hunts: the "visible" hunt of the hunter seducing the elk and, preceding this, the "invisible" hunt in which the hunter's *ayibii* seduces the animal's master-spirit. Each is the shadowy mirror image of the other.

I will return to comment on the various phases of the seductive process of the hunt in the following chapters. Here, however, I will mainly reflect on the relationship between mimetic practice and seduction, love, and metamorphosis. Gebauer and Wulf have noted that "seduction depends on lending form; the seducer's weapon is an image. . . . As soon as the object of seduction becomes fascinated by this . . . image she falls under the power of the seducer. . . . Only because the object of seduction desires herself does she let herself be seduced" (1992: 213). Thus, the success of the seducer rests on his ability to create an image of the seduced—which, however, is not an exact image of how his victim experiences herself, but rather an ideal representation, a fantasy image of what she could become. Seduction is in this sense inherently narcissistic. It is rooted in the attraction of like to like, in the mimetic exaltation of one's own image, or rather an ideal mirage of resemblance. Indeed, this

Figure 8. A Yukaghir dressed in traditional hunting clothing.
Photo by Uffe R. Christensen.

seems to be the reason why the Yukaghir hunter's fur clothing traditionally had to be carefully and beautifully made (cf. Chaussonnet 1988:
208–26). When imitating his prey, the hunter would set in motion an
ideal reflection of the animal, which in its turn could not resist submit-
ting to such self-reflection. Even today, items of a hunter's dress (for
example, the ammunition belt) are often highly decorated with bands
and beadwork of different colors. Also, their sheath knives are beautifully ornamented with metalwork. Hunters say that the animal may be
so pleased by what it sees that it "gives itself up" (Rus. *otdat'sya*) to
them.

A slight detour is necessary at this point to obviate any possible misunderstanding. In emphasizing that the animal "gives itself up," Yukaghirs

Figure 9. Hunter's ammunition belt and knife. Drawing by Mads Salicath.

do not mean to suggest that it generously presents itself to be killed by the hunter. Anthropologists often assert that animals are perceived by northern hunters as allowing themselves to be killed if shown proper respect, and are thus seen as assuming a willful part in their own deaths. As Rasmussen puts it with regard to the Inuit, "Animals have in reality no objection to being killed by human beings, as long as the rules of life are observed by the latter. It may even happen, and not infrequently, that an animal will approach a human being, actually desiring to be killed by a particular person" (1929: 58). This is also the view of Sharp (1991) in relation to the Chipewyan Indians of the Canadian boreal forest. He writes, "[They] often explain, in English, the willingness of animals to die, by saying of a specific hunter that 'they like him.' . . . [The Chipewyan] depend upon the willingness of prey species to yield their own physical existence on behalf of the maintenance of human physical existence" (1991: 186, 187).

As Brightman (1993: 189) has appropriately pointed out, ethnographic accounts such as these bear an obvious resemblance to images in Western food industry advertising, which represent animals as being eager to become food or as participating actively in the cooking process. However, I do not know any Yukaghir who would regard this as an accurate representation of the hunter-prey relationship. As a matter of fact, Yukaghirs are very much aware that the interests of prey not only differ from their own, but indeed conflict with them. They clearly express this when they say that, from the animals' point of view, they are the ones who are humans, while human hunters are seen as cannibalistic spirits. Still, the Yukaghirs do have sayings such as, "Only if the elk likes the hunter will he be able to kill it." What they mean to suggest by this, however, is not that the animal willingly gives itself up as food. Rather, the idea is that of sexually exciting the animal so that it draws near enough to be shot. In order to achieve this, the hunter must appear sexually attractive to his prey, and thus friendly and harmless. Indeed, this is why he undergoes the long process of preparation by which his body is modified into the image of the animal. The animal will then come to perceive him not as an evil spirit or a predator, but as a harmless lover and a member of its own species. We might say that the hunter, by taking on his prey's identity and acting in a manner that resonates with its behavior and sensibilities, establishes an empathetic relation with it. Because of this empathy, the animal suspends its disbelief and inherent hostility toward him and "throws" itself at him.

Surely, we ourselves experience the powerful mechanisms of empathy in our everyday lives when, for example, we watch Hollywood romantic comedies. They tend to be concerned with people whose lives are filled with love, with problems caused by love, and with the drive to achieve and retain love. The characters—rich, beautiful, and likeable—establish an empathetic relationship with us as spectators. Through this empathy, we are seduced into abandoning our own universe and incorporate, empathetically, the universe of the characters in the film, and we begin to experience as completely as they do their desire for love, and their propensity to sacrifice everything for love. This occurs no matter how simple and banal the storyline might be, and despite the fact that we may consider ourselves to be "realists," and despite the emotional orgies that the films present.

My point is that empathy functions even when there is an objective conflict of interests, and this is exactly what makes it such an efficient weapon. Animals have no objective desire to yield up their own physical existence on behalf of human beings, but they are manipulated into doing so by the hunter, who, by establishing relations of empathy with his prey, transforms its perception of reality into a manipulated fiction. It follows from this that what the Yukaghirs have in mind when they say that a hunter will be able to kill the elk if it likes him is not the hunter as human predator, but the hunter in his animal disguise, playing his deceitful role as harmless lover.[11]

With these observations in mind, I now return to the issues of seduction, love, and metamorphosis. Seduction, as we have seen, is basically a game in which the seducer, by playing on his victim's narcissistic inclinations, seeks to excite her to the highest pitch, so that she is willing to sacrifice everything to him, even her life.[12] The seducer himself, however, must remain emotionally unavailable. That is, although he needs to show his victim empathy or affection, he should not allow himself to fall in love with her. Love is rather like metamorphosis. It is self-surrender, the consignment of self to another. "The goal of love," write Gebauer and Wulf, "is the broadening of the self, the assimilation of the self to a counterpart" (1992: 287). In this sense, love is very different from seduction, which, at least in its ideal form, is nothing but pretended love on the part of the seducer and vanity on the part of the seduced. The boundary between love and seduction is, nevertheless, uncertain. The game of seduction always runs the risk that real emotions of love will develop between the two parties. Thus, hunters told me how they might feel pity and even love for the animals they kill. However, they always emphasized that such sentiments are dangerous and should be banished. Still, they argued that it does occasionally happen that a hunter becomes so absorbed in some enticing trait or action observed in the elk that he forgets about the task at hand until it is too late and the animal is out of range. They explained failure of this kind as the hunter falling in love with his prey. Consumed by this love, he cannot think about anything else, stops eating, and after a short time dies. His *ayibii*, hunters explained, will then leave the cycle of human rebirth to be reincarnated as an animal and so go off to live with his former prey. This, they said, is the reason why one occasionally comes across an animal that behaves in an extraordinary way. If, for example, an elk walks right into an encampment of hunters, it is likely to be the manifestation of an animal with a human *ayibii*. It retains traces of memory from its former life, which is why it seeks the company of humans. What we might conclude from this, then, is that the actual killing of prey does more than simply provide the hunter with meat. It prevents his game of seduction from transforming into uncontrolled feelings of love for the animal, thus making it possible for him to secure his boundaries and to preserve his human personhood.

MIMETIC EMPATHY AND PERSPECTIVISM

Let us now return to the issue of perspectivism. What I have sought to show is that the perspectivist quality of Yukaghir animism, as expressed in myths and other types of discourse, has a practical side, or at least that these narratives contain within them the traces of a practice. This practice, I have argued, is mimesis, or what might more appropriately be characterized as mimetic empathy. The latter term emphasizes the fact that what we are dealing with is not just some outward mimicry, simulation, or aping, but instead something deeper and more intense, that is, the ability to put oneself imaginatively in the place of another, reproducing in one's own imagination the other's perspective. To say that such adoption of another's perspective is imagined suggests that I cannot experience another's viewpoint directly. I can only take it up in an imaginative manner, because to see the world through another's eyes in an original fashion would require that I actually inhabit the other's body. I can therefore never know for certain what the world is like from the viewpoint of another being. However, by mimicking another's bodily behavior, senses, and sensibilities empathetically, I can assume the quality of the other's perspective, because although the experiences that I come to share with the other through the practice of mimetic empathy are imagined as shared, they are not fictive. By this I mean that they are not pure fantasies, but acquire a sense of "reality" through their connection to my lived body. This might be exemplified by my own fieldwork experience, during which I learned to be painfully watchful for tracks and other signs of prey whenever I was out hunting, and during my nightly dreams I occasionally had sexual encounters with spiritual beings. My adoption of a Yukaghir hunter's perspective was not mere representation, but it had a materiality grounded in my bodily experiences of their lifeworld—which, through my mimetic mirroring of their behavior, senses, and sensibilities in day-to-day events and routines, became our shared lifeworld. Mimetic empathy, we might say, then, does not imply simply representation or imagination, but it has a decisively corporeal, physical, and tangible quality from which the former ultimately emerges and from which it derives its "material."

Now, it might be argued that it is one thing to claim that we can understand other humans by empathetically projecting ourselves into their lifeworlds, and quite another to make this claim with regard to other life-forms. Even with regard to fellow humans, our understanding of what it is like to be them can only be partial, and when we move to species whose corporeal nature is very different from our own, it seems obvious that a much lesser degree of understanding will be available. As Vendler (1984) writes, "It requires some imagination to make sense of such positive contexts as: 'Now I understand this jaguar,' or: 'Try to understand my washing machine.' No such effort is needed to appreciate similar contexts about people: It is possible to understand Castro or Gadaffi if one tries" (1984: 203).

Yet it might be easier than we suppose to transcend interspecies barriers with the aid of our embodied imagination. In his well-known paper "What Is It Like to Be a Bat?" Nagel (1997) suggests, "Blind people are able to detect objects near them by a form of a sonar, using vocal clicks or taps of a cane. Perhaps if one knew what that was like, one could by extension imagine roughly what it was like to possess the much more refined sonar of a bat" (1997: 172). I believe that a similar argument can be made with respect to Yukaghir hunters, who undergo a process of corporeal dehumanization in order to be reshaped into the image of their prey. Surely, their understanding of the animal's viewpoint cannot in any way be complete (indeed, they do not intend it to be complete), but I consider it plausible that, when using their own bodily experiences to achieve a vicarious understanding of an animal's experience, they can, at least roughly, form a conception of what it is like to be that animal. In making this claim, I take it for granted that higher mammals, such as the elk, have conscious mental states—a standpoint that is supported by much evidence of animal researchers, as will be pointed out below. Personally, I do not wish to speculate about what, precisely, is the nature of the elk's conscious experience. Following Nagel, I hold simply that "the fact that an organism has conscious experience *at all* means, basically, that there is something it is like to *be* that organism" (1997: 166; emphasis in the original), and it is this "something" that hunters attempt to assume when they project themselves, through practices of mimetic empathy, into the lifeworld of their prey.

In any case, I believe that there is reason to suggest that in mimetic empathy we have found the type of practices that mediate between perspectivism as an abstract cosmological principle and everyday perceptual experience. Without mimetic empathy, perspectivism, as represented in myths and other types of narratives, would bear no resemblance to the world of lived experience, and would be nothing but a cosmological abstraction. Practices of mimetic empathy provide the entrée to the perspective of the other. In fact, this is the closest one can come to experiencing another's point of view without being that other in an absolute sense.

This last point highlights the fact that mimetic empathy registers not only similarity, but also difference. Indeed, feelings of empathy arise precisely because the other's experiences are *not* mine, because we are different beings that, in the face of our dissimilarity, possess similar access to basic bodily and sensory experiences. This recognition of difference as something that is maintained rather than totally annulled is, it seems to me, what distinguishes empathy from uncontrolled feelings of love. Falling in love, as I have already argued, can be experienced as the sacrifice of one's self-being, the surrender of self to another. In this sense, falling in love is closely related to metamorphosis. In mimetic empathy, by contrast, the investment of the self is far shallower and burns at a much lower emotional temperature than in love. It does not involve the dissolution of the whole of me into a counterpart. Rather, when I empathize with someone, I single out particular bodily states, feelings, or conditions in another, which I then reproduce in my imagination. Therefore, while mimetic empathy *does* imply that I identify with another, taking on the other's experience as if it were my own, the boundary between myself and the other, between my experience and that of the other, does not vanish. At its most intense, I might come to occupy an ambivalent position in between identities, but I do not altogether lose sight of my own incarnate being.

It is this aspect of "incomplete copying," inherent in practices of mimetic empathy, which connects it to seduction as an instrument of power. As already described, what the seduced sees in the seducer—the unique object of her attraction—is her *own* seductive, charming self, her lovable self-image. Thus, the game of seduction is essentially mimetic; the one seduced finds herself in the person of the seducer, whom she is therefore compelled to embrace mimetically. However—and this is the key point—for the seducer to succeed, he is *not* supposed to create a truthful mirror image of how his victim sees herself, but instead an ideal representation or a fantasy image of what she could become. This, in turn, causes the seduced to desire this image and to do everything possible to obtain it. In other words, the seducer has to act as an ideal reflection of the seduced, that is, as an *incomplete* copy of her, and practices of mimetic empathy, as we have seen, provide him with this ability to be like, yet also different from, his victim.

Among Yukaghirs, the hunter's encounter with the elk is the ultimate example of such mimetic empathy, but it is also strikingly apparent in Yukaghir dancing and singing. Jochelson writes, "The dances of the modern Yukaghir represent a mixture of the circle dance of the Tungus, with movements mimicking animals . . . sometimes interrupted by a guttural rattle and by other sounds in imitation of the cries of various animals. . . . This . . . discloses how carefully the Yukaghir observe the ways of animals. It is performed with great vivacity and grace" (1926: 129–

39). In one dance, for example, the participants mimic male swans paying court to the females while imitating the sounds with which the birds
call to each other in the mating season. Unfortunately, I did not under-
take an in-depth study of Yukaghir dancing during my fieldwork. I now
regret this, because such a study might have provided a clue to female
experiences of animals as persons. Although women are no longer
directly engaged in hunting (as I shall describe below), they are often very
keen dancers. Thus, there is reason to believe that it is roughly in the
lived experience of dancing that Yukaghir women's perspectival notions
are situated.

Another field in which we observe the empathetic imitation of animals
is in trapping, where the hunter, as I have described, tries to think like the
sable. However, the impact of trapping on hunters' experiences of animals as persons with a (subjective) point of view is, I believe, less intense
compared with elk and reindeer hunting. This is because in trapping the
animal is taken while the hunter is far removed in time and place. It does
not, then, involve the same physical, sensual, and emotional connection
between the hunter and his prey as in elk and reindeer hunting, in which
the hunter uses his own body to experience vicariously an animal's perspective. This difference between the two hunting techniques might be
one of the reasons why hunters tend to conceptualize the elk and the
reindeer as being closer to human persons than the animals that are
trapped for their fur, the sable, fox, wolverine, and wolf.

Moreover, in the minds of hunters at least, chance plays a greater role
in trapping than in hunting. Hunters talk about trapping not in terms of
sexual seduction but as a "game of cards" (Rus. *kartochnaia igra*). The
spirits of the forest, they say, are constantly playing cards with one
another. Their stakes are the sable and other fur-bearing animals, which
may have to pass from one animal master to another when the game is
over. This accounts for the sables' highly unpredictable and ever-chang-
ing migration routes. Likewise, having a number of well-placed traps is
referred to as "holding a good hand of cards" (Rus. *khoroshii rasklad
kart*). Furthermore, the dreams of hunters while trapping tend not to be
of a sexual nature, as during elk and reindeer hunting, but deal instead
with receiving gifts of money from the spirits. A young hunter, for example, explained to me that when going trapping, the spirits come to him in
dreams and give him rubles. If they give him coins, he always asks them
for bills, because the amount of money given indicates the number of
sable he will catch.

In any case, the point I want to stress is that when both hunting and trapping, the aim of the hunter is not to become an animal and adopt its point of view absolutely. Rather, the hunter uses acts of mimesis to achieve a double perspective that allows him to assume the point of view of his prey while still remaining a human person with the intention of killing it. Thus, perspectivism among Yukaghirs is not really about moving from one point of view to another. Rather, it is about not surrendering to a single point of view. It is concerned with action in between identities, in that double negative field that I have characterized as not animal, not *not* animal.

HUNTING AND SEX

But how are we to understand the linkage between hunting and sex, and the apparent assimilation of animal prey as an erotic object, which the link implies? This translation of hunting into a sexual act is by no means unique to the Yukaghirs, but is widely reported among other groups of hunter-gatherers from the circumpolar north (Tanner 1979; Brightman 1993; Saladin d'Anglure 2001), across the Amazon (Århem 1996; Reichel-Dolmatoff 1971) and Africa (Guenther 1999; Morris 2000: 112), and in Southeast Asia (Valeri 2000: 317).[13] Take, for example Reichel-Dolmatoff's classic account of hunter-prey relations among the Tukano of the Colombian Amazon: "The relationship between man the hunter and his prey has . . . a marked erotic component. The hunt is practically a courtship and a sexual act. . . . The verb to hunt, *vaí-merä gametarári*, [is] translated as 'to make love to animals.' . . . [The hunter] is always conscious of the erotic aspect and the essentially sexual relationship that unites him and his prey. . . . When I asked if the hunter felt sexually excited, the informant answered dryly: 'to kill is to cohabit.' " (1971: 220, 225)

One of the most influential approaches for exploring the connection between sex and violence is the psychoanalytic theory that love and rage, desire and hatred become entwined at a deep psychological level through the infantile experience of absolute dependence on the mother (this also explains, or claims to explain, why women are prototypical objects of both desire and violence). However, this approach has been heavily criticized by feminist scholars such as Cameron and Frazer (1994), who write, "there are different forms of violence with differing histories and meanings, and the assumption that all of them have the same ultimate source in the infant's contradictory impulses towards her mother seems to us hopelessly reductive and unrevealing" (1994: 168). I tend to agree with their criticism. Even if, for the sake of argument, we were to take it as axiomatic that violence and sexuality are inescapably conflated, this would tell us little or nothing about the processes whereby the potential for eroticized violence is taken up in specific cultural practices, such as in Yukaghir hunting.

Perhaps this is the reason students of hunter-gatherers have largely refrained from taking on board the psychoanalytic argument, but instead ascribe to a Durkheimian model in which the sexual imaginary of hunting is seen as modeled on relationships between men and women within the human social domain, so that the hunter is said to relate to his prey as a man to his wife or female lover (see, e.g., Tanner 1979: 136; Århem 1996: 192). Also, among the Yukaghirs there seems to have been a neat correspondence between how hunters conceptualized their relations with prey and their relations with potential female lovers back in the village. As Jochelson writes:

> Any one who remains for some time in a Yukaghir village at the present time may observe the free intercourse that prevails among young people before marriage. . . . A girl, having reached the age of puberty, is given a separate sleeping-tent, and becomes quite free to receive visitors. When the lights in the houses of the Yukaghir are put out and the people retire, the youths quietly leave their homes and find their way to the tents of the neighbouring girls. Unmarried young men very rarely pass the nights at their own homes. Certainly these visits are mostly founded on the mutual attraction of the young persons; but cases of unfaithfulness are frequent. The vacant place of a youth who has left the village for a hunt or to fish, is at once occupied by another one. When a young man finds a rival in the girl's tent, he compels him to come out and fight. The vanquished one goes off home, and the conqueror re-enters the tent. In olden times, according to the tales of the Yukaghir, rivals used to go away from the tents, and fight until one or the other was killed. (Jochelson 1926: 62–63)

From this description, it seems that Yukaghir women had a "sexy" rather than a "reproductive" image (see Collier and Rosaldo 1981: 267) and that a basic theme in Yukaghir society was male sexual rivalry, fired up by the fickleness and sexual manipulativeness of women. We find this imagery repeated in the context of hunting, in which the hunter does everything within his power to attract the favorable attention of his prey, conceived as a female lover who has to be sexually seduced into "giving herself up" to him. Still, it would be quite wrong to see such analogy simply in terms of symbolic schemas, provided by the human social domain for metaphorically constructing hunters' relations with prey. The fact that the traditional gender relations among the Yukaghirs were systematically distorted throughout the Soviet period simply rules out any such Durkheimian model of direct correspondence.

Prior to Soviet rule, Yukaghir men and women lived and worked together. They would spend winter in their permanent homes and follow game migrations in summer and autumn. Thus, the "kinship unit" and the "productive unit" overlapped or were identical. During the 1960s, however, the Soviet authorities made special efforts to sedentarize the women, who were seen as not directly involved in hunting and therefore an "unutilised labour resource" (Vitebsky and Wolfe 2001: 84). They were removed to the village of Nelemnoye, where they were given jobs, such as that of cook, administrator, bookkeeper, and teacher. Since then, virtually all women have lived in the village full-time. Only those who are closely involved with their husbands' work as hunters may join them in the forest for a few weeks during summer and autumn. But there is more involved than just a spatial separation of the genders. Many younger women came to regard the hunters' way of life in the forest as "uncivilized" (Rus. *ne tsivilizóvanoe*) or "uncultured" (Rus. *ne kul'turnoe*), and they started to form temporary or permanent relationships with Russian "frontiersmen" who came to the region in the 1960s and 1970s as skilled laborers (working as radio operators, tractor mechanics, boilermen, etc.). The young Yukaghir men, who as hunters had low status in the eyes of the women, for the most part remained bachelors, either in fact (they stayed unmarried) or else in effect (they lived away from their wives and children for eight to ten months of the year). After the collapse of the Soviet Union in the beginning of the 1990s, the large majority of the Russian workers returned to the cities of European Russia, leaving their native lovers behind.[14] However, although the general economic crises have forced many women once again to take part in subsistence activities, many of them still prefer to live on their own together with their children rather than forming partnerships with local hunters. As reported by Anderson (2000: 199) with regard to Evenki reindeer herders, who face a similar situation, this has lead to much resentment among the young bachelors, who occasionally describe the women as "prostitutes" or "bitches." Even so, the offspring of the Russian-Yukaghir partnerships are generally accepted as "Yukaghir" in the settlement and given the surnames of their mothers.

Originally, I had intended to divide my time in the field equally between the men in the forest and the women in the village, and to explore the interplay between these two domains of Yukaghir existence. However for reasons I explained in the preface, I came to spend considerably more time among male hunters in the bush and thus never got a full picture of present-day gender dynamics within Nelemnoye. However, from what I detected, they appear to be characterized by a kind of conflict and antagonism similar to that recently described among other Siberian indigenous groups (Vitebsky and Wolfe 2001; Kwon 1997; 1993; Anderson 2000: 197–200; Ssorin-Chaikov 2003: 182–93), and which I have briefly outlined above. However, to further develop this argument would require deeper research into the gender relations than that in which I engaged.

The argument I want to pursue here is that at present we are, in effect, dealing with a situation where the sexual imagery of hunting exists quite independently of the social dynamics of society. There is no longer any apparent correspondence between the interaction among the genders in the human lifeworld and the symbolic parallels between hunting and sexual seduction. We therefore need to approach the connection between hunting and sex from a different angle than that of the Durkheimian model. I suggest that perhaps we should consider what it is about the hunter's actual, perceptual experience of hunting that evokes in him feelings of a sexual nature. It seems to me that the mimetic empathy that is manifest in hunting is fundamentally significant. We have seen that, during the mutual imitation of hunter and prey, a momentary transcendence of bodily boundaries occurs. The hunter and the animal identify with each other, so that "me" and "not me" for the moment blur into "*not* not-me*." Accordingly, the hunter comes to experience a crisis of self-image, not only in terms of his species identity, but also in terms of his gender identity: he is neither male nor female, as he is neither human nor animal. He becomes, so to speak, polymorphous. Sexual intercourse affords a similar kind of experience. Here, male and female bodies are locked in an erotic struggle that blends them to a point that makes them of the same kind. That is, otherwise singular bodies collapse into some kind of "erotic polyvalence." As Casey writes with regard to "myself-*cum*-other-in-erotic-interplay-together," "it is difficult to draw any strict dividing line . . . between myself-as-being-touched by the other and the other-as-touching-me. The two of us form a dyadic pair who collaborate in the experience. . . . The members of this dyad are so intimately interlocked that I cannot say for sure where one leaves off and the other begins: the touched and the toucher merge in a phenomenon of interpersonal 'reversibility'" (Casey 1987: 158).

However, as in hunting, this transgression of bodily boundaries during sex can be experienced not only as thrilling and exciting but also as somehow intimidating—a rupture of one's bodily autonomy or even a feeling of self-abandonment in the sense of becoming self-less. Indeed, this seems to be the reason why sexual intercourse is often followed by a careful scrutinizing of the partner's body (or one's own body), to make sure that the other is a different being or person after all: "I was looking at everything in the other's face, the other's body, coldly: lashes, toenails, thin eyebrows, thin lips, the luster of the eyes, a mole, a way of holding a cigarette; I was fascinated—fascination being, after all, only the extreme of detachment" (Barthes 1990: 72).

My point is that there is reason to see the linkage between hunting and sexual seduction in quite literal terms; that is to say, perhaps they are sentiments that emerge from the hunter's actual, perceptual engagement with his prey and are not derived metaphorically. Moreover, as long as we follow Durkheim in assuming that hunter-gatherers relate metaphorically with animals and more generally with the natural world, their animist beliefs are bound to be nothing but conceptual projections and therefore not factually true. In other words, indigenous claims about having sexual and other types of relations with nonhuman persons become pure representations, evolving not from the condition that anything such as genuine nonhuman persons exist, but solely from the condition that human societies exist.

HUMANS AND ANIMALS: A DIFFERENCE OF DEGREE

This Cartesian attitude, which takes the qualities of personhood to be the single cutoff point between humans and the rest of the animal kingdom, has faced increasing challenge from evolutionary biologists. In an important book on human-animal relations, Noske (1997: 126–60) reveals how recent ethological studies of a variety of mammals—primates, whales, dolphins, wolves, and elephants—have proven that qualities that we usually consider to be uniquely human, such as sociality, intentionality, self-awareness, tool use, and above all language, are, in fact, found to various degrees in the animal kingdom. She thus reaffirms the essential ideas of Darwin, who more than a hundred years ago wrote, "Some naturalists, from being deeply impressed with the mental and spiritual powers of man, have divided the whole organic world into three kingdoms, the Human, the Animal, and the Vegetable, thus giving to man a separate kingdom. Spiritual powers cannot be compared or classed by the naturalist: but he may endeavour to shew, as I have done, that the mental faculties of man and the lower animals do not differ in kind, although immensely in degree. A difference in degree, however great, does not justify us in placing man in a distinct kingdom" (Darwin 1882: 146–47).

It is possible that such studies of animal behavior, which invalidate a clear-cut phylogenetic boundary between nature and culture, animal and human, can provide anthropology with the solid evidence needed to make a shift away from understanding animism simply as the projection onto nonhuman worlds of the thoughts and feelings that "primitive" people recognize in themselves, and instead see it as based in real empirical knowledge, directly derived from people's actual engagement with their environment. However, the problem is that these ethologists, who set out to free animals from their object status, are themselves trapped in an anthropocentric bias. In asserting *differences of degree,* they cannot help posing a universal scale of progress, in terms of which animals are judged "more" or "less" human (Ingold 1994: 30). Hence, in their attempt to show that human-animal differences are far from absolute and that animals can do things that at least resemble what humans can do, they present animals as somehow "quasi-human" (Noske 1997: 157). However, an animal such as an elk is not an incomplete human, but a complete elk. When compared with us, therefore, it is scarcely surprising that it will not be very good at being human.[15] Even the Yukaghirs recognize this fact when they say that animals, while impersonating humans, retain some of their former species-specific qualities, which identify them as nonhuman persons acting in a human way. The same criticism can be raised against much animal language research, where, as Fudge points out, the conventional question, "can animals learn to speak human language?" in reality needs to be turned on its head, so that that we start asking "can humans learn to speak animal language?" As he writes, "Why is it that our language is primary? Why not attempt communication in the other direction. If we are so superior, surely we should be able to speak ape. . . . We judge things on the basis of whether or not they are like us; and they fail on that basis too. This hardly seems a fair contest" (Fudge 2002: 128, 138). Basically, the researchers of animal behavior face a dilemma in that they cannot impose upon animals either object or *human-subject* status, and yet there seems to "exist in [their] thinking little room for the notion of a non-human Subject and what this would imply" (Noske 1997: 157).

HOW TO UNDERSTAND ANIMAL PERSONHOOD

How, then, are we to come to grips with the claim of Vasili Shalugin and other Yukaghirs that elk and other animals are "people like us?" Are we to understand Yukaghir animism as a figurative use of categories pertaining to the human social domain to conceptualize the domain of nonhumans, as the sociocentric models of the Durkheimian tradition would have it? Alternatively, are Yukaghirs simply pointing to what biologists are now starting to realize: that the human-animal discontinuity is far from absolute? I believe that neither is the case and that something very different is at issue.

First, I shall argue that there is no such thing as Yukaghir perception with a capital "P," based on a central unifying principle—what Durkheim called "the elements of the social structure" (1976). Among Yukaghirs, as among other groups, perception is a plural phenomenon, not a unitary one. There are different modes of perception, and the animist framework provides only one of several ways of perceiving animals and the environment. When, for example, a hunter is buying his yearly hunting license from Russian or Sakha officials in the regional center of Zyrianka, he talks about elk and reindeer not as persons but simply as material entities to be killed and consumed. Likewise, when he is evaluating the cost of furs with fellow hunters or traders, sable and other fur-bearing animals are discussed purely in terms of their marketing criteria: fur color, density, and size. In contrast, when chasing prey, hunters often relate to animals as persons who have distinctive modes of behavior, temperaments, and sensibilities that the hunters take into account in their practical dealings with them.

The same animal—an elk, for instance—thus has a quite different meaning depending on the context in which it is experienced. It is not, as Durkheim would have it, that regularities in social organization provide an overarching animist cosmological schema for perception in general. Rather, different frameworks of perception flourish side by side, and the same individual will move in and out of those frameworks depending on the context. I should therefore move at once to correct the misleading idea to which the "-ism" in "animism" is apt to give rise, namely, that the term refers to a coherent cosmological schemata for perception in general. Among the Yukaghirs—and, I suspect, among other hunter-gatherers, too—animism is nothing of the sort. Rather, it is a particular way of perceiving animals and the environment that is brought into play in specific contexts of practical activities. Outside these particular contexts of close involvement with prey, Yukaghirs do not experience animals as persons any more than we do, but instead live in a world of ordinary objects in which the distinction between human subjects and nonhuman objects is much more readily drawn. This is exactly the reason why Old Spiridon would deny elk and other animals personhood when I interviewed him in the village, yet, when hunting in the forest, he would talk about them as intentional subjects with powers of language and sociality. In short, for hunters, the person status of animals is context-dependent. It is within situations of actual, perceptual engagement with prey that nonhuman entities are experienced as persons.

This leads me to my second point, which has to do with the concept of the person as it is understood among the Yukaghirs versus among Western scientists. Among the latter, personhood is usually discussed in relation to permanent dispositional characteristics of particular entities: "Here is X. Is it a person or not?" The answer is, "That depends on whether X has intentions, consciousness, language abilities, etc." (Gell 1998: 21). The question of personhood is thus brought up in a purely classificatory context, as all the things in the world are classified as those that are valid as persons and those that are not, based on intrinsic properties that they may or may not possess in common. This classificatory exercise gives rise to the familiar tree diagrams of taxonomy, with their roots in the lower, most inclusive levels and reaching up to higher levels of ever-finer discrimination (Ingold 2000: 138–39). While mainstream animal scientists believe in the existence of only one such class of persons, namely the human kind, a few—those who argue for a difference of degree between humans and animals—would add some of the higher mammals to a lower class of persons. In both cases, however, humans and animals are compared by virtue of their essential natures, irrespective of their position with respect to one another. This way of thinking of personhood—as something totally self-sufficient, without the need of any mediation of the real world of others—has its roots in Cartesianism, which lies deep in Western thinking.

For Yukaghir hunters, however, personhood is not understood in anything like this manner. For them, personhood is innate only in the sense that all entities in their environment are considered *potential* persons by virtue of their shared inner essence, *ayibii*, which provides them with similar rational capacities. Whether or not an entity *actually* reveals itself as a person depends on the context in which it is placed and experienced. I have especially focused on one such context: the mutual imitation of hunter and elk (other contexts, such as dreaming, will be added in the following chapters). A critical feature of this example is that the hunter recognizes himself in the image of the animal and therefore is forced to see it as a person. The personhood of the elk, in other words, is not experienced as a property of the animal as such, but of its position within the relational field of mutual mimicry. In fact, the hunter's experience of the animal as a person is highly ambiguous. He cannot say for certain that the elk really is a person, with a (subjective) point of view, but due to the situation of mutual mimicry in which he is caught up, he cannot afford not to regard it as such, because, in denying it powers of consciousness, intentionality, and emotionality, he would, by the same stroke, deny himself these qualities. This, however, does not mean that the elk's personhood can be reduced to a simple projection of the hunter's own personhood onto the animal, because, as we have seen, his experience of the animal as a person, with a perspective similar to his own, is fundamentally conditioned by its capacity to "act back," or rather interact with him. It is because the elk starts to imitate him imitating the animal that the "snare for thought" is created and the hunter is forced to see the elk as a person. Therefore, the animal's personhood results from the coming together of the hunter's own awareness as a person and his experience of the prey animal acting as a reflection of his own body, or as his double. In short, we are by no means dealing with the classificatory sense of the person as a "thing-in-itself" or with a downright metaphorical projection of human consciousness onto nonhuman entities. Rather, in the world of Yukaghirs, entities gain personhood by virtue of being practically bound up together within specific contexts of real-world engagement.

I shall take this point to an even more fundamental level of analysis in chapter 8, where I deal with hunters' knowledge about the more "imaginary" creatures of their environment, the spirits. For now, however, we shall attend to the institution most commonly associated with animistic beliefs and practices, namely shamanism.

CHAPTER 6

Shamanism

YUKAGHIR SHAMANSHIP

The word *shaman* has become one of the most heavily worked terms among scholars of anthropology and religious studies. *Shaman, shamanism,* and *shamanship* are also terms with a major presence within neo-religious movements all over the world. What are we to understand by this word *shaman,* which originated in Siberia, but which has come to be applied much more widely to those people in tribal societies throughout the world who are otherwise known as medicine men, witch doctors, sorcerers, or magicians?[1] The notion that shamans constitute an early type of priesthood is common in the classical literature on the topic. This is the view of Eliade (1964), for example, in his widely read work on shamanism, in which he uses the phrase *religious elite* interchangeably with *shaman,* thereby reducing a very diverse and complex set of phenomena to an ideal type of religious expert. Soviet scholars also adopted the idea of shamans as representatives of an embryonic priesthood, classifying them alongside churchmen. The appearance of shamans, they argued, had been part of the process by which "primitive Communism" was destroyed by a more hierarchical form of society (Anisimov 1963; Vdovin 1978; Mikhailov 1990). Indeed, this interpretation of shamanism as being interlinked with abuse and exploitation provided the historiography needed for the Soviet campaign to eradicate shamans in Siberia.

In this chapter I shall provide a very different view on shamanism.

Referring to the hunter's experience of merging with his prey, which closely resembles the experience of the shaman during his ritual performances, I suggest that shamanism among the Yukaghirs should be understood as a broad-based activity practiced to varying degrees by common hunters rather than as a form of "mysticism" under the control of a religious elite. Before beginning my analysis, however, it needs to be said that the information that I succeeded in obtaining on shamanism is both limited and fragmented, and I have nothing like a complete picture of the Yukaghir shamans' various practices and their importance in social and religious life. The main reason for this is that there are no living shamans among the present-day Yukaghirs, and there have not been since the 1970s, when the last one is said to have died. Hence, I could not make any firsthand observations and was restricted to writing down the accounts of people who attended a shamanistic performance in their youth. What is more, I soon realized that eyewitness reports of former shamans and their practices were extremely difficult to obtain since people systematically avoided the topic. It was not unusual, for example, that an old man or woman whom I was told had a shaman among his or her relatives would refuse to discuss the matter with me, claiming to "know nothing" or "not remember anything."

I can only speculate about the reasons for this, but I assume that it results from a combination of factors. First, there is the historical impact of the Russian Orthodox mission, which launched its first crusade in northeastern Siberia at the beginning of the eighteenth century (Slezkine 1993: 17). Although the mission had rather limited success in converting the indigenous peoples as a whole to Christianity, its influence is very apparent among the Yukaghirs, even after seventy years of communism.[2] Thus, despite the fact that virtually none of the present-day Yukaghirs has been baptized, reads the Bible, or has even encountered a priest, many still carry crucifixes and claim to be Orthodox Christians. Likewise, I would occasionally hear hunters appeal to either God, Jesus, or some Orthodox saint for luck in hunting—a practice that was also noticed by Jochelson, who writes, "At the present the saints of the Orthodox Church . . . are to some extent rivaling the ancient Yukaghir 'masters.' Thus, St. Nicholas is considered the protector of quadrupeds and St. Peter that of fishes" (1926: 63). The impact of Christianity is also evident in the Yukaghirs' attitude toward the former shamans. Several of the old people to whom I spoke referred to the shaman by the Russian word *satana,* meaning "Satan," a view that they probably adopted from the Orthodox priesthood, who deemed the spirits addressed by the shamans to be devils and the shamans themselves to be devil worshipers (Jochelson 1926: 162). In addition, an elderly woman told me that before beginning a shamanic ritual, people used to take off their crosses and turn representations of the Orthodox saints toward the wall in order to prevent them from frightening away the shaman's helping spirits.

In addition to the impact of Christianity is that of communism. It is important to point out that no Yukaghir shaman, nor any other person from Nelemnoye for that matter, was ever the subject of concerted persecution during Stalin's antireligion and anti-*kulak* (rich peasant) campaigns of the 1930s and 1940s,[3] as were shamans in many other parts of Siberia. The reason for this, I believe, is that the Yukaghirs in general, and the Upper Kolyma Yukaghirs in particular, came to occupy a special place in the Soviet imagination. Because they had no domesticated herds of animals, because their social relations were largely egalitarian, with females playing a great role in decision making, and because no "suppressive" traditions, such as bridewealth, existed among them, Soviet intellectuals came to see them as a sort of contemporary prototype of a largely "classless society," packed, as it were, with "survivals" from the "primitive communist formation." Moreover, the fact that the Yukaghirs were on the verge of extinction and heavily oppressed by their much more stratified neighbors made them the exploited native underclass par excellence. Thus, in the massive ethnographic work *The Peoples of Siberia (Narody Sibiri),* originally published by the Russian Academy of Sciences in the mid-1950s, the Yukaghirs are described as follows: "there was, on the average, only one gun and one net at the disposal of three Yukagir families. They had neither reindeer nor dogs. A hunter departing to hunt had to be outfitted in warm clothing collected from several people, who remained at home in light suede clothing, or without any. The steps taken by the local [tsarist] government were inadequate and placed the Yukagirs in a position of dependence on the Yakut upper classes, which already held the Yukagirs in a state of debt peonage" (Stepanova, Gurvich, and Khramova 1964: 790). Moreover, "Within the [Yukaghir] encampment there were many survivals of primitive-communal relations. Thus, the hunter's quarry—the carcass of the meat animal he killed—was distributed among all the residents. The hunter's family received an equal share, and only the pelt went to the man who killed the animal" (1964: 796).

So, although the Yukaghirs were considered among the least advanced of all the native northerners along the Marxist scale of historical progress, they were also the purest, simplest, and most socialist in character. It was even suggested that, just as they lacked a class system, they had no shamans of their own, although they used those from neighboring peoples (Spiridonov 1996 [1930]).

Because of their somewhat privileged status as "aboriginal communists," the Yukaghirs were by and large saved from the ubiquitous processes of systematic persecution that marked the Stalin era, as many anthropologists and historians working with Siberian indigenous peoples have stressed (Grant 1993: 100; Vitebsky 1997; Humphrey 1998: 414; Ssorin-Chaikov 2001). This, however, is not to say that the antireligion campaigns of the 1930s and 1940s had no impact on the Yukaghirs' attitude toward shamanism. In the Soviet propaganda of this period the shaman, like the Orthodox priest, was generally presented as a charlatan who purposefully deceived and cheated his fellow men in order to live luxuriously at their expense (Forsyth 1994: 288–90; Kwon 2000: 44). I encountered this perception among a number of old people, especially those who had been active members of the Communist Party. For example, when I asked the former leader of Nelemnoye's collective farm, an old Yukaghir named Alexsei Dyachkov, if he had ever come across any shamans, he answered, "No, but if I meet one, I'll beat him and throw him in the river. They are nothing but vicious showmen and conjurors."

Unlike the Sakha, who believe that one of a person's three souls, the *yör*, hangs around in the Middle World to afflict its living relatives with sickness and misfortune, and who therefore avoid abandoned camps and burial grounds, the Yukaghirs are not normally afraid of their deceased. However, with respect to the ghosts of their dead shamans, they expressed much unease. In the words of my informant Vasili Shalugin, "You know that I'll do anything to help you. I don't keep any secrets from you. But I can't talk about the shamans. It'll put both of us in great danger. In Yukaghir, we call a dead shaman *le'nde a'lma*, which means 'the eating shaman.' He can kill people just for mentioning his name."

Thus, the old people among the Yukaghir have all kinds of reasons for not wanting to talk openly about the former shamans or to reveal what they know about them. Nevertheless, over time I succeeded in collecting a number of personal accounts that might help us shed light on the character of Yukaghir shamanism. Before presenting my data, however, it is worth summarizing what Jochelson writes about the subject.

In eighteenth-century Yukaghir society each clan had its own shaman who presided over the cult of the ancestor-shaman after whom the clan was named (Jochelson 1926: 163). After his death, the shaman himself found a place in the clan's ancestral cult: his body was cut into pieces, the flesh and bones distributed among members of the clan as amulets, while the skull was placed on a wooden body as a spirit effigy, which was "fed" daily and "asked" for advice by the living clan shaman (1926: 164–65).[4] During the mid-nineteenth century, however, this shaman-ancestor cult entirely disappeared, and when Jochelson carried out his fieldwork at the turn of the twentieth century, only a few old people could vaguely recall it. The modern Yukaghir shamans, Jochelson writes, "have lost their original clan affiliations and have become ordinary professional shamans, like the shamans of the Tungus and Yakut, whose main function is the curing of the sick. Even in matters pertaining to the hunt, the very source of Yukaghir life, the significance of the shaman, as a priest and mediator between the spirits controlling the animals and the hunters, no longer exists" (1926: 168–69). In addition, he states, "At the present time, no women-shamans occur among the Yukaghir [and] women-shamans are nowhere mentioned in the folklore" (1926: 193).

The information I succeeded in collecting not only adds to but also opposes Jochelson's account on several central issues. First, there is much evidence to suggest that, as a direct response to devastating epidemics of smallpox, measles, and other European diseases, which killed native peoples in the thousands, a class of so-called "professional" shamans arose all over Siberia during the nineteenth century. They were not attached to any social group in particular and, as Czaplicka suggests (1914: 167; see also Vdovin 1978: 409; Hutton 2001: 118), they served a wide circle of clients and lived mainly on their earnings from fighting outbreaks of disease. But my data clearly reveal that, at least among the Yukaghirs, a type of "family" or "household" shamanism also existed. In fact, these family shamans eventually outlived the professional ones. While the latter virtually disappeared with the consolidation of Soviet power in the 1930s, I was told that the family shamans, including both female and practitioners, continued to perform, at least occasionally, until some time in the mid-1960s. This group of shamans, however, was not clearly distinguishable from ordinary people. Outside their role as shamans they participated in everyday work such as hunting and fishing. Moreover, they tended to serve only their kinsmen and did not receive payment for practicing their art. In fact, many of them did not even possess drums or any special dress. In this respect, it seems, they were rather similar to the shamans of the Chukchi, who, Bogoras tells us, "have nothing similar to the well-known type of coat covered with fringes and images" (1904–9: 457–58). What is more, while the family shamans would occasionally engage in healing and the curing of diseases, this was mainly left to the professional shamans. Instead, the main role of the family shamans was related to their expertise in hunting magic: when hunting luck deserted the group and famine set in, they would use their magical powers to compel an animal to approach the hunters.

Why is it, one might wonder, that Jochelson failed to notice this type of shamanism during his field studies among the Yukaghirs? One important reason, I believe, rests in the very term *shaman*. Humphrey (1996: 30, 48–49), in a useful critique of the literature on north Asian shamanism, has pointed out that the anthropological extension of the word *shaman* seems to suggest a professional specialization equally present in all societies with shamanistic practices. However, it is clear, she argues, that this is fundamentally misleading, since "having to do with spirits, ancestors, and so on was not the prerogative of shamans alone" (1996: 30) and "there were always several kinds of 'shaman'" (1996: 49). In other words, by imposing on Yukaghir society the term *shaman*, with all its implications about the existence of a specialized religious elite or an indigenous priesthood with a consistent set of practices, Jochelson made the matter of "being a shaman" out to be much more cut and dried than it actually was. Although the Yukaghirs *do* speak about the shaman as a person with particular skills and powers, they do not recognize any formal office of shaman. Nor do they recognize any explicit procedures for determining who is a shaman and who is not. As Nikolai Likhachev, who himself underwent years of shamanic training, kept telling me, "Virtually everyone can shamanize; it is just that some are better at it than others." What he is quite clearly pointing to is the fact that, for the Yukaghirs, shamanic specialization is a question of *degree*. That is, the shaman's activity and experience, rather than being some kind of mysticism at the disposal of a particular religious elite, is a specialized form of what any other member of the society is capable of doing. This is also the argument put forward by Vitebsky (1993: 21–22) with regard to the Sora, a small indigenous group of eastern India. Drawing on Atkinson's suggestion (1989: 17) that the term *shamanism* be replaced by *shamanship*, he writes, "Like craftsmanship or musicianship, [shamanship] is a talent or inclination as much as an activity and is spread variously among persons who practise it to varying degrees" (Vitebsky 1993: 22).

Below, I shall link this notion of degrees of specialization to the differentiation between the hunter and the shaman, and I shall argue that the Yukaghir hunter is in fact at a halfway stage toward full shamanship. For now, however, I will simply point to the fact that the term *shamanship*, with its epistemological primacy of concrete bodily processes of perception and experience rather than an exaggerated or enhanced control of abstract religious representations, signs, and symbols, is something that resonates with Yukaghir understandings. For them, shamanism is not a theory for "thinking" about the world, nor does it convey anything like a coherent symbolic structure. As a matter of fact, a great deal of Yukaghir shamanic practices, as we shall see, does not involve mere symbols (things standing for something else in an arbitrary fashion) as such, but consists of actual bodily imitations of animals with the concrete objective of taking control over them. This essentially pragmatic view is also reflected in the Yukaghirs' own word for a family shaman, *a'lma*, which means "to do."

COMPARING THE SHAMAN WITH THE HUNTER

Among the many friendships that I established with people in Nelemnoye, the most affectionate was with the elderly Yukaghir couple Akulina and Gregory Shalugin. Akulina sewed most of my fur clothes—reindeer boots, gloves, jacket, trousers, hat, and ammunition belt—and Gregory made the skis, covered with sleek elk leg skin, on which I went hunting in winter. Over time they even started calling me their "son," a role that I fell into easily. Whenever I returned to the village from the forest Akulina cooked for me, while I, for my part, provided their household with meat from my hunting expeditions. One evening, when eating with the old couple, I raised the question of shamanship. Akulina replied that although she knew that some shamans had lived in the village, she personally had never witnessed any of their performances. Gregory said nothing on the subject, and the topic of our conversation soon changed. When I returned the next day, however, Akulina told me that after I had left, Gregory had revealed to her that his mother had in fact been some sort of *a'lma*. "He has never told anyone about this, not even me," she assured me. "But he'll tell you because you are our son, and he knows that this kind of information is important to you." This is what he told me:

> When I was a child, my family lived at the Shamanika River. It was before we moved to Nelemnoye. At times, the men had no luck in hunting and we starved. Then, my father would ask my mother for help. "Do you want me to sin again?" she replied. She was not keen on using her powers, but only did so when we had nothing to eat. All the members of the family gathered in one room. A willow bush with four branches was placed on the floor. Then my mother started walking around on her hands and knees, mimicking the movements of an elk. On her neck was placed a small child.[5] After a while, she would go into some kind of trance [Rus. *kamlanie*], grunting and swinging her head back and forth like an elk. Eventually, she would

Figure 10. Gregory and Akulina Shalugin. Photo by Rane Willerslev.

approach the willow bush and begin to eat its shoots. At this point, my father would give me a small bow and arrow and say, "you see the elk, go and shoot it in the heart." So I did, and she fell to the ground, kicking her legs like a dying elk. My father would then help my mother to bed. She was exhausted. All she said was that the hunters should go to a particular spot in the forest, where a willow bush with four braches was standing. There she had tied up [Rus. *priviazat'*] an elk. She said that they should shoot it in the heart so that it wouldn't suffer. It worked every time. The men always returned with elk meat. My mother never ate of the meat, saying that she would die if she ate it. Also people in general were afraid of eating it. In fact, some people would rather starve than eat the meat.

This narrative is representative of others I recorded in which the *a'lma,* by means of imitating an animal, takes control over it. Now, while the hunter and the *a'lma* are alike in possessing this ability, such that no absolute division can be drawn between the two, they do differ with respect to the amount of power they possess as well as their capacity for metamorphosis. While the hunter, as we have seen, gives in to the alien perspective of his prey and changes in the process, his human sense of self is not entirely expelled. He moves, as it were, in between human and animal perspectives. The *a'lma,* by contrast, goes into a state of trance or ecstasy and surrenders to the single viewpoint of the animal imitated. In other words, in the shaman's own experience as well as in that of the spectators, she actually transcends the human-animal interface and becomes an elk. This greater capacity for metamorphosis is also dramatically revealed in an account related to me by Nikolai Likhachev:

> As part of my training as an *a'lma,* I followed my grandfather around the forest. Most of the time we did nothing, just walking around without talking. One day, he took his huge knife and pointed it at me. His eyes were wild and I thought that he was going to kill me. But instead he stuck it into a fallen trunk. "Don't remove it," he said. "I need it to make it back." Then he started moving around like a bear. It was scary. He hummed heavily like a bear and sniffed the ground as a bear does when looking for food. Then, he jumped over the knife and I saw how his body had become covered with a bear's coat. He turned into a bear and ran into the forest. We didn't see him for a long time. When he came back, he was himself again. He said that he had been living with friends. I suspect that the master of the bears was his helper [Rus. *pomoshchnik*], because every time people asked him for help in hunting, he always gave them a bear in addition to some other animal. That is, they would not only go and kill an elk or reindeer, but also a bear. He himself never ate of the bear's meat. He would just sit in silence and drink tea while the others were eating.

I have already pointed to the fact that the hunter may at times experience real feelings of moral anxiety when killing and eating his prey. This, as we have seen, is grounded in the fact that during hunting the boundary between self and other, human and nonhuman, is somewhat dissolved, and the hunter comes to experience himself ambiguously as both hunter and animal. Killing the animal, then, is for him rather like killing a fellow person, although it is not the same as killing someone identical to himself. However, for the *a'lma* who takes up the subject position of prey absolutely and actually becomes one with the animal he or she imitates, this moral anxiety is much more intensely felt. For the *a'lma* to eat the animal's flesh would be to engage in an obscene act of cannibalism or even auto-cannibalism. He or she must therefore renounce the meat.

What is slightly more puzzling, however, is the fact that the others in the group also express unease about eating the meat obtained with the help of an *a'lma*'s magic. In my view, this has to be understood in relation to the conceptual world of hunters. I have already described how the hunter-prey relationship among the Yukaghirs tends to be idealized as a process of sexual seduction. Although the hunter does not refrain from using various deceptive techniques to make his prey "give itself up" to him, there is nevertheless an element of voluntary surrender on the part of the animal, as it "throws" itself at the hunter out of sexual desire. It is thus the animal and *not* the hunter that permits the killing to occur. When the *a'lma* is responsible for attracting the prey, however, this element of voluntary surrender seems absent. Instead, we are dealing with a process of mere coercion; that is, the *a'lma*, using magical powers, compels an animal to come against its own free will. Indeed, this is what Gregory seems to point to when he tells us that his mother would "tie up" the elk so that the hunters could go and kill it with ease.

Such a strategy of coercion, however, poses considerable danger. To be short of hunting luck is seen by the Yukaghirs as an indication that the animals' master-spirit refuses to nourish human beings because they have in some way acted immorally. Thus, for the *a'lma* to step in and take an animal by force is, in effect, to kill it without the consent of the spirit— an act that carries the threat of retribution in the form of sickness or misfortune. Insofar as one takes part in eating the animal's flesh, he or she will inevitably be an accessory to its involuntary death and thereby become a target of the spirit's revenge. For some people, as Gregory pointed out, this fear of spirit attacks would exceed their hunger and they would reject the meat. However, it is the immediate family of the *a'lma* who face the greatest risk of being preyed upon in retaliation. As Nikolai Likhachev commented, "My father had twelve siblings and they all died young. I, for my part, had eight brothers and sisters, and there are only two of us left. Even my own children died before me. We have all been paying for the sins [Rus. *grekhi*] of my grandfather."

Thus, the animal's master-spirit takes the lives of the *a'lma*'s relatives as compensation for the game he steals, and such acts of retribution may run over the course of several generations. It is therefore no wonder that the ethnographic literature on Siberian shamanship repeatedly reports that people were exceedingly reluctant to obey the call of the spirits and take up the position of shaman, as this would put not only themselves but also their kinfolk in great danger (see Bogoras 1904–9: 418–19; Eliade 1964: 72; Vitebsky 1997: 8; Hutton 2001: 66).

What is important to stress, however, is that the *a'lma* is not unique in risking the threat of vengeance from the spirits of the animals. The common hunter, too, faces such danger when killing his prey. As I illustrated in chapter 3, among the Yukaghirs we find a number of narratives describing how the predatory violence of the hunter is reciprocated by

Figure 11. The author with a butchered elk. To his right, above the elk's head, hangs the miniature wooden model of the "animal killer," which is also represented in the drawing to the right. Photo by Rane Willerslev. Drawing by Marie Carsten Pedersen.

the animal's master-spirit, causing a series of deaths in his family. Kwon (1998) has pointed out that this "perilous interchange-ability" of the roles of predator and prey is a common concern among hunters throughout the Siberian north: "In Siberia, the position of the human hunter is insecure. As soon as he succeeds in a predatory act, the hunter falls into the position of prey. . . . hunting [therefore] involves not only the skill of finding and pursuing the animal but also the equally important skill of avoiding being preyed upon in turn" (Kwon 1998: 119).

With regard to "avoiding being preyed upon in turn," it is interesting to note that Yukaghir hunters employ various tactics of displacement and substitution to cover up the fact that they are the ones responsible for their prey's violent death. Immediately after killing an elk, for example, they will roughly carve a small wooden figure, which they paint with lines of blood from the dead animal. The figure is said to be a miniature model of the animal's killer. It is hung from a string above the meat and serves the double purpose of protecting the meat from ravens while the hunters are out of sight as well as attracting the attention of the raging spirit of the killed animal. The spirit, hunters say, will smell the blood of its "child" painted on the figure's body and attack it. Meanwhile, hunters can safely butcher the animal and transport its meat back to the encampment. The wooden figure is then left on the spot of the kill in order to leave the animal's "murderer" behind.

The ritual performed after killing a bear follows a similar pattern, but it is more elaborate because the danger and fear are greater, and the cost of error more terrifying. Before removing the skin of the bear hunters will blindfold it or poke its eyes out while croaking like a raven. This will make the bear believe that it was a bird that blinded it. Moreover, they will address the bear, saying, "Big Man! Who did this to you? [Who killed you?] The one who eats of the willow bushes [the elk] was here." In this way, the hunters seek to blame the bear's violent death on the elk—a misdirection that is underscored by the fact that the hunters themselves move around and smell like elk. They might also blame the killing on other humans. Spiridon, for example, would say, "Grandfather, I wasn't the one who killed you; it was a Russian [or a Sakha] who killed you." Moreover, while skinning the bear, he would say, "Grandfather, you must feel warm. Let me open your coat."

Having removed the flesh from the bear's corpse, the hunters then deposit its cleaned bones on a raised platform or in the cleft trunk of a tree, with the animal's skull facing west toward the setting sun, which is said to be the direction of the Land of Shadows. As a last safety measure they will bind its jaws with willow twigs to prevent the bear's spirit from preying upon them in return. Thus, by various means of trickery, hunters seek to direct the anger of the animal master-spirits against non-Yukaghirs—humans and nonhumans alike.

An *a'lma* would use trickery similar to that of the hunter when engaging with the spirits of prey. Nikolai Likhachev told me that whenever his grandfather traveled to the Owner of the Earth, Lebie'-po'gil, to ask for the *ayibii* of prey animals, he would bring with him small figures of humans made out of snow and grass, which he would present to the spirit as his "children." The spirit would then take these figures in exchange for its own "children," the animal game. Later, when the figures of snow dissolved, the spirit would realize that it had been tricked and fly into a rage. By this time, however, Nikolai Likhachev's grandfather would have returned to his own domain, safely out of the reach of the spirit.

My point in all of this is to show that the world of the *a'lma* is not categorically distinguishable from that of the hunter, and that the practices and experiences of the former are only a specialized or intensified form of those of any hunter. My argument finds further support when we turn to

Figure 12. The skull of a bear after the completed ritual. Photo by Rane Willerslev.

what in the ethnographic literature are known as "familiars," or "guardian," "assistant," or "helping" spirits. These are supernatural agents with whom the shaman establishes special relationships and who assist him. They might warn him about obstacles and enemies, or support him in removing or fighting them. They might also serve as messengers that are able to contact other spirits at greater distance, such as the masters of animals. Moreover, Nikolai Likhachev told me that it is the helping spirits (Rus. *pomoshchniki;* Yuk. *e'iye*) who first call the person who is to become an *a'lma,* and that they do this "out of love for him" and "because they want to live with him." Although Nikolai Likhachev did not provide anything near a complete picture of the kind of relationship that is established between the *a'lma* and his or her helping spirits, it is clear from what he told me that the acquisition of shamanic power is essentially conceptualized as a process of establishing intimate sexual relationships with a selected number of spirits. He described how his grandfather received much of his power from marrying the *ayibii* of two dead girls, Anna and Marpha, who would "sleep next to him in the bed" and "with whom he would have intercourse."[6]

The important point for my argument, however, is that the Yukaghir shaman does not differ from the common hunter in his quest to establish and maintain intimate sexual relations with spiritual beings. As a matter of fact, many hunters claim to have one or more helping spirits with whom they copulate during their nightly dreams and who provide them with hunting luck in return. We might thus conclude that helping spirits are not an exclusive attribute of the shaman, but are instead part of a more general system for obtaining magico-religious powers and might be shared by other members of society. The *a'lma*, however, differs from the rest of the community with respect to the degree of intimacy that he can establish with his spiritual assistants. Thus, while the *a'lma* might marry one or more of them, as did Nikolai Likhachev's grandfather, for the common hunter this would prove lethal. In fact, I will later show how the hunter must make sure that feelings of sexual pleasure do not evolve into actual feelings of love between him and the spirit, which would cause the latter to keep his *ayibii* as its spouse and thus prevent it from returning to his body.

The last similarity between the hunter and the *a'lma* to which I shall draw attention is concerned with the latter's experiences during his initiation, which closely resemble those of the hunter during the hunting process. Both cases involve a two-phase deconstruction and reconstruction process involving the symbolic death of the person and his subsequent rebirth. For Nikolai Likhachev, for example, his shamanic initiation was experienced as a process of bodily dismantling. He told me how he was put into a wooden coffin by mystical beings who then sawed his body into pieces. When his body was reassembled by the spirits, they granted him an extra rib. In the case of his grandfather, he experienced a death, represented by his temporary loss of human speech. As Nikolai Likhachev remarked, "My grandfather lived alone in the forest for three years. When he returned he couldn't talk with humans, only with birds and animals. Only gradually did he learn to speak in the human tongue again." The resemblance of these experiences to those of the hunter is striking. We have seen how the hunter, during his preparations for the hunt, must undergo a process of skillful "dehumanization," the removal of his human bodily qualities in order to be reshaped into the image of his prey. Among other things, he must abandon ordinary human speech, first by adopting a special linguistic code that conceals his intent to kill, and later, when in the forest, by refraining from speaking in the human tongue and instead adopting the language of his prey. In contrast, when returning to the encampment, as will be described in chapter 8, the hunter is obliged to engage in storytelling—an act that is believed to "humanize" him and marks his rebirth into the ordinary sphere of human existence.

Now, while the experiences of the hunter and the *a'lma* are similar in this regard, they do differ in degree. Although the hunter transforms from one identity to another, his transformation is only temporary: at the end of each hunt, he reenters ordinary life just about where he left off. The transformation of the *a'lma,* by contrast, is permanent. During his initiation he takes on an ontologically new identity as shaman and can, therefore, never completely return to his previous state. This is not to say that change never occurs within the hunter or in his social status. My point is rather that, for the hunter, such change happens only gradually, whereas for the *a'lma* it happens immediately. Let me illustrate this point with a concrete example.

The leader of my hunting group, Old Spiridon, is said to be capable of forcing prey into submission. This is one reason why people call him by the Yukaghir name for hunting leader, *xani'ce,* from the verb *xa'ni,* which means "to persecute" or "to harass" [an animal]. In fact, I myself once witnessed how he forcibly drove an elk into our encampment, where it collapsed from exhaustion right in front of the fireplace. The others in the group expressed not only admiration for Spiridon's skills, but also much fear that his brutal behavior toward the animal would upset Khoziain, the animal master-spirit, and one hunter in fact renounced his share of the animal's meat in much the same way as some people would reject the meat taken by the force of an *a'lma*. What is more, Spiridon claims to have a relationship of particular intimacy with the Owner of the Omulevka River, from whom he derives his extraordinary hunting luck and skills. Hence, there is a real sense in which Spiridon resembles an *a'lma* with respect to his social status, skills, and spiritual powers.

Still, in Spiridon's own opinion as well as in the view of others, he is *not* a shaman. The reason for this, I suggest, is that whereas Spiridon has acquired his expertise and power in an ordinary way, that is, gradually during the course of his lifetime, the *a'lma,* by contrast, receives his extraordinary capacities at once during his initiation. From the very outset, then, the *a'lma* displays consummate spiritual potency, which Spiridon, as an ordinary hunter, does not. However, in time, and with age and experience, the hunter can reach a level of expertise close to that of the *a'lma,* and the two become almost indistinguishable. Thus, I contend that the difference between the hunter and the shaman is really a difference of degree, not a matter of absolute opposition, and there is an important sense in which the common hunter is in fact at a stage that is halfway toward full shamanship.

SHAMANS IN BILATERAL VERSUS PATRILINEAL SOCIETIES

In making this claim, I take a position opposite to that of Humphrey (1996), who, in her comparison of the "shaman" and "elder" *(bagchi)* among the Daur Mongols (as well as among various south Siberian groups such as the Buryats, Tungus, and Nanai), argues that they represent two fundamentally distinctive and often antagonistic kinds of knowledge. Thus, the elder, who is also the leader of hunters, represents "straightforward" or "plain" knowledge about the world (p. 54), whereas the shaman's knowledge is founded on "particular flagrantly non-realist premises" (p. 39), which "contradict in different ways people's most fundamental knowledge of ordinary things" (p. 38). While I do not doubt that this dichotomy between shaman and elder/hunter holds true for the Daur and various south Siberian groups, matters are different among the Yukaghirs. Here the shaman's experiences and knowledge are, as we have seen, to a significant degree simply intensifications of those of any ordinary hunter, and therefore no absolute division in kind can be drawn between the two. What is more, Humphrey's analysis rests on a prior distinction between "natural categories" and "counter-intuitive unnatural images"—the first of which she associates with the elder/hunter, who "tended to eulogize the actual world in its ideal order," and the second with the shaman, who "disturbed that order, presenting images of hostile, invisible currents that would undermine the solidity of the known world" (pp. 58–60). To me, however, such an analytical dichotomy seems unhelpful, since among Yukaghirs—and, I suspect, among the Daur too—the world is not seen in terms of such antinomy between two closed and irremediably opposed realities. Rather, the world is for them perceived as both material and spiritual at once. Likewise, technical know-how is intertwined and fused with spiritual know-how, and the two domains of knowledge are not conceptually distinguished. Hence, it seems quite wrong to try to separate them analytically.

Having said this, I find it likely that Humphrey's and my conflicting views can be at least partly explained by examining the basic organizational differences between the societies that we study. It seems to be no coincidence that the Daur, Buryats, Tungus, and Nanai, with their lineal structures of rigid patriclan organization, strict rules of residence, and clan exogamy, define the social position or office of shaman much more clearly than does a bilateral band society such as the Yukaghirs. Krupnik, along with other anthropologists, has related the widespread bilateralism in the circumpolar north to an economic need for organizational fluidity (Krupnik 1993: 83; Graburn and Strong 1973: 84; Thomas 1974: 18). The argument goes that the harsh environment and the comparatively low level of technology under which the arctic and subarctic peoples secure the material basis of life require flexible bands that constantly change in size and in membership, and this has in effect precluded them from taking on a unilineal descent ideology with strict residential rules. Whether or not one agrees with such an explanation, which emphasizes environmental and technological conditions as decisive in shaping social relations, it seems clear from the ethnographic literature that in bilateral band societies, such as the Chukchi, the northern Naskapi and Athapaskan (or Dene) Indians, and many Inuit societies, the social position of the shaman, as that of the bilateral band itself, is of an ad hoc nature, similar to what I have described among the Yukaghirs. Thus, with regard to the position of shaman among the Chukchi, Bogoras writes, "every adult Chukchee will occasionally take his drum . . . singing his melodies to the rhythm of the beats. . . . The transition from such songs to shamanic performances is quite imperceptible, and in this way it is fair to say that every Chukchee may play the shaman in all branches of the craft as far as his skill and inclination permit him to do so" (Bogoras 1904–9: 413).

We find a somewhat similar argument by Smith (1998) in an essay on the ontology of the Athapaskan Indians: "The egalitarianism of bush sensibility and the fact that thought categories are open-ended militate against the idea of the shaman as categorically distinguishable from, and superior to, other persons . . . *inkonze* [medicine-power] is something that can come and go regardless of one's level of ability. It is quite impossible to specify, at any given time, who has major abilities with *inkonze*" (Smith 1998: 424). What the above statements quite clearly point to is that in these bilateral band societies, although there is a role of "shaman" in the social network, the position of the shaman depends not on the assumption of an office but entirely on the attitudes of the people, and that virtually anyone can act as shaman.

What we seem to be dealing with, in effect, is two qualitatively different shamanic configurations, which can be seen, at least in part, as reflections of rather different types of social organizations: the patrilineal clan structure of the Mongols and some south Siberian groups, with their strict rules of residence and clan membership, and the bilateral groupings of the Yukaghirs and other circumpolar peoples, marked by a flexible band organization and constantly changing in size and membership.[7]

THE DISAPPEARANCE OF THE YUKAGHIR SHAMANS

I have already pointed to the fact that there are no shamans among the present-day Yukaghirs, and I would be surprised if any shamans were to be found among the neighboring groups of Evens, Sakha, and Russians in the district of Verkhne Kolymsk Ulus. Nor have I encountered any "self-proclaimed" or "would-be" shamans among these groups, a widespread phenomenon in the capital of the Sakha Republic, Yakutsk, where many people, as Vitebsky tells us, "live in a state of eager expectation which almost demands that new kinds of shamans should appear," and where "many people now claim to be descendants of shamans and some imply that this makes them, too, some sort of a shaman" (1997: 9). Among the Yukaghirs, however, one does not get the feeling that shamans are in demand, or that people have any desire for their return. In fact, people seem to manage quite well in their everyday dealings with the world of spirits and other nonhuman dwellers without shamanic support.

Why is it, one is led to wonder, that the Yukaghirs express such indifference about the fact that their shamans are gone, and make no attempt at rehabilitating them in post-Soviet society? I have already pointed to the fact that Yukaghir shamanship, rather than being a religion that entails a coherent and explicitly articulated theory about the world, is seen quite simply as a concrete technique for manipulating the environment, and it is with reference to this essentially pragmatic view that I believe we should approach the questions raised.

I shall start by addressing the decline of the so-called "professional shamans." They were, as already noted, a special class of socially detached shamanic healers that arose as a direct response to devastating epidemics of smallpox, measles, and other European diseases, which killed off native peoples in the thousands. During the Soviet regime's antireligion campaigns of the 1930s and 1940s, these shamans were easily singled out on account of their conspicuous and spectacular clothes decorated with fringes and images. Virtually all of them were eliminated during this period, either killed in labor camps along with thousands of other Stalin-era gulag prisoners, or forced to abandon their profession. Hence, the Soviet regime was, in effect, responsible for the final disappearance of this type of shaman. However, there is reason to suggest that they had already been rendered largely superfluous by that time. The Soviet system, shortly after establishing its power in northeastern Siberia in the mid-1920s, effectively succeeded in putting an end to the dreadful epidemics that caused this class of shamans to develop in the first place and that had kept them in place for more than a century. As Gregory Shalugin commented, "We clearly saw that smallpox could be eradicated by vaccination, so why go and pay the Sakha shamans, who only occasionally did well in curing us?" Shalugin points to a situation in which the Soviet doctors, with their scientific knowledge and technology, decisively displaced a group of shamanic healers who were competing in the same curative space. Modern medicine and its treatment of disease simply proved superior, causing this particular class of shaman to lose ground about a decade before they were purged by the Soviet authorities.

If we turn our focus toward the so-called "family shamans," or what the Yukaghirs tend to understand by the word *a'lma*, their fate was altogether different. As noted earlier, none of them was subject to concerted persecutions by the Bolsheviks, presumably because they lacked all the standard attributes of shamans, such as special clothes and a drum, and because they were careful to exercise their skills only in the company of close and trusted kin. Hence, this group of shamans kept practicing various kinds of hunting magic until the mid-1960s. When I asked people why they stopped, they always responded with something like, "Food was in abundance, so there was no need for the *a'lma* any more." What they seem to point to is the fact that the Yukaghirs at this point had been effectively integrated into the Soviet state economy, with its waged employment and centralized delivery of consumer goods. Obviously, this process of economic integration had begun much earlier, but in the 1960s it acquired a precipitous character. People no longer depended on hunting for subsistence. Wild meat, although still cherished by the Yukaghirs, came to constitute at best a minor part of their diet relative to domesticated reindeer and cow meat, which was delivered in large quantities to the village shop by the *sovkhoz* (state farm). Rather than hunt for wild reindeer and elk, the Yukaghirs were expected to provide sable furs to the *sovkhoz*, in return for which they were given hard cash so that they could buy foodstuffs and other necessities in the village shop.

What is more, during this period the population of elk increased to a point of abundance. Before the mid-1960s it was considered a rare event indeed to kill an elk anywhere in the Kolyma Region, and people hunted mainly for wild reindeer, which could be found in small herds of less than a hundred, or even only a few dozen. However, because of large-scale forest fires in the 1950s and 1960s, which burned off the lichen on which the reindeer depend, this animal moved away. Instead, the elk began migrating into the Kolyma valley in large numbers, attracted by the young willow bushes that flourished in the soil after the forest fires. Within a few years, in fact, the elk became so numerous that, on a trip of any distance from the village, it was quite normal to come across several animals and to see the tracks of many more.

My point is that in such an environment of material plenty, where virtually all threat of famine and disease had been effectively eliminated, there was no longer any need for the a'lma. After all, shamanic practice is essentially about eliminating human suffering, whether in the form of bad hunting luck, hunger, or disease. This is not to say that the Yukaghirs stopped having faith in shamanic powers, but as long as things went smoothly, there was simply no need to pay them much attention. As a result, the office of shaman, insofar as we can talk about an office at all, faded out and the remaining shamans simply lived as ordinary people, doing ordinary things.

What is interesting, however, is that this development did not seem to upset the shamans. When I asked Gregory Shalugin how his mother reacted to the fact that her shamanic skills were no longer needed, he answered, "She was very pleased indeed. For her, to employ her powers was both sinful and dangerous, so she was truly happy that she didn't have to do this any more." And he added, "Although my mother was old, she was a devoted communist. She often said, 'our previous father [the Tsar] didn't care for us the same way as our new father [Stalin] does. Our new father never lets his children [the Yukaghirs] go hungry.'" What this reveals is that the Yukaghirs did not necessarily experience shamanic thinking and communist thinking as incompatible. By stressing the incompatibility of "shamanism" with "communism," or the gulf between "tradition" and "modernity," we risk missing those mechanisms that enabled the Soviet authorities to recruit loyal communists among the Yukaghirs, even within the ranks of the shamans. Instead, we need to consider what it is about shamanic thinking that makes it accept, or at least find room for, an ideology that holds a basic premise that all religion is false. The answer, I believe, rests in the fact that shamanship is *not* a religion, but merely a system of techniques intended to cause concrete things to happen. As such, success and failure is the essence of shamanic practice, but it requires no personal commitment to any single metaphysics, religious cosmology, or political ideology. Humphrey points to exactly this when she writes, "It is quite possible to go to a shaman for various kinds of problems and at the same time think of oneself as a Buddhist or even an atheist. . . . Shamanism demands nothing (as Buddhism, for example, does, even in the form of the most elementary precepts) which must be taken into the rest of life as a personal commitment" (1998: 417).

In other words, to engage in shamanship does not require any personal commitment to religious or ideological belief—something that is underscored by the fact that Russian Orthodox priests and even Communist Party members and officials have been reported to consult shamans (Jochelson 1926: 162; Vitebsky 1992: 239; Humphrey 1998: 417). Rather, what seems to be at the heart of shamanic practice is efficacy. That is, the attention of both the shaman and the audience is directed toward the performance itself—whether it is forcefully carried out and whether it has the intended effect on the physical world. This is also what Humphrey and Laidlaw seem to be pointing to when they state, "The question most insistently asked of [shamanic practices is], 'Has it worked?'" (1994: 11). It is also, I believe, the reason why shamanic performances often involve miraculous tests of various sorts, such as the shaman cutting his own stomach with a knife and the cut immediately healing (Jochelson 1926: 201; Humphrey and Laidlaw 1994: 10), or licking red-hot iron (Vitebsky 1997: 9). Such tests seem to have no purpose except to convince the audience, and perhaps the shaman himself, that his techniques are both powerful and effective.

This leads me to yet another point: if it holds true, as I have argued, that Yukaghir shamanship is *not* a system of belief but merely a system of techniques for manipulating the environment, and that these techniques, rather than being attributes of shamans alone, are specialized forms of abilities that may be practiced by all members of society to varying degrees, then it follows that we cannot simply judge the legacy of Siberian shamanism by the presence or absence of shamans themselves. Rather, the shamans were just the tip of an iceberg, so to speak, sustained by a much broader and more pervasive set of everyday shamanic practices, such as, for example, dream sexuality with spirits and the mimetic seduction of prey. Far from dying out with the shamans, this "do-it-yourself" shamanship has been sustained and is an essential part of contemporary Yukaghir life, being practiced in everyday activities like hunting (Willerslev 2001). Vitebsky appropriately refers to this as the "shamanic impulse" (1997: 9). He talks about its having a "chameleon-like" character, which takes on "different forms according to the political and cultural climate." During the communist era, he argues, this impulse passed through various transformations and emerged in forms that do not immediately present themselves as shamanic, such as rock music and various kinds of theater play. I would add that another essential trait of the shamanic impulse is that it switches in and out of focus along with the overall material and physical condition of the community. Thus, it is kept dormant during times of stasis, even to the point of ceasing to exist in people's awareness altogether, but germinates rapidly in times of crisis. As one middle-aged hunter commented:

> Ten years ago, we had everything. We could go to the village shop and buy what we needed. Hunting was like a hobby to us. It didn't really matter. Now, it is totally different. We have no money and there is nothing to buy. When I go hunting now, I'm really anxious. If I fail, it is a disaster. I would have wasted my wife's pension on fuel. Therefore, I refrain from having sex before going to the forest, don't let women touch my weapons, and so on. All these things didn't really matter before. In fact, I didn't give a damn. But now I do anything to keep my hunting luck.

With the steady trend toward a more subsistence-based lifestyle, and with the elk population declining because of overhunting, we see the shamanic impulse building up once more among the Yukaghirs. Hunting is carried out with great care and according to strict rules, and the spiritual awareness of prey is nowadays acknowledged by virtually everyone, even the younger generation of hunters. People simply cannot afford to be careless about these matters. The question is whether this movement back to a subsistence lifestyle will eventually see the return of the office of shaman in one form or another. We shall have to wait and see.

CHAPTER 7

The Spirit World

In his classic study of the Yukaghirs Jochelson devoted a major part of his work to what he called their "religious concepts." In the opening chapter of his description of the Yukaghir's pantheon of spirits, he writes, "I propose to analyze the elements of the ancient Yukaghir religion in the sense in which I understand that term and to the extent to which it was possible to reconstruct the religious system of the Yukaghir in its present state of degeneration" (1926: 140). Having said that, he begins the ambitious task of classifying all the various kinds of "owners," or "fathers" and "mothers," as Yukaghirs (past and present) prefer to call them. According to Jochelson, the Yukaghir pantheon can be divided into two elementary categories: benevolent spirits and evil spirits. Within each of these two groupings, there exist spirits of varying degrees of authority and power, so he goes on to classify them into taxonomic pyramids. The result is a complicated hierarchical ordering, consisting of no less than five levels, within which each spiritual being is allocated its fixed place.

Now, it happens that this complicated hierarchy of spirits proposed by Jochelson requires knowledge of what spirits *exist*, as well as their ordering, interrelations, and distinguishing characteristics. During my fieldwork among Yukaghir hunters, however, I found no one who demonstrated such an elaborate knowledge of spiritual beings. In fact, hunters' notions of spirits seemed mostly vague and confused, and they found it

41

very difficult to put them into any order whatsoever. In everyday speech they did not even differentiate between different kinds of spirits, but simply referred to them with the general term *khoziain,* which means "owner" or "master" in Russian. Although they acknowledged the existence of various kinds of spiritual beings, associated both with locations in the landscape and with animals, they were generally incapable of naming them, either individually or by type. Nor could they give any substantial information about their individual characteristics. The comment of a middle-aged hunter in my hunting group serves as an example of the overall state of affairs:

> They [the spirits] are around. One can meet them in dreams. One time it is a child the size of my hand, another time it is a woman. They give you things, presents. . . . But do not ask me who they are. They do not tell. My father did not explain it to me. He just said that people exist that you cannot see when you are awake. If they like you, they will provide you with prey, so do not upset them. . . . Probably they [the spirits] want it to be in this way, they do not want us to know too much.

A few old people who still speak the Yukaghir language could recognize some of the names of the larger classes of spirits described by Jochelson, such as Lebie'-po'gil (the Owner of the Earth), *mo'ye* (the owners of various animal species), and *pejul [sic]* (the owner of each individual animal). However, their statements revealed considerable disagreement about the characteristics of these spirits and their respective domains, and there was a general overlap between the different spirit categories. Some of the old people were able to describe in some detail the personalities of a few specific spirits associated with the local rivers where they hunted or with a particular animal species, but they were just as ignorant as the rest about the pantheon of spirits as a whole.

The statements of Yukaghirs also revealed an attitude of conspicuous ambivalence about whether spirits were good or bad, a basic distinction for Jochelson. When, for example, I asked an old man about the Owner of the Earth, Lebie'-po'gil, who in Jochelson's spirit hierarchy is among the highest of the benevolent beings, he described, to my surprise, the looks and character of the Grandfather with the Pointed Head, Yiodeiis'ien'ulben. In Jochelson's pantheon the latter is the head of the evil spirits, who resides in the underworld and lives on human souls (Jochelson 1926: 152). Moreover, the old man denied that any benevolent spirits exist: "All the spirits we know," he assured me, "want to kill us. The good ones, we don't know about." Others again would describe Lebie'-po'gil as a lustful young woman whom hunters must persuade to provide them with prey animals by seducing her in their dreams. In short, it seemed as if the Yukaghirs did not regard classes such as benevolent and evil as mutually exclusive, and this moral ambiguity was mirrored in the gender of the spirits: they were in general conceptualized as ambi-gendered.

Although hunters perform a number of everyday rituals, such as the burning of offerings and the reverent deposition of animal remains in trees, that are intelligible only from the perspective that spiritual beings exist, their interpretations of these practices were generally vague. When I asked them to whom these ritual practices were addressed, most often they would shrug their shoulders and say, "Who knows!" Or they might simply give a short explanation without even mentioning the spirits, such as, "I do so and so, otherwise I will have no luck," or, "This works for me, so this is how I do it."

COMPARING THE YUKAGHIRS WITH THE YUPIK

My overall impression, then, was that Yukaghir ideas about the spirit world were essentially confused, contradictory, incoherent, and vague. I found nearly nothing that resembled Jochelson's clear-cut outline of the Yukaghir pantheon of spirits. Could it be that the people had lost this knowledge during the hundred years that had passed since Jochelson did his fieldwork? Given the ubiquity of processes of "acculturation," which many anthropologists and historians working with Siberian indigenous peoples have stressed followed the period of Soviet rule (Forsyth 1992; Slezkine 1994; Grant 1995; Schweitzer and Gray 2000: 17–37), one would indeed expect such an erosion of central spiritual ideas.

The Soviet school system had a particularly severe impact on Yukaghir life. After a few years of experimenting with small-scale classes for Yukaghir children, the Soviet system of education shifted to a fixed curriculum, with emphasis placed on Russian language, literature, and history (Vakhtin 1991). Yukaghir children were moved to a permanent boarding school, first in the village of Balygychan in Magadan and later in the regional center of Zyrianka. Moreover, the number of years to be spent in compulsory education was continuously increased: from three to four years in the 1930s, to seven to eight years in the 1950s, and to eight to ten years in the 1970s.[1] The teachers in the boarding schools were virtually all Russians, while the students were ethnically mixed. This meant that the children could not speak with each other or with their teachers in their native languages (see Krupnik and Vakhtin n.d.). Consequently, more and more Yukaghir children returned to their families completely fluent in Russian, but with only an elementary or passive knowledge of the Yukaghir language. As a result, by the end of the 1960s, Russian had gained a firm foothold as the principal language among the Yukaghirs. Today only the oldest generation is competent in the Yukaghir language. For everyone under sixty, the primary language is Russian or Sakha (Vakhtin 1991). Not until the mid-1980s did Nelemnoye get its own village school, and only in 1986–87 did the Yukaghir language become part of the compulsory school curriculum. However, from my own experience, the local children hardly ever speak Yukaghir among themselves or with their parents, switching instead to Russian the moment they leave the classroom.

Could it be that the people's knowledge of spiritual matters had become distorted by new ways of thinking, in much the same way that Russian had replaced the Yukaghir language? Of particular interest here is a survey carried out by Krupnik and Vakhtin (1997; n.d.) among the Siberian Yupik (Inuit), a group of sea mammal hunters whose land lies northeast of the Kolyma River where the Yukaghirs live, and whose linguistic situation is similar to that of the Yukaghirs.[2] The survey attempted to document the extent to which the Yupik's traditional spiritual knowledge had changed over one hundred years of intense cultural contact. They conducted a large number of interviews with Yupik people from various generations and asked them about issues central to their traditional worldview, such as the reincarnation of dead souls, the treatment of animal bones, ideas about human relations to the world of spirits, and so on (1997: 239). They then compared the statements with classic ethnographic accounts about Yupik religious ideas, primarily in the work of Bogoras (1904–9), to evaluate the extent to which the people's "intellectual culture," as they called it, had undergone change or been lost altogether (Krupnik and Vakhtin 1997: 238). To their surprise, they discovered that contemporary Yupik adults showed no significant difference in their traditional knowledge than adults of earlier generations. They concluded that current knowledge about the spirit world and various ritual practices did not, as they had expected, decrease in direct relation to the loss of the indigenous language or the extension of formal schooling (p. 236). What had happened instead, they claimed, was that the formally recognized universe of spirits had shrunk. Whereas the environment of the Yupik used to be populated quite densely with various spiritual beings, the people today recognize many fewer spiritual entities (p. 244). Moreover, Krupnik and Vakhtin argue that the Yupik have "filled in" the (spiritually) empty gaps "by actively incorporating values, explanations, and beliefs from outsiders' cultures (mainly Russian/European) with their focus on non-spiritual interpretations and practical reasoning" (Krupnik and Vakhtin n.d.). So, whereas many of the traditional practices still prevail, their former spiritual meanings and interpretations have to a large extent been replaced with more secular ones (1997: 237). The authors conclude that the accumulation of knowledge by the Yupik people now proceeds via the creation of a new cultural blend that they call "mixed culture": "the mixed culture which emerges from several interviews with modern Yupik adults is not just a combination of some old (indigenous) and some new (borrowed) components. It is, rather, a specific reconfiguration of the pieces of an old legacy with the paradigms of another cognitive system. The analogy with the modern definition of mixed language, a concept now broadly accepted by linguistics in describing similar reconfigurations in language interactions, is revealing" (1997: 249).

My observations suggest that the situation of the Yukaghirs strongly resembles that of the Yupik. In both cases there seems to be no major difference between adults from different generations in terms of their knowledge of the spirit world. Both the older Yukaghirs, who still speak the indigenous language, and the younger adults, who lack proficiency in the language, make almost equally incoherent, vague, and fragmented statements about spiritual matters. Likewise, in both Yukaghir and Yupik societies we see what could be interpreted as a diminution of a former abundance of different spiritual beings. Contemporary Yukaghirs have thus ceased to distinguish between different classes of spirits, but simply refer to them by the general term *khoziain*. Moreover, just like the Yupik, my Yukaghir informants would often provide what we would call secular rather than spiritual explanations for why they carry out particular rituals.

Still, I am somewhat uneasy about the methods and conclusions of Krupnik and Vakhtin's survey. First, there exist major problems with using classical ethnographies as the basis for a direct comparison with contemporary indigenous statements about the spirit world. The studies of both Jochelson and his friend Bogoras were deeply rooted in the intellectual traditions of the late nineteenth century.[3] Both were strongly influenced by the "new" antievolutionist anthropology of Franz Boas. While Boasian anthropology shared with evolutionism the goal of elucidating development over time, it did this by focusing in the first instance on cultural variability (Miller and Mathé 1997: 21). Boas thus insisted that

detailed historical reconstruction of specific cultures had to precede any
attempt to derive laws of general cultural development (Nash 1977: 4).
Devoted to this idea of historical reconstruction, both Jochelson and
Bogoras saw it as their main task to reconstruct in their writings the
indigenous cultures of Siberia in their original form, before they were
completely displaced by the pressure of Russian civilization (Miller and
Mathé 1997: 22). For this purpose, the behavior of the present was
understood to be less important than the informant's memory of the way
things had been. The shamans, in particular, were understood to be the
bearers of ancient spiritual knowledge, so these "religious experts" provided most of the ethnographic material about indigenous religious ideas.
"Common people," Bogoras briefly notes, "only know little of spiritual
matters" (1904–9: 290). However, his observation did not prevent him
or Jochelson from taking the various disconnected statements of
shamans and weaving them together so as to produce ideal models of the
indigenous peoples' pantheons of spirits, which they then presented, with
all the rough edges and contradictions edited out, as the "religious ideas"
of "the Yukaghirs," or "the Yupik," for example. My point is that these
ideal mappings of the spirit world are more likely to belong to the imagination of the two anthropologists than to the thoughts of the indigenous
peoples themselves (with the possible exception of the shamans). It is
thus highly dubious to use these accounts as the basis for evaluating the
extent to which spiritual ideas have changed or been lost among "ordinary" people today, as Krupnik and Vakhtin do in their survey.

However, the main focus of my criticism is concerned with the very
object of their study, which is "indigenous spiritual knowledge" per se.
They define this in terms of what they call "intellectual culture": "It is
culture, *intellectual* culture in particular, that converts the physical environment into a cognitive organized or formatted space (i.e. into a cognitive environment)" (1997: 237; my emphasis). "It is this very knowledge
(intellectual) that constitutes the core of every culture's legacy and one
that is crucial for the stability and continuity of every human community.
It explains to people in appropriate and understandable terms how the
universe is built. It shows people their place in the world, both physically
and spiritually; it deals with birth and death, rationalizes communal and
individual success and misfortunes, and regulates human behaviour. As
such, this is the most vital component of the indigenous environmental
knowledge, by all means" (Krupnik and Vakhtin n.d.).

"Intellectual culture," as proposed by Krupnik and Vakhtin, is thus
something like a worldview or a cognitive model for perceiving the

world.[4] At the heart of this approach is a representationalist view of knowledge, according to which people can neither know nor engage with the world directly, but only indirectly through the medium of their cultural representations. People acquire these representations as they develop the use of language, and they are thus reproduced every day by everyone who shares that language. This means that the way people perceive the world—the very categories and concepts that provide a framework of meaning for them—is provided by the language that they use. "Our internal perception of the world around us," writes Leach, "is greatly influenced by the verbal categories which we use to describe it. . . . We use language to cut up the visual continuum into meaningful objects" (Leach 1976: 33). Burr, in her book on constructionist theory, takes a similar stance: "If our knowledge of the world, our common ways of understanding it, is not derived from the nature of the world as it really is, where does it come from? The social constructionist answer is that people construct it between them. . . . Therefore social interaction of all kinds, and particularly language, is of great interest to social constructionists" (Burr 1995: 4). And she continues, "Language . . . is a necessary pre-condition for thought as we know it" (p. 7).[5]

Despite these somewhat varied approaches to the issues of knowledge and perception, their basic assumption is the same, namely, that people come to know what is "out there" in the world by representing it in the mind, in the form of culturally specific "mental models." These models are the result of linguistically based categories and concepts, which give shape and meaning to what is taken to be the otherwise chaotic and formless flux of sensory experience. It follows from this line of theorizing that it is above all as a result of language that the knowledge of a particular cultural tradition is shared between people. With the loss of the language, the worldview that is expressed in it will inevitably also be lost. Indeed, this is the reason that social scientists and linguists often exhibit much anxiety about the disappearance of ancestral languages, since they believe that cultural knowledge, handed down from time immemorial, will be lost forever with the last generation of speakers.[6]

THE DWELLING PERSPECTIVE

But if it does, in fact, hold true that language in some fundamental fashion determines how we perceive and understand the world, why is it then that the older generation of Yukaghirs and Yupik, who still speak their native languages, do not demonstrate a significantly more coherent and

elaborate knowledge of spiritual matters than the rest of the adult population, who lack proficiency in their indigenous languages? It is here that
we touch upon the contradictory view that Krupnik and Vakhtin appear
to entertain. Although they hold that "intellectual culture" is the most
vital component of traditional knowledge, and, as I have outlined, such
knowledge is understood to be grounded in language, their field data
reveal quite the opposite: it suggests that the knowledge of spiritual matters and ritual practices does not deteriorate in direct relation to the loss
of native language.

To come to terms with this paradox, I will propose a radically different approach to the issue of spiritual knowledge, one that sets aside the
traditional view of perception as a matter of conceptual representations
or cognition and instead proceeds by focusing on the way things show up
in the flux of people's everyday activities. What I propose, in other
words, is to reverse the order of analysis, so to speak, and begin from the
assumption that people's practical engagement with things is the crucial
foundation upon which "intellectual culture," that is, abstract cognition
and conceptual representation, is necessarily premised. Ingold, drawing
on the phenomenology of Heidegger, calls this the "dwelling perspective," which he contrasts with the "building perspective" of representationalist theory (2000: 172–89). "We do not dwell because we have to
build, but we build and have to build because we dwell, that is, because
we are *dwellers*" (Heidegger 1993: 350; see also Ingold 2000: 186). Like
Ingold, I take this to be the fundamental principle of the dwelling perspective: "What it means is that the forms people build, whether in the
imagination or on the ground, arise within the current of their involved
activity, in the specific relational contexts of their practical engagement
with their surroundings" (Ingold 2000: 186). Thus, the dwelling perspective does not deny the fact that people interpret their experiences and
construct representations of them, but it emphasizes that people do not
do so on the basis of an original detachment of the intelligent subject
from his environment and the construction of the world in his mind
prior to any attempt at engagement with it. A dwelling perspective holds
that it is because we are, from the very outset, beings-*in*-a-world, which
affords meanings to us in contexts of current action, that we can produce
representations of it.

Even if Heidegger's philosophy is not without its own biased commitments and ethnocentric stances (see my criticism in chapters 1 and 9), it
is an approach that has the advantage of taking seriously the actual experience of those who practice it. In other words, what is particularly valu-

able in his philosophy is its insistence that abstract knowledge always emerges from contexts of practical engagement. For Heidegger, a knowable object is a *tool:* we know the world not contemplatively, but as tools, which are experienced as "ready-to-hand" elements in our everyday practical projects. Knowing, therefore, is deeply related to doing. It is exactly in this respect that his approach rejoins Yukaghir hunters, for whom spiritual knowledge begins with lived practical experience. By moving away like this from high-level linguistic theorizing toward the concreteness of everyday practical experience, I believe we can come to grips with why it is that the hunters seem to reduce to a shambles any attempt to bring the world of spiritual beings inside the bounds of a neatly ordered classificatory system and instead tend to lump them all together under the general term *khoziain.*

SPIRITS AS "READY TO HAND"

Although we in the West usually describe the culture that we live in as "scientific," we do not in fact usually use scientific thinking in our everyday lives (Worsley 1997: 6). Rather, we simply assume that we "know" about science because we use technological devices, such as cars and computers, that have been developed through the use of modern science. Our knowledge, however, is what could be called "recipe knowledge," since it does not require any understanding of the underlying scientific principles (Schutz 1971: 95; Worsley 1997: 6). The fact that we do not understand why and how these technological devices work does not usually hinder us from using them. Thus, a driver is not required to be familiar with the laws of mechanics in order to drive a car, and a computer user does not need to understand electronics in order to write an email. Instead, these and other objects we use daily fit naturally into our ordinary activities.

What is more, we make use of all these diverse tools in our daily lives without paying them any attention as such (Costall 1997: 76–86; Ingold 2000: 407). When, for example, I am writing on my computer and it is functioning as usual, I do not explicitly perceive the machine. I might perhaps pay attention to the keyboard, but if my typing is going really well, I do not even pay attention to that. Instead, I fully concentrate on what I am writing, while my typing simply continues in a "transparent coping" mode (Dreyfus 1988: 257–58). The point I wish to make is that when we look at our everyday ways of being with things, we do not find conscious subjects directed toward independent objects at all. Rather, the objects of our daily use are absorbed into the current of our activities, becoming in a sense transparent, wholly subordinate to the "in-order-to motives" of our tasks at hand.

Shifting our focus back to the hunters and the spirits they address in their rituals, I suggest that something similar is going on. However, before I begin my analysis, it needs to be pointed out that among the Yukaghirs we find no major public rituals concerned with, for example, initiation, childbirth, or burial of the dead. In fact, a remarkable feature of Yukaghir society is its paucity of ritual (see Jochelson 1926: 89). Yukaghir rituals are all of an everyday type and related to hunting. The rituals are performed individually or by the small group of hunters who happen to be together. They are often carried out in a matter-of-fact fashion, and are rarely formulated explicitly in conversation, still less reflected upon in the abstract. They are simply the "ways in which one does things" (Schutz 1966: xvii). A young hunter, who was somewhat annoyed at my perpetual questions about spirits, expressed it this way: "It is like the way you use your computer.[7] You write on it, but you do not think about how it actually works. You have told me this yourself. You just need to work on it, not to understand how it works. It is the same with me. I need to do so and so to kill an elk, but I do not think about its deeper meaning, and I do not need to know."

By describing how his knowledge of spirits and mine of computers are thoroughly situated in practical involvement, the hunter points to how our fundamental sense of things is not as objects of abstract thought but as instrumental objects for practical use. Whether computers or spirits, they are employed to get something done, and so they manifest themselves as "tools" that are used in a prosaic and matter-of-fact fashion in order to accomplish concrete objectives.[8]

Taking as an example the practice of "feeding the fire," which is a ritual carried out before every hunt, I hardly ever heard hunters talk about which spiritual entities were being addressed when they threw tea, tobacco, bread, and sugar into the flames. When I asked them, they either would not know or would simply say "to *khoziain.*" In other words, when feeding the fire, hunters do not typically reflect on the wider cosmological meanings of this ritual practice, nor do they consider the nature of the spiritual entities to which they are making the sacrifice. They simply feed the fire. Instead of focusing on the spirits, their attention is directed toward the activity of hunting itself, toward their concern with where and when to search for prey so that they can support their hungry relatives, exchange meat for fuel, and so forth. Thus, when feeding the fire, the hunters' intentions seem to pass through the spirits addressed toward the goals and purposes of their activity. One could say that in the midst of such a sacrifice, the spirits present themselves to hunters as a kind of available being, what Heidegger calls "readiness-to-hand" (1962: 99) and Dreyfus renders as "availability" (1991: 60). By this, I mean that spirits serve their instrumental functions in such a matter-of-fact fashion that they almost cease to exist altogether in the hunters' awareness. The same can be argued about "nonspiritual" tools, such as knives, axes, traps, and guns, when they are skillfully employed by hunters in some practical project: "The peculiarity of what is proximally ready-to-hand is that, in its readiness-to-hand, it must, as it were, withdraw in order to be ready-to-hand quite authentically. That with which our everyday dealings proximally dwell is not the tools themselves [material as well as spiritual]. On the contrary, that with which we concern ourselves is the work" (Heidegger 1962: 99; my insertion).

Each spiritual being has its perceivable properties, of course; every hunter would agree with that. However, the point is that a hunter does not, for the most part, explicitly notice or think about these properties. Indeed, it could be said that during everyday practices such as "feeding the fire," the spirits have a tendency to "disappear." Hunters are not aware of them having any characteristics at all, and this is why in conversation they simply refer to them by the general term *khoziain*. Their indifference to distinguishing between the various kinds of spirits does not necessarily reflect a loss of traditional knowledge, as implied by Krupnik and Vakhtin. Rather, this apathy toward the spiritual realm is intrinsic to their practical mode of being, in which the spirits effectively vanish as objects of attention in favor of pragmatic concerns. It comes as no surprise, then, that when asked about the meaning of their ritual practices, hunters tend to provide secular rather than spiritual explanations, for, as we have seen, their orientations toward the world in the course of such practices are not mystical or magico-religious. Quite the contrary: it is work rather than spirits that concerns them, and their frame of mind is just as sensible and empirical as that of any worker engaged in some practical project.[9]

This essentially pragmatic attitude of hunters toward the spirit world and their environment in general is not unique to Yukaghir hunters but is also reported among other indigenous peoples. A prosaic mindset thus seems to underlie Lee's observation that "Ju [a group of Bushmen] do not spend their time in philosophical discourse in the abstract. Instead, people get on with the concrete matters of life and death, health and illness in their daily lives" (1993: 114). Similarly, with regard to the Daur Mongols, Humphrey notes, "For ordinary people living their lives, entities and processes in the world are not the object of thinking in the abstract. In fact, occasions of context-less contemplation are so rare as to be virtually non-existent" (1996: 57). However, it is important to note that the practical mindset does not refer to a primitive stage in human intellectual development that can be contrasted with abstract "civilized" thinking. Rather, it is our most basic way of being, shared by all humans, irrespective of time and place.[10] The pragmatic motive also dominates Westerners' everyday lives, as revealed by Schutz in his account of the "common-sense world": "Man in his daily life is not particularly—and we dare say exceptionally—interested in the clarity of his knowledge, i.e., in full insight into the relations between the elements of his world and the general principles ruling those relations. He is satisfied that a well-functioning telephone service is available to him and, normally, does not ask what laws of physics make this functioning possible. He buys merchandise in the store, not knowing how it is produced, and pays with money, although he has only a vague idea of what money is" (Schutz 1971: 94).

While these statements point to how our original understanding of things (whether spirits or technological devices) is not theoretical but grounded in practical concerns, we should not lose sight of the fact, however, that even "ordinary" people do, in certain situations, reflect upon the world and their relations with it. The question is how, from the point of view of my dwelling perspective, this kind of abstract thinking is to be understood, and how does it differ from the concept of "intellectual culture"? The latter concept, as we have seen, starts from the assumption of an imagined separation between subject and world, so that the subject has to construct the world in his mind by means of concepts and categories provided by his language, prior to any meaningful engagement with it. Here, then, is the essence of what Ingold refers to as the "building perspective": "that worlds are constructed before they are lived in; or in other words, that acts of dwelling are preceded by acts of world-making" (Ingold 2000: 179). The route I take is exactly the opposite: supposing a primordial condition of direct perceptual engagement, of dwelling, I argue that the subject has to then disengage himself from the current of his activity in order to reflect upon it in the abstract. Only when he has achieved such a mode of contemplative detachment will he begin to ask such questions as "Who are the spirits?" or "Why are we doing this ritual?" It is this state of being, which Heidegger calls "present-at-hand" and Dreyfus translates as "occurrentness" (1991: 60), to which I will now turn.

WHEN THINGS GO WRONG

According to Heidegger a shift from an attitude of practical engagement to a contemplative one always implies some experience of "shock." It is when our ongoing coping with things runs into trouble that we will encounter a "changeover" in the way things reveal themselves to us (1962: 102–3). If, for example, my computer fails to turn on, the whole project of my writing grinds to a standstill and I am put in the position of simply looking at the computer to determine what to do next. A temporary breakdown of this kind thus forces me to shift into a mode in which what was previously transparent becomes explicitly manifest. Instead of focusing on my writing I now focus on my computer, which appears to be of a particular kind with specific properties. If the breakdown persists, an object's unusability may be thrust upon the subject, who may then begin to look at it from a purely theoretical perspective. It is then, according to my understanding of Heidegger, that we catch a glimpse of the web of the functional relations in which the malfunctioning object plays its part. When, for instance, my computer continuously fails to turn on, I become aware not only of the computer itself, but also of the network of relations in which its instrumental functioning is embedded. I see the printer with which the computer is connected, as well as the many other pieces of equipment that I use for writing. I may even become painfully aware of my own dependency on all these various objects for the realization of my in-order-to motives of writing. "[It is] when an assignment has been circumspectively aroused," writes Heidegger, "[that] the world announces itself" (1962: 105). Thus, in a sense, breakdowns make it possible for us to catch sight of the essential properties of things and our relations with them.

I believe that Heidegger's insights can be employed in our study of the Yukaghirs, and in particular they illuminate an incident that took place while I was living in the forest with the hunters. More than two weeks had passed without any hunting luck. We saw elk tracks everywhere, but we never got close to any of the animals. Then one hunter, Yura, succeeded in shooting an elk. The animal fell to the ground but then stood up again, and despite the fact that Yura kept shooting at it, it walked away. When Yura returned to the cabin he was very upset. "Just ten meters!" he cried. "I shot it five or six times, but it walked away.

Khoziain came to me last night [in a dream] and gave it to me. So why did he [the spirit] take it back? We had no such problems at the Omulevka River." "Yes," the others agreed, "Khoziain of the Omulevka had no problem with us." Yura, when he failed to succeed in killing an elk that had been offered to him in a dream, experienced the kind of "shock" that Heidegger described. When the elk got up and walked away, there was a shift in Yura's perception: he suddenly abandoned his practical attitude and adopted a kind of theoretical standpoint toward the hunting activity in which he was engaged. He started to regard spirits not just as an anonymous group, but as separate beings available for reflection, and he began to seek causes for his failure in their distinctive senses and sensibilities. This is not to be misunderstood as Yura undergoing some kind of cosmological illumination. Instead, he simply gained a quick insight into the web of human-spirit relations. For many hunters, their knowledge of spiritual beings and their relations with them does not extend beyond such brief moments of clarity.

MAKING INQUIRIES INTO THE SPIRIT WORLD

A situation of continuous failure, like that experienced by the members of my hunting group, may inspire further inquiry into the reasons for the failure. Hunters are likely to resolve their questions through experience as well as in conversations. In dreams, for example, a spirit often reveals its reasons for being insulted. It turned out that Yura dreamed that a woman with a child approached him. Both were clothed in dog fur, and a tiny stream of blood was running from the eye of the child. We all knew that Vasili, a Russian who had joined our group for the winter, had killed a pregnant dog in Nelemnoye before leaving for the forest. Yura's dream convinced the hunters that this was the reason behind our failure. They argued that the Owner of the Olguia River, where we were hunting, was most likely upset by the presence of the "polluted" Russian and that we would have no luck as long as he lived among us. The hunters never explicitly agreed to get rid of Vasili, nor did any of them ask him to leave. Instead, they simply "froze him out" by ceasing to pay him any attention whatsoever. Eventually, he decided to leave and live in the village.

The point I wish to stress is that although the hunters sometimes feel a need to make inquiries into the spirit world, these inquiries always concern specific elements of that world and never its totality. The hunters simply single out those elements that will help them overcome some obstacle. A hunter's interest in the elements that make up the spirit world is therefore always specialized and limited (Humphrey 1996: 83). No one is inspired to become familiar with the spirit world as a whole. Moreover, when making inquiries, hunters do not necessarily have clear insights into the particular characters of spirits. In most cases, they simply do not know the spirits well enough to say anything specific about them. Instead, they will draw from typified notions of how spirits are supposed to react to events (see Boyer 1993: 121–43). None of the hunters could thus explain to me why killing a pregnant dog in the village should upset the Owner of the Olguia River in particular. In fact, the dog is usually said to be the only nonhuman creature that does not have a guardian spirit, but only its human master. In other words, it seems that the killing of the dog was accepted as a valid explanation for our bad hunting luck on the simple grounds that killing a pregnant creature is generally seen to be a sinful act.

I do not want to overstate this image of hunters' knowledge as confused and lacking in depth and insight. The chief purpose of relating this episode has been to illustrate that their ideas about the world of spirits are not systematic. For the most part, their ideas are incoherent and rife with contradictions. To be sure, some increased insight about *certain* spirits may be achieved over the course of a person's life. Yukaghirs claim that, through years of repeated encounters with certain spiritual beings, one can gain deeper knowledge about the character of a few selected spirits. Many old people, for example, are said to have a *pomoshchnik* (helping spirit), or a particular spirit that favors him or her. It can be the spirit of a place where the person has hunted for decades, or it can be that of an animal species with which he or she has developed an intimate friendship through years of practical engagement. Younger persons, like Yura, may encounter various spiritual agents, but it is said that the spirits tend to develop permanent relations only with old people whom they have known for years.

The leader of my group, Old Spiridon, for example, claims his helping spirit to be the Owner of the Omulevka River, who comes to him in dreams in the shape of an old woman. She gives him presents, such as a piece of bread and butter. If the layer of butter is thin, he will try to persuade her to put more on, because the butter indicates the fatness of the elk being offered to him. "She loves to be sweet-talked. I say she is beautiful despite her age and tell her other pleasant things. In this way, I almost always succeed in persuading her to give me a thick layer," he explained. Thus, old people like Spiridon can give detailed descriptions of the character, mood, and sensibility of their helping spirit. They are capable of interpreting what the spirit means when it offers things to them, and to forecast its actions and reactions to events that may happen. But their knowledge does not extend beyond those particular spirits with whom they have intimate relations and a personal interest. Although Spiridon insisted that each spirit has its own distinctive character, he could never specify the ways in which spirits are different from one another: "How the devil should I know about the Owners of Popova and Shamanika?" he asked. "I hunt at the Omulevka River."

OPPOSING THE NOTION OF "WORLDVIEW"

In the light of these observations, let me return to the concept of "world-view" (i.e., intellectual culture), which is employed by Krupnik and Vakhtin in their study of indigenous spiritual knowledge. I want to explain why this concept is fundamentally misleading. The concept of a worldview rests on the assumption that the religious representations of a given group—a "culture" or "society"—constitute an integrated and consistent set of abstract principles (Boyer 1994). To say that they are integrated implies that the various ideas entertained by different individuals about spiritual beings are in fact connected and constitute an overall system, a cosmology. To say that they are consistent implies that the system in question is based on some kind of underlying pattern or structure, a sort of "cultural grammar" (Hoebel 1972: 541). The analogy with linguistics is thus obvious. Cultural knowledge is conceived as similar to linguistic knowledge, and by some authors as identical with it (see, for example, Goodenough 1951; Leach 1976: 51). Like the linguist who assumes that the language of a community already exists, complete with grammar and lexicon, implanted in the minds of its speakers, the concept of worldview thus implies that a body of context-free, propositional knowledge about spiritual beings, their characteristics and interrelations, lies fully formed inside people's heads, like a "cosmological map" simply waiting to be applied in particular situations of its practical use.

From what I have described, however, the existence of such a cosmological map is most likely an artifact of analytical abstraction. I have shown how hunters' ideas about spirits, far from being a corpus of stable conceptual knowledge imported into various contexts of experience, are in fact generated within these contexts in the course of people's everyday practical activities. Hunters' conceptions of spirits are, in other words, not simply *expressed* in activity, as the notion of worldview implies. Rather, they *subsist* in the flow of the activity itself (Ingold 2000: 162).

We have thus seen that, so long as the hunters' ongoing engagement with things goes smoothly, spirits simply cease to exist in their awareness altogether. It is when "absorbed coping" is somehow thwarted that a switch to deliberation is evoked. Hunters will then make an attempt to bring the spirits within the bounds of some kind of ordered classificatory system in order to locate the agent causing them trouble. However, even in such situations of "crisis," their attempt to classify the sprits is indeed a very limited undertaking. First, the hunters concern themselves only with a small subset of the universe of spirits and never with its totality. Their allocation of spirits into distinctive groupings, then, does not add up to anything like a cosmological map, a synoptic whole that encompasses all spiritual beings and their distinctive characteristics and interrelations. Moreover, in most cases, all that hunters have to go on are prototypical notions of what spirits are like. Thus, the concept of a spirit X is not necessarily a series of characteristics particular for that spirit, which can be codified as dictionary entities or as checklists of features. In most cases it is simply a loosely associated group of features, linked by a general idea of what a typical spirit is like (Boyer 1994: 36). The moment hunters identify the causal agency disturbing their lives and overcome it, their interest in the spirit usually ends, and they do not feel that it is necessary to further explore the nature of its agency. The spirit then returns to its former anonymity and becomes *khoziain,* everyone and no one. In short, although we might say that there are spirits and that hunters have experiences with spirits, there hardly exists a cosmological map.

I would like to point to yet another unfortunate consequence of the concept of worldview. It is precisely because it rests on the notion that the indigenous person's view is structured—that is, that all the attitudes, values, and beliefs form an integrated system—that the concept has an ingrained inability to deal with ambiguity (Guenther 1979: 102–27). Ambiguity is simply not acknowledged as an element of religion, or any other domain of culture for that matter, and is argued away in one fashion or another.[11] One such way is to treat what is ambiguous as "noise," that is, as elements incidental to the core of the religious cosmology as it has been defined by the anthropologist (see the criticism raised by Barth 1987: 77; Guenther 1999: 226–37). This was the approach pursued by Jochelson and Bogoras in their attempts to reconstruct, in their writings, the Siberian indigenous societies in their original state. Another approach is to see what is confusing, vague, and contradictory as evidence of distortion by external cultural forces. This latter line of reasoning is the one used by Krupnik and Vakhtin, who see the Yupiks' essentially fragmented and prosaic statements about spiritual matters as evidence of the emergence of a mixed culture, a new cognitive system of thought, which Krupnik and Vakhtin compare with mixed languages. My point is not to deny that changes have occurred in the ways Yukaghirs and other Siberian peoples think about spirits and their environments more generally. (Indeed, changes in knowledge are inevitable.) Nor do I dispute that the Siberian peoples have been victims of processes of acculturation (whatever that means). What I am saying is simply that ambiguity, contradiction, and vagueness is not in itself evidence that a rupture of tradition has occurred. However, the reason that anthropologists like Krupnik and Vakhtin are led to make what is, in my view, a false assumption is now clear: it is grounded in their approach to knowledge, which fails to situate perception and cognition within the practical contexts of people's ongoing engagement with things, and naively assumes that knowledge about spirits actually exists (or at least used to exist) in a worldview format.

CHAPTER 8

Learning and Dreaming

KNOWLEDGE AND REINCARNATION

A question that still needs to be explored is how we can account for the somewhat puzzling fact that the Yukaghirs' paucity of spiritual knowledge does not seem to be bound up with their loss of indigenous language. One explanation, I suggest, is that among the Yukaghirs very little knowledge about spiritual beings is explicitly transmitted between generations. Instead, people are largely left to think independently, and this gives rise to highly heterogeneous ideas about spiritual matters. Moreover, I will show that the hunters have a general attitude of mistrust, at times even hostility, toward information conveyed through language, which, on a fundamental level, is grounded in an ontology that considers verbal accounts to be an inferior way of knowing compared to lived experience.

Let me begin with an episode from my fieldwork that might serve as an example of what I am talking about. Once, when I was out hunting with Yura, we came across some tracks made by an elk, and Yura asked me in which direction the animal had gone. I bent down and took a close look at the tracks. They were not difficult to decipher. Countless numbers of small snowballs had been pushed to the right side of the track, clearly indicating that this was the direction in which the animal had moved. I told this to Yura, who, to my surprise, replied, "Wrong!" Again I examined the track carefully, but there was nothing about it that could change my opinion: "It went to the right," I insisted. "No," he replied in a firm voice, without even looking at the track. This obscure conversation went on for half a minute or so, and in the end I was both angry and confused. Then he suddenly smiled. "Don't worry, you are right," he said. "I'm just testing you. . . . Remember never to let anyone tell you what is right and wrong. Every hunter should say, I know . . . only I know what is right!"

I experienced many similar incidents in which I was told never to accept what people told me without examining the matter myself. The point is not that hunters do not listen to what others have to say or that they should keep what they know to themselves. On the contrary, knowledge about hunting, both its practical and its spiritual aspects, is regarded by the Yukaghirs as a communal resource, and hunters are instructed that "you must tell what you know" (Bodenhorn 1995: 171). The point is that for the individual hunter, knowledge about hunting should only be recognized as such when it has been tested for himself. In other words, the crucial test for knowledge is personal experience. This was made quite clear to me by a hunter who, in response to my question about whether he believed in the existence of the spiritual agents described in Yukaghir myths, replied, "I believe in those I myself have encountered. The rest I don't know about. They might exist or they might not." In other words, verbal information is never seen as sufficient; firsthand knowledge is "an epistemological *sine qua non*" (Smith 1998: 417). This is why hunters tend to speak only for themselves and of the things that they have learned through experience. For example, I never heard any-body say, "My father or grandfather did this or that." All that matters is what a person himself has experienced. This is closely related to the hunters' desire to be autonomous. As the older hunters often empha-sized, "To be a hunter, you must know everything yourself." Each is also cautious not to impinge upon another's autonomy, what they call "his matter, not mine" (Kwon 1993: 78). Goulet (1998: 36), who reports the same for the Dene Tha, describes this pattern of behavior as an aspira-tion to "consistently maximize the number of occasions in which one can learn by oneself and for oneself what it is to live an autonomous life com-petently." This ethos of the right to one's autonomy and the obligation to respect the autonomy of others is also evident among other circumpolar peoples, such as the Ojibwa (Hallowell 1960: 25; Black 1977), the Chipewyan (Smith 1998), and the Inuit (Guemple 1991).

What we are dealing with, however, is not simply a "native phenome-nology," as suggested by Black in relation to the Ojibwa, who, just like the Yukaghirs, only credit as knowledge "that which is revealed through their own experience" (1977: 93). Rather, we are talking about an entirely different notion of how people become knowledgeable persons in the first place. I described in chapter 2 how Yukaghirs are inclined to view an infant as a reborn dead relative. At some moment during the mother's pregnancy, the soul, or *ayibii*, of the deceased person is believed to enter the mother's womb through her vagina and possess the child. The two then become the same person, and the child is said to share with the deceased his or her personality, including such attributes as temper, humor, and drinking and eating habits. The child is also believed to possess the same range of skills and relations with spiritual beings. Thus, all the elements of character and knowledge that we usually understand to be accrued throughout a lifetime, the child receives all at once, in finished form, even before it is born.

However, in gaining access to language, a failure in the child's memory is said to occur. The child's knowledge is not lost as such, but the child is no longer explicitly aware of who it is and what it knows. Its knowledge comes to exist in a sort of encapsulated form, which needs to be drawn out through processes of personal rediscovery. We are not talking about some kind of self-reflection of a Cartesian kind. Rather, a person gains access to what he or she knows through living out a life. To engage in everyday activities such as hunting, fishing, and dreaming, then, is said to be engaging in acts of remembrance. This, however, is understood as a matter not only of calling up internal images from one's former life, as when children start to talk from the vantage point of the deceased person they are said to be, but also of engaging with things and people, which are believed to be pregnant with clues to one's past knowledge. It follows from this that in the world of the Yukaghirs there is no such thing as a child, at least not in our sense of a blank slate that needs to be instilled with knowledge. A person knows from the very beginning everything he or she will ever come to know, and is therefore not in debt to anybody for this knowledge.

This outlook has major implications for understanding what learning means among the Yukaghirs. Rather than simply involving the transmission of information "from the top down," learning requires assisting or guiding people in practical activities through which they will come to realize what they are already believed to know. Thus, I hardly ever saw children having things explained to them, especially with regard to spirits and ritual practices. The transmission of such knowledge consists largely of hands-on training in specific ritual techniques, such as feeding the fire, cutting off the chin beard of a slain elk, and avoiding feeding its interior organs to the dogs. So, although an adult might be highly con-

cerned that a youngster gets the ritual techniques right, each child is generally left to reach his or her own conclusions about the meaning of
these ritual practices. Judging from the material of Krupnik and Vakhtin,
the same seems to be the case among the Yupik, who share with the
Yukaghirs ideas of reincarnation: "Each and every elder's recollection
stressed that adults had never told the children what to do or how to do
something directly, but that the kids simply watched and repeated what
the adults were doing" (Krupnik and Vakhtin n.d.). This model of
knowledge transferal could be described as "doing is learning and learning is doing."

Another instructional method is to allow the child to teach him- or
herself. A Sakha schoolteacher in Nelemnoye gave me a rich description
of what this implies:

> Obviously, these people [the Yukaghirs] don't care about the well-being of
> their children. You see how they let small boys take guns and run into the
> forest on their own. . . . Last year, two drowned. . . . If they don't feel like
> going to school, their parents don't tell them to. When I ask them why
> Stephan and Nadia are not in school, the parents simply say they didn't
> want to go. . . . One time, I witnessed how a little boy reached for a burning
> stick and got terribly burnt. His parents watched it happening but did noth-
> ing to prevent it. They just laughed as the child came running screaming
> toward them.

Yukaghir children, then, are allowed almost complete freedom to explore
their environment on their own, with little or no intervention from their
parents. If children place themselves in a dangerous situation, the parents
generally leave them to work out the situation on their own, because children are supposed to know what they are doing, even though they might
not be explicitly aware of it. Goulet (1998: 39–42), who reports the
same attitude among Dene parents, describes how they allow their children to play with both alcohol and chainsaws while observing silently
from a distance. He summarizes this ethos of minimal intervention by
writing, "Because Dene consider true knowledge to be personal, firsthand knowledge, they learn in a manner that emphasises the nonverbal
over the verbal, the experimental over the exposition of principles"
(Goulet 1998: 58).

LANGUAGE, KNOWLEDGE, AND IDENTITY

But what is it about language and explicit instruction that the Yukaghirs
and other circumpolar peoples seem to oppose so strongly? As we have

seen, the Yukaghirs hold that children, at least until they learn to talk, know everything. They also say that the child's body at this stage is "open" (Rus. *otkryt*), which is their translation into Russian of the Yukaghir *ongdsjotjunäi sjoromok*, which means "raw meat." The moment the child acquires speech, however, its body "closes" and it has to spend the rest of its life rediscovering its knowledge through practical engagement with things and people. In other words, there is a sense in which the Yukaghirs see language as distorting people's proper understanding of things.

To come to terms with this idea, I shall return to Lacan's theory of the child's passage from the "mirror stage" to the symbolic world of language (1989 [1966]). We can follow Eagleton's (1983: 166) semiotic take on Lacan and think of the small child looking at itself in the mirror as a kind of "signifier," something capable of bestowing meaning, and of the image it sees in the mirror as something "signified." The image the child sees in the mirror, or in any other object for that matter, is somehow the meaning of itself. Signifier and signified are here harmoniously united. There is no gap between subject and world. The two ceaselessly reflect themselves in each other, and no real differences or divisions are yet apparent. In Yukaghir terms, one could say that the child truly knows the world because it is simply a clearing or an openness in which things can manifest themselves and thus "be" in accordance with its own limits instead of in accordance with the limits imposed on it by linguistic constructs.

In gaining access to speech, however, the child falls victim to the symbolic world of language, by which Lacan means a system of signification, that is, a system of difference (1989 [1966]: 165–66). The child unconsciously learns the Saussurean point that identities come about only as a result of difference—that one sign, thing, or subject is what it is only by excluding another (Saussure 1959: 102–22). The child must now resign itself to the fact that it will no longer have any *direct* access to the world, what Lacan calls the "real" (1991 [1953–54]: 66). Although it will attempt to bridge the gap between self and world by producing meanings or signifiers, the world will always be beyond its reach, always outside the symbolic order of language, because the effect of language is essentially to divide and differentiate everything. Heidegger makes a somewhat similar point when he says that language is not a mere instrument of communication, but instead the very dimension in which humans "build" or construct the world (1962: section 34).[1] "Building" and "language" are therefore all but synonymous. In this sense, language by its very nature opposes "dwelling," which, as we have seen, rests on the principle of similitude between subject and world, not unlike the child's relations with the world in the "mirror phase." Since dwelling is the basis for all experiential knowledge, which by and large is seen by hunters as the only proper way of knowing, there is a sense in which language is a direct threat to their very existence as knowledgeable subjects. Knowing for them, therefore, becomes a matter of overcoming the boundary between self and world, initially created by language. This, as we have seen, is attempted by refraining from using explicit instructions when teaching children, but instead allowing them to (re)discover meanings in the world on their own. The same principle is apparent during a hunt when the hunters deliberately seek to temporarily suspend their separation from their prey by abstaining from talking in human language. Not surprisingly, hunters refer to this process of dehumanization as an attempt to "open their bodies."

Despite the fact that hunters see language as an inferior way of knowing that distorts people's true understanding of things, its significance for their human sense of self cannot be overstated. Just as movement and smell are seen as identifying markers of human personhood, so the hunters' self-awareness of belonging to the human species is inseparably bound up with human speech. Dwelling does, after all, entail the danger that the subject's involvement with the world becomes so complete that differences appear to vanish altogether, and, as I described in earlier chapters with regard to human-animal transformations, such complete dissolution of the self should be avoided at all cost. Entry into the symbolic order of language is therefore seen by Yukaghirs as necessary for the development and growth of the person, for without human language the subject-world relation would be an enclosed, circular relationship that would make any distinctive human identity impossible. In this sense, human language provides hunters with security against self-dissolution or metamorphosis.

In fact, hunters often told me about a kind of hybrid creature that roams the forest. They call them *hairy ones* (Yuk. *syugusuy suroma*) or *wild people* (Rus. *dikiie liudi*). Although these creatures are human in appearance, their bodies are covered in fur, like animals. They live a solitary existence and keep their distance from each other, as well as from humans and other creatures of the forest. Hunters' conceptions of these essentially antisocial creatures are interesting because they represent a gray area, mediating the narrow gap between the human and animal worlds. The creatures are believed to be hunters who, after failing to find their way back to the encampment, lost the fundamental aspects of their humanity but did not become animals in any absolute sense. They therefore remain alien to human and animal societies alike. In other words, while hunters see animals and spirits as "cultural beings," *syugusuy suroma* are conceived as "wild" because they are neither fully human nor nonhuman but somewhere in between—rather like the hunter when he is imitating his prey. Persistent isolation from human communication is said to cause the transformation of lost hunters into these wild creatures. "You can't live without talking," a hunter explained to me. "This is why I always bring a radio with me to the forest if I go on my own. It is not for safety, if that's what you think. Who could save me if I had an accident or fell ill? There are no helicopters left in the region. No, I bring it to talk with other hunters. One needs to talk or one will go wild!"

Thus, when hunters return from the forest to the encampment, they are obliged to engage in storytelling. And as I will show, the hunters' narrative mode is not so important as an instrument for exchanging knowledge, but is instead a "magical" tool for "humanizing" hunters, a method for withdrawing from the betwixt-and-between state of hunting and reconstructing their self-identities as human persons.

STORYTELLING AND SPATIAL ORIENTATION

When they arrive at the cabins in the encampment, the hunters hang their fur clothes outside, then light the cabin's small metal stove and boil water for tea and meat. Within a few hours the air is thick with wood and tobacco smoke and the smell of cooked food. During their meal and afterward, the hunters talk nonstop about the day's hunt. Their speech forms narratives, and everyone takes a turn telling one: "Running, running along Ivan's *protoka* [place along the riverbank].[2] Nothing, damn! Oh, over there [tracks from elk]. Running along Yura's *protoka*. Running, running. Nothing. What a clever [one]. . . . Oh, there, moving away from the water. Running. Damn, this morning there was a hare's trail. Didn't have time [to lay snares], damn. Running, damn. . . . Three of . . . [tracks from elk]. Making a circle. The kind of impossible wind . . . [moving his hand back and forth over his head]."

Numerous stories of this kind filled the many evenings I spent with Spiridon and his hunters. The stories could be termed "minimalist" (Rosaldo 1986) in that the sentences are short, fragmented, and often incomplete. Either the subject or another part of the sentence may be missing, and one has to guess the meaning according to the general context of the story or according to the previous or following sentences, or by deciphering the bodily gestures of the speaker. Moreover, the story-teller is not guided by any strict chronology, but might jump back and forth between various events that occurred at different times and places during the day. Although virtually everyone narrates in the Russian lan-guage, older hunters like Spiridon would occasionally intermix Yukaghir and Sakha phrases, ignoring (or pretending to ignore) the fact that most of the others in the group do not understand these languages well. The others, then, would have no choice other than to sit patiently in the hope of picking up some parts of the narrative or just get bored. No narrator, however, expects to hold everyone's attention from beginning to end. People drift in and out of the conversational community, paying atten-tion to the parts that interest them most or that happen to be presented when they are around or awake.

What are we to make of these minimalist accounts of the hunt? What purpose does the storytelling serve, and why does it take such an ellipti-cal form? With regard to the latter question, Rosaldo (1986: 108) has suggested that in small-scale societies storytellers speak to people who share enormous background knowledge about their hunting practices and their landscape. Consequently, hunting stories can communicate information in "telegraphic shorthand," because the speakers can safely assume their listeners' "depth of background knowledge": "Ilongot hunting stories relegate to the subject matter of composite accounts (what all hunts have in common) to silence or, more precisely to tacit background knowledge.[3] Ilongot storytellers and their interlocutors no more need repeat what 'everybody' already knows about hunting than a group of avid sports fans need to bore each other by reciting the basic rules of the game" (Rosaldo 1993: 129).

I shall return to comment on Rosaldo's statement in a moment. For now, I will turn to Kwon (1993; 1997), who in his study of storytelling among Orochon hunters, a Siberian indigenous group living on Sakhalin Island, makes an assumption similar to Rosaldo's. Kwon accounts for the maddeningly elliptical nature of Orochon hunting narratives by referring to the depth of the hunters' shared background knowledge:

> Whether the talk is narration or conversation, or whether it is about the present or the past, it is impossible to keep up with it, unless one has a certain shared map. (p. 67)

> For me as an outsider . . . it was not possible to comprehend these stories coherently, for the referent landmarks within the story were spatially un-known (e.g., the highland) and temporally inaccessible (e.g., the *duia* [home

of the past]). Secondly, the terrain where the web of landmarks is present and the complex motions and actions take place seemed to me so vast that I would never be able to get a picture, especially if I had to sit around in the camp all the time. (p. 10)

Kwon then goes on to suggest that hunters' storytelling serves primarily as an "intellectual-organisational technology" (1993: 59), a medium by means of which information obtained by individual hunters on the land are translated into a shared cognitive structure, a mental map of some sort, for navigating the landscape: "The hunters go out to the territory perhaps with a fragmentary map but bring back informative resources for further mapping to their conversational community" (Kwon 1997: 146; see also Kwon 1993: 4).

But does the hunters' storytelling really amount to a kind of modeling of reality, a mental representation of the landscape that they might consult in the same way as Westerners would consult a map? I think not. Kwon, like other mental map theorists, seems to hold that technically sophisticated navigation based on maps and everyday way finding are essentially similar processes. The only difference is that the native hunter's map is not held in the hand but in the head, in the form of a comprehensive mental representation of his spatial surroundings. At any given moment he can, it is assumed, access this mental map and determine his location in terms of it. This, however, is not very true in our own experience of what it is like to know one's whereabouts, which is something quite different from using a map. As Bourdieu, among others, has pointed out, in real life the question of using a map arises only when people do *not* know how to accomplish a journey or find their way around a landscape (1977: 2; see also Ingold 2000: 219). A person familiar with a landscape has no need of a map, but instead gets his bearings from attending in a nonconceptual and habitual manner to the landscape itself, rather than to some abstract representation of it. The same, I suggest, holds true for the Yukaghir hunter, who has lived and worked in the same territory for years and whose powers of perception and action have been fine-tuned to pick up the sights, sounds, and even smells that constitute the specific atmosphere of its various locations. He knows quite well where he is, or in what direction to go, without having to consult any mental map. For him, practical way finding is informal, subjective, and based on habit and familiarity with his home ground. Thus, whatever goes on when one uses a map does not correspond to what goes on in the mind of a Yukaghir hunter navigating effortlessly without one.

Now, it is true that not all hunters know the landscape like the back of their hand. As I have already described, a hunting group typically consists of not only men with long-standing experience in a particular territory, but also a wide range of other hunters who join the group for a short period of time. Could it be that hunters' storytelling provides these "strangers" with a comprehensive description of the landscape's landmarks, locations, and names, which they might then consult as we would consult a map? Surely not. As my Sakha friend Ivan bluntly admitted to me, "When Spiridon or one of the others talk about this or that *protoka*, I hardly ever know what locality they are referring to. To know these things one must have been hunting along the river for years." Thus, to people unfamiliar with the local landscape, the places and landmarks mentioned in hunters' narratives remain as obscure as they did to Kwon. Indeed, this is the reason why a novice hunter unfamiliar with the landscape usually accompanies a more experienced one, the latter pointing out specific locations as they walk around. The novice hunter is also encouraged to discover other things on his own, because, as Yura assured me, "The one who simply follows in the footsteps of his mentor becomes like a robot who just walks along. To become autonomous, you need to go hunting on our own. Only then do you really start noticing the myriad of details around you."

The type of learning we are dealing with here is what Lave (1997: 310) has called "understanding in practice," to which she counterposes the "culture of acquisition." The latter phrase denotes the theory of learning, long favored by cognitive scientists and adhered to by Kwon, according to which mastery of one's spatial environment depends on the practitioner having acquired a body of abstract representational knowledge, a maplike structure of the world by means of which he can find his way around in it. "Understanding in practice," by contrast, implies that everyday skills of orientation and way finding are realized through practice and experience (i.e., what I have called "doing is learning and learning is doing"). This does not involve "talking about" the landscape so much as acquiring practical skills for *direct* perceptual engagement with it. In fact, the transmission of such skills can take place even when the coparticipants fail to share a common linguistic code, because the novice's ability to learn from his mentor depends not on their possessing the same conceptual representations, but rather on their being caught up together in the same current of activity (Ingold 1993: 222–23).[4]

Similarly, the mentor's effectiveness as an instructor is not dependent on his ability to implant in the novice his own representations. Rather, it depends on his ability to demonstrate and support—that is, to set up situations in which the novice can develop his own "feel" for the landscape. What the experienced hunter gives to the inexperienced one, then, are specific contexts of experience through which the novice can develop his own powers of perception and action. This is what Ingold has appropriately called "an education of attention" (2000: 354). It involves moving around in the landscape, exploring it, attending to it, and adjusting one's senses to pick up the signs by which it is revealed. It is not about building mental images of it in the mind from verbally transmitted information, which is what Kwon seems to suggest when he maintains that hunters' storytelling serves as "an intellectual organisational technology" for cognitively mapping the landscape (1993: 77). In fact, one might question what use hunters' narratives could possibly have as maps if they are largely unintelligible to all but those who are so familiar with the landscape as to manage quite well without devices of this kind.[5]

PURGING OTHERNESS FROM THE SELF

I do not believe that hunters' storytelling fulfills an educational function. If the main purpose of their narrative mode were to transmit knowledge about the landscape, then why would their stories take such a minimalist and elliptical form? This discord cannot simply be explained away, as Rosaldo does (1986: 108; 1993: 129), by the people's "depth of shared background knowledge." A group of hunters, as we have seen, consists of people from many different backgrounds, ranging from experienced hunters with a long-standing relation to a particular area, to inexperienced beginners. Hence, the social distribution of knowledge within a group of hunters is necessarily "plural," for not every hunter holds the same amount or same kind of knowledge. I therefore find it hard to accept that their conversational community should be based on a body of "shared background knowledge" about "the landscape and hunting practices," which the "speakers can safely assume" (Rosaldo 1986: 108). For what we are dealing with is, in effect, "*knowledges,* not simply Knowledge with a capital K" (Worsley 1997: 10; my emphasis). In addition, one might question what value the narratives of older hunters such as Spiridon could possibly have as "knowledge," when he deliberately uses Yukaghir and Sakha phrases that are largely unintelligible to most people in the group. If Spiridon's aim were to communicate and pass on knowledge, he would presumably do so in a language that the others could understand.

These points, however, constitute only part of my argument, which I shall attempt to bring to a more fundamental level of analysis. I will begin by returning to Lacan's theory of language (1989 [1966]), and his view that meaning in language is basically a matter of *difference*. The signifier "dog," for instance, communicates to us the concept or signified "dog" because it divides itself from, let us say, the signifier "cat." Thus, the signified "dog" is the product of the difference between two signifiers. But it is also the product of the difference between a great many other signifiers, such as "horse," "chap," "coat," and so on. This fundamentally questions the Saussurian view that the signifier and signified constitute an indissoluble unity (Saussure 1959: 112–13). For the signified "dog" is defined by reference to other signifiers, which in turn require definition by reference to yet other signifiers—an endless chain with no end point. Thus, for Lacan, meaning in language is the outcome of what is essentially an endless play of signifiers rather than a concept tied firmly to the tail of a particular signifier (Lacan 1989 [1966]: 165–66). What is more, there is no fixed distinction between signifiers and signifieds either. Were I, for example, to look up the meaning of the signifier "dog" in my Oxford dictionary, it would tell me that a dog is "a domesticated carnivorous mammal probably descended from the wolf." Thus, all that I am given is yet more signifiers whose signifieds I can look up in turn. The process with which we are dealing is therefore not only infinite but also somehow circular: "Signifiers keep transforming into signifieds, and *visa versa*, and you never arrive at a final signified that is not a signifier in itself" (Sarup 1988: 35).

The implication of all this is that meaning is not immediately *present* in a linguistic sign. Since the meaning of the sign is a matter of what the sign is *not*, its meaning is always somehow absent from it. Meaning in language, if you like, is scattered or dispersed along the whole chain of signifiers: it cannot easily be nailed down because it is never fully present in one sign alone. Language is therefore not a well-defined, clearly demarcated structure containing symmetrical units of signifiers and signifieds, as Saussure would have it. Rather it is, as Eagleton puts it, "like a sprawling limitless web, where there is a constant interchange and circulation of elements, where none of the elements is absolutely definable and where everything is caught up and traced through by everything else" (1983: 129).

If this is so, then it strikes a serious blow at theories, such as that employed by Kwon, that hold that the function of peoples' linguistic communication is to convey facts about the world. For, according to the view I have just outlined, nothing can ever be fully present in language. It is an illusion to believe that one can reveal through language what the world is really like, because the meaning of a word is always somehow dispersed, divided, and never quite one with itself. Indeed, this is what Lacan is pointing to when he writes that to enter language is to be detached from the "real" (world), which is always beyond the reach of signification, always outside the symbolic order of language (1991 [1953–54]: 66). This is also, I believe, the reason why a philosopher of language such as Rorty remarks that there is no such thing as a language in the sense of a medium that can represent or express facts about the world (1989: 10), for there are, as we have seen, no such facts that can ever be fully present in the chain of signifiers, whose effect is to divide and differentiate all things. Rorty suggests that instead of thinking about words as conveying intrinsic meaning, we should think of them as ways of producing *effects;* that is, language is to be seen not as a medium but as a *tool* that works better or worse for concrete tasks at hand (1989: 12–13). As Hobart notes, "We are back not just to what words 'mean' but what people *do* in using them" (1986: 12; my emphasis).

I am aware that this view of language raises a number of epistemological and other problems. Nevertheless, what we are offered, I believe, is a view of language that resonates well with Yukaghir understandings of both language and knowledge. In their view, what imparts meaningfulness to a person's experience is *not* language, but instead the act of direct perceptual engagement with things—an act that is believed to occur independently of language itself. For them, in other words, meaning is something that predates language; language is no more than a secondary activity that gives names to meanings, which the person is believed to already possess. In fact, they claim that verbal instruction might even distort a person's proper understanding of things. Talking obstructs rather than promotes genuine knowledge about the world.

Still, the Yukaghirs *do* regard language as a marker of identity, as something inseparably bound up with what it means to be a human person, and it is with reference to this aspect of language that I believe we should understand their narrative mode. What I am suggesting, in other words, is that hunters' storytelling is not about conveying knowledge about the world, since knowledge for them is something that is embedded in contexts of nonlinguistic modes of being-in-the-world, that is, in practical activities of dwelling. Rather, they engage in storytelling and are obliged to do so in order to bring about certain "humanizing" effects.

I have already pointed to the fact that among the Yukaghirs we do not find any initiation ritual to mark the transition from boyhood to manhood. Instead, manhood is reckoned when a youth becomes a "four-legged animal-killer man" (Yuk. *ye'lokun-no'ineyebon ku'de'ciye coro'-mox*), that is, when he has killed his first big game animal, such as an elk, reindeer, or bear (Jochelson 1926: 63). This lack of formal initiation ritual is, however, no accident, since the hunting process itself can be sub-divided into a succession of three stages that recall those classically associated not only with initiation rites, but with other rites of passage as well (Van Gennep 1960 [1909]). The first stage, that of "separation," I have already described in some detail. Basically, it serves to break down the hunter's identity, making him a tabula rasa on which an animal identity can be inscribed. As noted earlier, hunters call this stage in the hunting process "opening one's body." The hunter's ordinary human identity that gives sense and order to his everyday life no longer applies, but is in a way suspended. The second phase, that of "liminality" or "transition," I have also described. In this stage the hunter gives in to an alien perspective and changes in the process: he is not the animal whose perspective he is assuming, and yet he is not *not* that animal either. While this state of being betwixt and between perspectives enables the hunter to do things he cannot ordinarily do, such as seducing an animal into "giving itself up," it also causes him certain feelings of anxiety about losing his human personhood. This is the reason he must return to the encampment at the end of the day when the hunt is over. The return to the encampment marks the final phase of the hunting process, which is that of "reincorporating." What life in the encampment does, in effect, is to transform the hunter back to his ordinary mode of existence as a human person, so that he is not left hanging in the liminal stage, as are *syugusuy suroma*, the wild men of the forest who are trapped in between the human and animal worlds. Thus, the hunting process as a whole is, in effect, an act of temporary transformations—not only the transformation from "me" to "*not* not-me," but also back to "me" again.

Talking plays an important part in this final stage of the hunter's return to his starting place. The narrative mode and the endless exchange of words, together with the smell of human presence, "humanizes" hunters and the space of the encampment. Speech and smell—both of which are seen as identifying markers of personhood—are thus to be seen as everyday types of "magical" tools for purging otherness from the self and reconstructing one's human identity. However, it is not so much the meaning of the words uttered as the talking itself that brings hunters back to their ordinary spheres. Whether the narrator talks in the Yukaghir, Sakha, or Russian language, and whether he is fully or only

Figure 13. Storytelling in the encampment. The man on the right is Yura
Spiridonov. Photo by Rane Willerslev.

partly comprehensible, is of secondary importance. The listeners are not
expected to attend too closely to his words for meaning. Rather, it is the
act of talking that brings about the intended effect. It confronts—almost
engulfs—hunters with the paramount reality of human social life from
which they had previously withdrawn, and it forces them to examine the
hunting event in these terms. To this extent, their narrative mode is
directly involved in the promotion of reflexivity. Hunters are, through
their engagement in storytelling, provided the opportunity to reflect back
on the day's hunt, to stand apart from it and to "look" at it from within
the human social sphere of the encampment. The result is that they are,
in Turner's words, made conscious of their own consciousness (1982: 75;
see also Kapferer 1984: 186). They come to see that they are neither reindeer nor elk, but rather genuine human persons.

THE DREAM WORLD

We have seen that among the Yukaghirs very little knowledge about spiritual beings is explicitly transmitted between generations. However, I
believe that this only partly explains why a person's spiritual knowledge
does not seem to depend on the language he or she speaks. In fact, I will

attempt to make an even stronger point, namely, that conceptions of spiritual beings are not in any fundamental way based in language. At first this might seem to be a flawed claim. How can we possibly have conceptions of things that do not exist outside our imagination? Is it not language that somehow provides us with these concepts? It is this line of thinking that seems to be the reasoning behind Humphrey's assertion that, among the Daur Mongols, "A concept such as . . . *endur* [spirit of meritorious old man] . . . could not develop without language, and although it might well also be based on intuitive assumptions . . . its use would depend on definitional principles. Terms like *endur, barkan* (shamanic spirit), or *mudur* (dragon) will always depend on conventional definitions" (Humphrey 1996: 108).

Humphrey, in her analysis, is drawing on recent findings within cognitive science that show that basic concepts do not come from language learning but instead from experience and practice, and they are not codified as dictionary entries, nor as checklists of features (Bloch 1998: 5–7, 47–48). Children, then, will have a basic concept of, for example, "house" long before they can actually say the word, and this concept is not the product of a series of definitions (such as a roof, walls, and a door), but rather a loosely associated group of "houselike" qualities, none of which is essential but all of which are linked by a general idea of what a prototypical house is like. Moreover, these cognitive studies show that the acquisition of lexical semantics by children is largely a matter of trying to match words to concepts already formed prior to the development of language (Bloch 1998: 6). Accepting all this, Humphrey argues that the felt authenticity of religious representations is guaranteed primarily by nonlinguistic and direct modes of experiencing natural phenomena, such as mountains, rivers, and animals (1996: 106, 108). However, the concepts of the spirits that represent these natural phenomena cannot be formed without language, because spirits do not, after all, really exist, unlike a house or a mountain, but are instead supernatural creatures fostered by the human imagination.

While this seems to be common sense, when I consider the significance of dreams in the formation of concepts about spiritual beings, I am not so sure that her argument holds true. My idea bears some resemblance to that of Tylor, who more than a hundred years ago argued that "primitive" man's first doctrines of the soul or spirit developed on the basis of his dream life (Tylor 1929b [1871]: 356).

However, before proposing my argument, some words need to be said about the Yukaghirs' notions of dreams. Because the Freudian approach to dream interpretation is so dominant and familiar that it has become an ingrained part of our "folk knowledge" (see Gellner 1985: 5), I will reveal how Yukaghir ideas about dreams are different from our commonsense understandings of the phenomenon by briefly comparing them with Freud's theory. For Freud, dreams are the manifestation of the unconscious, those instinctual drives and desires that we need to repress in our everyday waking life. "The royal road to the unconscious is dreams," writes Freud. "Dreams allow us one of the few privileged glimpses of it at work" (1957: 156). Thus, for Freud, dream experiences exist only in the interiority of the unconscious mind, a mind that is freed during sleep from the psychological restrictions imposed on it during waking life. The Yukaghirs' vision of dreams is entirely opposed to Freud's. For them, the dreaming self, far from taking a break from the demands of coping with reality, sets out in search of meanings that will help it to accomplish concrete objectives in waking life. While the hunter's body is lying asleep, his soul, or *ayibii*, is said to penetrate beneath the surface of things into the "shadow world" so that he can encounter the invisible counterparts of the animals, their master-spirits, and seduce them into supplying him with prey. The following two dream experiences, recorded during my fieldwork, may serve as examples:[6]

Told by a middle-aged male hunter:
They live in a wooden house. There is a barn, too. I assume they keep the animals in the barn. They are always glad so see me, the three sisters. When I arrive, they are a little drunk [presumably, he is referring to the vodka offered when feeding the fire]. They start to play around with my penis, edging up to me. If I'm hunting at the upper part of the river, I'll take the oldest sister and we'll go to bed. If I hunt at the middle part, I'll pick the middle sister. And if I'm hunting at the lower part I'll go with the youngest one. When I wake up I know that in this season I will have good luck [in hunting].

Told by an old woman:
I was lying sleeping with my husband in the tent, when I suddenly heard a male voice calling me. "Stand up," it said. I stood up. "Go up the river," the voice said. It was as if I had started flying up the river. "Turn left," the voice said. I flew left, and there, in between the trees, stood a huge penis. [She laughs.] . . . I won't tell you any more. But next morning, when we got up, I said to my husband that I had had a dream. I didn't tell him what I had dreamt, but just said that we should go upriver and then go to the left. So we did, and there, at the very same spot, stood a huge bull [elk] that my husband killed.

So, what Freud ascribes to the realm of the unconscious, Yukaghirs see as real and conscious sexual engagements with spiritual beings. The important point about this contrast is that, in the case of the former, dreaming is seen as fantasy—a notion that is supported by the fact that sleep itself is understood to be a period of social inactiveness, a kind of "empty reality" (Riches 1995: 112). For Yukaghirs, in contrast, dream imagery reflects the experience of the soul, which is considered capable of influencing events to the person's advantage through sexual engagement with spiritual beings. This difference of interpretation has its roots in fundamental ontological assumptions: Freud, like many other Western thinkers, starts from the premise that the mind is distinct from the world, which is why dreams, in his view, only reflect one's inner state. For Yukaghirs, on the contrary, the mind always subsists in the very engagement of the person in the world, quite independently of whether he is asleep or awake. In their view, a person, therefore, always exists as a being-*in*-the-world, "caught up in an ongoing set of relationships with components of the lived in environment" (Ingold 2000: 101).

Moreover, and contrary to Harner's interpretation (1972: 134), Yukaghirs do not see any conflict between the world of dreams and that of the ordinary waking state. Harner asserts that the Shuar (Jívaro) of the Amazon see the normal world as an illusion, since the only real world is that of spiritual forces, which only the soul can reach through dreaming. This, however, does not reflect the Yukaghir understanding. They do not see the two worlds as opposed, but regard them as mirror images of each other, in much the same way as the soul, *ayibii*, is understood to be the reflected image of the person (remember that *ayibii* literally means "*shadow*" in Yukaghir). Therefore, in their view, the world of dreams and waking life are two sides of the same reality, which together constitute one world, and neither is therefore amenable to prioritization.[7]

It follows from this that among Yukaghirs the principles at work in the dream world are much the same as those at work in waking life. Thus, when a hunter seeks to approach and seduce the invisible counterpart of the animal, its spirit, the hunter's *ayibii* must take on the bodily appearance of an animal, in much the same way as the hunter himself does when he attempts to seduce his prey in waking life. The *ayibii*'s altered bodily form is also the reason why the spirit tends to be encountered in the shape of a human, because, as I argued earlier, this is how all beings that share the same body are believed to see each other. Still, just as in waking life, the dreaming hunter must maintain an element of self-awareness or reflexivity to safeguard his *ayibii* from being carried away by its animal body. Thus, a hunter described to me how, during his dreams, he would alternately see snapshots of himself in his ordinary

Figure 14. *Ioyä* (3.5 cm wide, 14 cm high).
Drawing by Mads Salicath.

human shape and in the shape of a fox. The reflexive element is also suggested by a small wooden figure that was given to me by a hunter to help me establish contact with spirits in my dreams. The figure, which is said to portray my *ayibii* during its nightly journeys, generally has the appearance of a human but also displays the horns of an elk. Moreover, it holds a crucifix in its hands, which serves to protect it against evil spirits. The hunter called the figure an *ioyä*, which means "the one that looks on your behalf," and I was told to put it under my pillow before I went to sleep. Whenever I killed something I should feed it with fat or blood as a way of repaying it for its services and to make sure that it did not abandon me for another body.

Moreover, Yukaghirs say that "if a spirit loves a hunter too much, it will kill him," referring to the tension, described earlier, between seduction and love. If the hunter's flirtatious game evokes in the spirit real feelings of love for him, the spirit will seek to keep his *ayibii* as its spouse and prevent it from returning to his body. In this case, the days of the hunter are likely to be numbered, unless his *ayibii* succeeds in overpowering the spirit and returning home. During my fieldwork I witnessed one such incident in which a spirit tried to kill a hunter out of love for him. It was our hunting leader, Old Spiridon, who ate some putrid butter while out hunting in the forest. It made a hole in his stomach, and he started to throw up blood. Soon he was so weak that he could not stand up and had to stay in bed. As the situation became more critical, he started screaming, while half-awake, "Go away, bitch!" At the time, I was too stressed by the situation to think about the meaning of this. Later, however, after we had succeeded in transporting Spiridon back to the village, where he miraculously recovered, one of the other hunters told me that it was the Owner of the Omulevka River, Spiridon's *pomoshchnik* (helper), who had tried to kill him. I went to Spiridon, who confirmed this. He explained that in his dreams, she (the spirit) had come with two of his dead relatives and one dead friend, and they had tried to persuade him to follow them to the Land of Shadows. He ended by saying, "She loves me, and therefore she gives me all the elk I want. But she is a tricky bitch. She wanted to kill me so that she can live with me. My mistake is that I've been too good to her." So, while the hunter has to sexually seduce the animal's spirit to provide himself with prey, he must make sure that pleasure does not evolve into actual feelings of love, which can prove lethal.

ARE SPIRITS REAL?

With these observations in mind, let me return to the question of dreams, spirits, and language. For Yukaghirs, as we have seen, dreams are understood as "doing," and they are part of conscious as well as self-conscious or reflexive life. In this respect, Yukaghirs are not unique. Carrithers, for instance, tells us that Singhalese dreams "are subject to the same principle of interpretation as that which rules the interpretation of all human action" (1982: 27). Likewise, Smith writes that for the northern Athapaskan (or Dene) people, "dreams are an aspect of the real world of perception" (1998: 417). We cannot, therefore, simply relegate dream content and meanings to the interiority of the unconscious mind. Instead, I will suggest that, from the standpoint of the experiencing subject, two assertions can be made. The first is that, whether one is awake or asleep, a person's encounters are always those of being-in-a-world and never an "empty reality." The second, which follows directly from the first, is that the awareness of the dreaming self is as phenomenally real as when the person is awake.

I derive these points from Ingold (2000: 100–102), who, drawing on Hallowell's writing on dreaming among the Ojibwa Indians (1955: 96; 1960: 42), has argued for a phenomenological approach to dreams. He writes, "Experiences undergone when asleep are just as much part of autobiographical memory as are experiences when awake" (Ingold 2000: 101). Neither Ingold nor Hallowell provides any evidence for their claims, yet evidence is available. Here I am primarily thinking about the book *Dreaming as Cognition* (1993), which reveals recent findings within experimental dream research. In the book's introduction, the two editors, Cavallero and Foulkes, write, "the data of empirical dream psychology . . . have suggested both that dreaming is a much more organised process than is generally imagined and that *it employs the same systems of mental representation and mental processing as are exhibited in the waking phenomena*" (Cavallero and Foulkes 1993: 3; my emphasis).

The experimental evidence they present for their statement is too vast for me to describe in any detail. Instead, I will summarize what I consider the most significant findings:

· Dreaming is not, as previously assumed, confined to REM sleep, consisting only of "active dreams," accompanied by rapid eye movements. Rather, people dream nonstop throughout their sleep (Cavallero and Foulkes 1993: 10; see also Empson 1993: 80–81). Consequently, I might add, humans are always "beings-in-a-world" and never find themselves in an "empty reality" in which all social engagement is suspended.

· Furthermore, experimental evidence has revealed that dreaming involves all the sensory modalities that we use in waking life, and apparently to a similar degree (Meier 1993: 62), and there is a significant correlation reported between dream imagery and waking perception (Kerr 1993: 27). Moreover, memory organization in dreaming and waking cognition is fundamentally the same, and access to various memory systems is comparable as well (Cavallero and Foulkes 1993: 144).

· Dreaming involves different levels of consciousness, including reflexive consciousness, that is, the possibility of considering oneself in a more or less decentered way, as if seen from the outside. Dreaming also involves the ability to evaluate emotional, interpersonal, or cognitive aspects of one's own behavior while dreaming (Meier 1993: 63; Montangero 1993: 100).

· Finally, evidence suggests that subjects can learn to control what they are going to dream about (Faraday 1972).

If these discoveries are correct and dreaming does, in fact, share basic cognitive structures and processes with waking life, then it is also likely that the processes for concept development in waking life are equally at work in dreams. In other words, if cognitive science is right in claiming that there is no inevitable connection between concepts and words, and that children develop basic concepts of things in their environment long before they develop language, then it is also conceivable that they can, through dream experiences, acquire notions of spiritual beings, in the form of prototypical concepts, well before they learn to speak. In this case, language would not be essential for conceptual thought about spiritual beings. My argument finds further support in the fact that REM sleep occurs from birth onward, and that children in particular fail to discriminate sharply between things experienced in dreams and in waking life: "[Dream experiences] still seem to children to have been real experiences" (Foulkes 1993: 115).

Still, when it comes to naming different spirits and bringing them within the bounds of a neatly ordered classificatory system, language is, of course, needed. But again, the degree to which people engage in such further structuring of non–linguistically based concepts varies cross-culturally. We have seen that unlike the Mongols, who seem to put great effort into differentiating between various kinds of spirits, Yukaghirs tend to lump them all together under the broad term *khoziain*. One explanation for this may very well rest in the differences between the two societies' hierarchies and power structures. As I explained earlier, Yukaghir society has always been small-scale and simple, that is, lacking in social segmentation, status differentiation, and religious specialists. We often see that simplicity in social structure has the effect of liberating the human propensity for structure, and this liberating effect plays itself out especially in the realm of religious representations (Woodburn 1982b: 206–8; Guenther 1999: 237). In any case, if what I have suggested holds true, namely, that concepts of spiritual beings can develop independently of language through the medium of dreams, then our conventional discrimination between the "natural" and the "supernatural," the "real" and the "culturally constructed," cannot easily be maintained. We will no longer be able to hold that conceptions of animals, trees, and mountains are more real than those of spiritual beings.

CHAPTER 9

Taking Animism Seriously

THE METAPHOR MODEL

This book is, in part, an extended reflection on the limitations of contemporary theories on animism and the inadequacy of the theoretical
tool kit available to the anthropologist who wants to take seriously the
attitudes and beliefs that indigenous peoples have about the nature of
such beings as spirits, souls, and animal persons and their relationships
with them. By "taking seriously," I simply mean taking seriously what
the people themselves take seriously. This is not usually done in anthropology. Spirits such as those the Yukaghirs claim to exist out there in the
world alongside humans and animals and with whom they interact in
both waking life and in dreams are generally not accepted by anthropologists as having any reality other than as mental representations,
imposed upon the world by indigenous minds as a means of grasping it
conceptually and appropriating it symbolically within the terms of a culturally constructed worldview. Consider, for example, Leach's classic
account of Katchin spirits in highland Burma. In typical Durkheimian
fashion, Leach writes that the various *nats* (spirits) of Katchin religion
"are, in the last analysis, nothing more than ways of describing the formal relationships that exist between real persons and real groups in ordinary human Katchin society" (1965: 182).

In other words, the awareness that the Katchin have about the existence of spiritual beings, an awareness that is central to their values and

goals and motivates much of their conduct, does not, we are told, arrive from the condition that genuine spirits exist, but solely from the condition that human social relations exist. When the Katchin assert the contrary—that they interact with spiritual beings as they would with people—they are said to be indulging in metaphor, and thus their discourse should not be treated like regular prose but understood as a symbolic statement. However, to claim that what the Katchin hold to be literally true about spirits is in actual fact only figuratively true, based on their inability to distinguish the "real" reality of the human social domain from its metaphorical construction in the "imaginary" domain of spiritual beings, is to reproduce the very Cartesian dichotomies between society and nature, human and nonhuman, and true and false knowledge that the indigenous view categorically rejects. In other words, the analysis takes our dualistic paradigm as axiomatic, and it is on this ground that we are reassured that spirits do not *really* exist, but are constructed as such only in the imagination of the local people. As we have seen throughout this book, this analytical attempt at reducing indigenous claims about the existence of spirits and other so-called "imaginary" creatures to conceptual devices or metaphors is still alive and well in the field of anthropology. Indeed, most contemporary studies of animism are variations of this Durkheimian theme (Tanner 1979; Nelson 1983: 239; Bird-David 1992, 1993; Århem 1996).

This strikes me as not only profoundly arrogant, but also problematic in a scholarly sense, as this mode of analysis obscures and denies the people's own modes of thought and discourse. According to those holding these animist beliefs, there are not two realities—one of actuality and one of metaphor—but only *one* reality, consisting of persons—both humans and nonhuman—and their relationships. Indeed, an irony of the anthropologist's explanatory model is that it yields much more insight into his own culture's ways of thinking, so centered on dualisms and binary oppositions, than into those of the people studied, for whom such oppositions have no place in their thought and practice. Moreover, by insisting that what the people themselves are saying about their relations with spiritual beings is nothing but a metaphorical reflection of those relations that obtain within their own human community, the anthropologist effectively prevents his own study of animistic understandings from telling us anything new about what the world is like. Instead, the anthropologist relies on a somewhat tautological process of deduction: he knows in advance how to explain the given reality of other people's animistic beliefs, and then relies on a thorough but predictable model to do so. But there is, as we have seen, no explanatory achievement here that goes beyond imposing an ontological dualism onto people where it does not apply, and on this ground implying that they themselves cannot really distinguish fact from fantasy or reality from metaphor.

RELATIVISM AS CARTESIANISM

Now it might be argued that my intellectual commitment to taking animism seriously rests on a fundamental misunderstanding of what social and cultural anthropology is all about. Its essential concern, it could be asserted, is not to understand the fundamental nature of reality—whatever that might be—but to set forth as accurately as possible the diverse ways in which it figures in the so-called "culturally constructed" worlds of human subjects. After all, it is an anthropological commonplace to assume that we cannot experience the world directly but only indirectly, through the medium of our cultural representations. Thus, for people who belong to different cultures, the same reality may mean quite different things: spirits might not be part of our reality, but this does not mean that they are not real to the indigenous peoples whose cultural conceptions for perceiving the world are different from ours.

Moreover, just like their beliefs, our Western assertions about the world are not derived from the world as it is in itself, but are mediated by our own cultural representations. Hence, there is no such thing as a single reality, absolute and universal, but rather multiple culturally constructed realities, each with its own unique set of beliefs, conceptualizations, and perceptual experiences (Nelson 1983: 239). This means that both their and our ways of perceiving the world are culturally relative, and it is therefore meaningless to make true/false judgments on a comparative basis, since each conception of reality can only be judged within its own cultural terms. This line of argument, commonly adopted by social and cultural anthropologists, is encapsulated by the following quotation from Burr: "All ways of understanding are culturally and historically relative. Not only are they specific to particular cultures and periods of history, they are seen as products of that culture and history. . . . The particular forms of knowledge that abound in any culture are therefore artefacts of it, and we should not assume that *our* ways of understanding are necessarily better (in terms of being nearer truth) than other ways" (1995: 4; emphasis in the original).

However, just here, in the claim to cultural relativism, lies the rub: to assert that every culture is locked into its own framework of constructed meaning, which can be measured only by the standards prevalent in that culture, means that the anthropologist offers a culture-transcending interpretation of *all* cultures, even though he himself is a member of *one* particular culture. This is logically contradictory as it involves making a nonrelativistic general claim about a relativistic assertion. The relativistic stance, therefore, must necessarily imply that the anthropologist himself has taken a step out of the worlds of culture in which the lives of all others are said to be confirmed, for "only from a point of observation beyond culture is it possible to regard [indigenous] understandings . . . as but one possible construction . . . of an independent reality" (Ingold 2000: 15). In other words, rather than undermining the primacy of Western epistemology over indigenous understandings, the anthropological claim to cultural relativism actually reinforces it. This is because it presupposes a prior, and essentially nonrelativistic, division between native peoples and the enlightened anthropologists who can apprehend their cultural worlds for what they really are, independently of any kind of cultural bias. As Ingold puts it, "If it is by the capacity to reason that humanity . . . is distinguished from nature, then it is by the fullest development of this capacity that modern science distinguishes itself from the knowledge practices of people in 'other cultures' whose thought is supposed to remain somewhat bound by the constraints and conventions of tradition" (Ingold 2000: 15).

We are, it seems, right back where we started with Tylor and Durkheim, who argue that the indigenous peoples themselves are essentially ignorant about the true nature of their animist convictions and that it takes the anthropologist's commitment to the supremacy of abstract scientific reason to deliver an authoritative account of how animism really works. The trouble is that the sovereign perspective of abstract scientific reason is itself a product of Cartesianism and its inherent dichotomies between modernity and tradition and true and false knowledge. In other words, the anthropological commitment to cultural relativism is essentially made on the terms of our Cartesian epistemology—an epistemology that, as we have seen, has no choice but to downgrade animism to some form of erroneous mental representation of the world.

MEANING IS GIVEN IN ENGAGEMENT

This book has been an attempt to break with this Cartesian legacy and provide an alternative starting point for the analysis of animism, one that follows the lead of the Yukaghirs in their perception of themselves and the world around them. Above all, this has meant eradicating the "representationalist" picture of human beings as subjects standing apart from a world of external objects about which they come to have beliefs by projecting onto it some kind of "cognized" system of mental representations.

For the Yukaghirs, as we have seen, the basic state of human existence is not that of a contemplating subject making abstract assertions about the world, but of a being immersed from the beginning in active perceptual engagement with others, humans as well as nonhumans, in the practical business of life. And the meanings that they find in the world, instead of being superimposed upon it by their own minds, are drawn from these relational contexts of everyday practical experience. So, if we were to ask where spirits reside, the answer would not be "inside people's heads," but "out there in the world," or rather in the relational contexts of people's activities. In this sense, spirits are not conceived as completely autonomous beings because they show up under conditions that are dependent on how they are put to use or realized by human subjects. Yet spirits are not altogether unautonomous either, because when they *do* show up, such as when "absorbed coping" runs into trouble or in dreams, they show up in their "essence" or "ownness," standing out from their ordinary anonymity as *khoziain* (everyone and no one) and becoming persons-in-themselves, with integrity and properties of their own. Spirits are thus both "found in" the world and "created" by people in the course of their active involvement with it. This may sound contradictory, but the contradiction disappears when we think about what is being said here. It is no more contradictory than saying that my computer's being depends not simply on its essential properties but also on how it is put to use *as* a computer. So, although both spirits and computers may well belong to the real world, they are constituents of that world according to their engagement in the activities of people. My point is that we must go beyond the Cartesian self-world dualism, and with it the claim that the real world exists independently of human experience. The world is not something apart from us, but the place in which we live—and it is because we are actively involved with it that it comes into being as meaningful. Indeed, this is why Yukaghirs insist on starting from immediate experience rather than from theoretical explanations of it—"for it is only from a position of such [lived experience] that they can launch their imaginative conceptions of what the world is like" (Ingold 2000: 60). Here, as we have seen, they find support from a persistent counter-Cartesian current within Western philosophy itself, most notably Heidegger and Ingold, who emphasize that meaning is primarily constituted in activity, not in thought, and it is only because we are actively involved with the world that we can think it at all (Ingold 2000: 60).

RELATEDNESS AND AUTONOMY

Among the Yukaghirs, however, it is not only spirits but all beings, including humans, that are understood in this relational and context-dependent way. The Yukaghir hunter, when out hunting, is both hunter and animal, and within the human community he is not simply himself but also a reincarnated deceased relative. There would be no hunters without prey, just as there would be no living persons without the souls of the dead. The Yukaghir person, therefore, is not isolated and self-sufficient in the Cartesian sense of the *cogito,* but essentially and inherently relational, having no existence of his own outside or separate from the relationships in which he participates. I have therefore employed the Heideggerian phrase "being-in-the-world"—a domain of interexistence, intercorporality, and interaction in which personhood lies in between entities rather than within any one of them. The somewhat paradoxical issue that we have to grasp, however, is that while the Yukaghir person is defined by the deep relationality of his being, he is also conceived of as a person in his own right, with intentionality and agency of his own. It is on exactly this basis that the hunter, although constituted and defined through the relationship to his prey, can still remain a human hunter with intentions of killing the animal. Likewise, the Yukaghir person, who attains his name and identity by virtue of the relationship he has with his *ayibii,* is at the same time capable of differentiating himself from his previous incarnation and making decisions and taking action of his own volition. How can we account for the somewhat puzzling fact that persons who are not thought to be separate from other persons, both human and nonhuman, living and dead, are at the same time conceived as possessing the capacity for intentionality and agency?

It is with regard to exactly this problem of accounting for the simultaneous dependency and relatedness of the person along with his evident autonomy and agency that the Heideggerian model of being-in-the-world reveals its explanatory shortages. Heidegger seeks to carry Western philosophy beyond the Cartesian dualisms of subject and object by showing how, through everyday activity, we can disclose the world and discover things in it without exhibiting any explicit or implicit awareness of ourselves as separate from it. Indeed, for Heidegger all states of being in which any element of separation inserts itself between self and world are predicated on this general structure of a primordial unity in which no real differences or divisions are apparent. Gurwitsch (1979: 67), a perceptive reader of Heidegger, captures this aspect of his philosophy adequately when he writes, "We find ourselves [in-the-world] and are interwoven with it, encompassed by it, indeed just 'absorbed' into it."

It should be said that Heidegger's claim that man and world belong together in an undivided unity is deeply colored by his rebellion against modernity, which he believed to be marked by a steadily more subject-centered metaphysics in which people appear as completely "rootless," with no essential bonds to anything in the world (Young 2002: 33). He frequently contrasts this state with the apparent harmony that "simple" rural people experience with respect to their home ground and the attitude of slavish self-abnegation that they express in relation to the world. In this respect, Heidegger's work is yet another expression of the widespread romantic condemnation of the alienation of modern humanity, which it is not my intention to discuss here. What I do want to point out, however, is that we find the same line of argument repeated in recent anthropological writings on hunter-gatherers. In these works indigenous animism comes to represent a basic affinity with the world and other beings that Western society has supposedly lost. This is apparent in Ingold's "dwelling perspective," but it is perhaps even more obvious in a recent article by Bird-David (1999) in which she proposes a revised understanding of animism as "relatedness." Yet, rather like Ingold, she predicates her notion of relatedness on the absorption of difference by sameness and togetherness with the world and other beings. Thus, she writes, "[Animism] grows from and *is* maintaining relatedness with neighbouring others. It involves . . . turning attention to 'we-ness,' which absorbs differences, rather than to 'otherness,' which highlights differences and eclipses commonalities. Against 'I think, therefore I am' stand 'I relate, therefore I am'" (Bird-David 1999: 78; emphasis in the original).

In the first chapter I raised some theoretical objections to this idea of a basic similitude between self and world, arguing that we can only have an experience of a world if we are conscious subjects of experience who can distinguish between ourselves as subjects and an external world that transcends our subjective experience of it. Otherwise, the experiencing subject and the object of experience would conflate, would become one, thereby making any experience of the world impossible.[1] This, I have argued, is the germ of truth in Descartes' doctrine of the *cogito:* there must be a reflexive awareness of the "I" built into perception from the very start or there could be no awareness of a world as such. Thus, the inference of Bird-David (along with Heidegger) that the *cogito* can be replaced by relatedness as "the absorption of difference" is fundamentally misleading. The *cogito*, or the self-awareness of being a subject who stands somewhat apart from the world, is a precondition for any attempt at engagement with it. All of this means that the notion of an absolute identity between self and world is not only a myth, but also a false one. The truth is that the ontological structure of our being is such that the otherness of the world, our difference from it, is part of the meaning the world has at the most primordial levels of experience.

Does this mean, then, that Bird-David is projecting her own romantic sentiment onto hunter-gatherers, suggesting what they are supposed to experience, when she suggests that animistic relatedness is predicated on the absorption of differences by "we-ness" as sameness?[2] There is, I believe, an element of truth in her argument. We have seen how the Yukaghirs, along with other hunter-gatherers, culturally endorse and elaborate such sameness with the world and with other beings. Indeed, it is on this basis that they consider language to be an obstacle to knowledge because words are dual logical elements, inherently discriminative and inadequate to express the nondual nature of perception as a direct and immediate relation with the world. Moreover, like other hunter-gatherers, Yukaghirs often address the spirits of the places where they live and hunt by kin terms and establish sharing relations with them on the precise grounds that categorically they are considered in some fundamental way to be the same. In fact, a general feature of the Yukaghir world is, as we have seen, an almost unbounded potential for identification with other beings: humans transform into animals, animals transform into humans, and one class of humans turns into another. There are no radical discontinuities here, only continuous substitutions of same becoming other and vice versa.

While all of this could be interpreted, following Bird-David, as revealing animism as based in some fusional identification between self and other, in fact the opposite is true. That the Yukaghirs do not postulate an insuperable ontological barrier between human and nonhuman or the living and the dead does not mean that they are not preoccupied with differentiating themselves from others. On the contrary, the lack of any guaranteed, a priori difference means that difference has to be created constantly through various everyday practices that demonstrate it.[3]

THE POWER TO DIFFERENTIATE

We saw how Yukaghir sociality, like that of other hunter-gatherers, is structured around the principle of sharing. The ethos of sharing, with its general disengagement from property and accumulation and thus from its potential for creating interpersonal dependency, establishes qualitative relationships of basic equality. Debt, credit, reciprocity, and asymmetrical relations of any sort are contrary to both the spirit and the practice of sharing. Instead, people who share with one another demonstrate unequivocal equivalence: "I can make claims on your possessions because you are, in some crucial respect, the same as me." Indeed, it is on exactly these grounds that Sahlins (1972: 193) calls sharing "the solidary extreme" and why Bird-David argues that hunter-gatherers through "reproducing sharing relationships with surrounding beings" override "differences . . . and [absorb] their sort into one 'we-ness'" (1999: 73). However, the trouble is that for the Yukaghirs, this condition of truly radical sharing with the natural agencies is ultimately unsustainable and indeed self-destructive. It always ends with the roles of donor and recipient being reversed, so that human predators fall prey to the spirits of their animal prey. We find the fear of this reversal again and again in Yukaghir dealings with the animal master-spirits, who are believed to share their abundance of game with their human "kinsmen" as a means of "killing" them out of "love" for them. On the whole, therefore, the "absorption of difference" as in "sharing" or "love" is viewed negatively: it stands for the loss of one's human identity and ultimately for "death," because without such distinct identity, there is no life for humans.

The hunters' solution is to accentuate difference by transforming the sharing transaction into "playing dirty tricks" (Rus. *pákostit'*), or what I have described as a game of sexual seduction. Yet here the difference is never so great that a key similarity is not kept in place. In other words, the game of seduction is characterized by a principle of "dissimilar similarity" with one's other: the hunter takes on the identity and appearance of his prey, thus projecting back to the animal (and its invisible spiritual counterpart) an image of itself. Just as the images of objects produced in mirrors are similar to real objects, without, however, themselves possessing reality on the level of the objects, so the image set in motion by the hunter refers to his prey without being fully identical with it. And it is exactly this aspect of noncoincidence or difference that gives the hunter power over the animal. First, it provides the hunter with a double perspective, that of seeing the elk as elk (as does a human hunter) and of seeing himself as elk (as seen by the elk he sees). Indeed, it is this duality of perspectives that makes the hunter so deadly, because it allows him to share the animal's fundamental "texture" while still retaining the distinction of existing as a perceiving subject with a perspective of his own—and a human one at that. Second, what the animal sees in the hunter, the object of its fatal attraction, is not an exact replica of itself but a fantasy image, exposing as "exterior" or visible what in reality is "interior" or invisible: its own infrahuman perspective. That is, by concealing his own humanness, the hunter exposes the humanness of the animal—that is, its *ayibii*—and this is what compels it to throw itself at him. Thus, the hunter's deceptive power lies not in being identical to the animal, but in being at once same and otherwise, similar and different. This opens up a space of play between visibility and invisibility, between actuality and fantasy, with which the hunter turns the animal's perception of reality into a manipulated fiction by means of which he kills it.

I could go on describing how an element of fission or noncoincidence between human and nonhuman, self and world, must always be kept in place—and is kept in place—by the Yukaghirs, and indeed this book has presented much evidence as to why animism is predicated not only on a principle of sameness, but also on difference. The point I want to make here is that what defines power in the Yukaghir world, where all beings continually mirror and echo one another and where the various boundaries between self and other are permeable and easily crossed, is the ability *not* to confuse analogy with identity. To exercise power is to steer a difficult course between transcending difference and maintaining identity, to see the world from the perspectives of various others, humans as well as nonhuman, yet avoid total participation and confusion. In this respect, it would seem that the power of animistic modes of relatedness rests on a paradigm of liminality—for "what is liminality but literally the 'threshold,' the space that both separates and joins spaces: the essence of in-betweenness?" (Schechner 1985: 295). It is this borderland where self and other are both identical and different, alike yet not the same, that I have tried to capture using phrases such as "analogous identification," "the double perspective," and "not animal, not *not* animal." What I mean to suggest by this is that if we are to take animism seriously, we must abandon the idea of total coincidence (the Heideggerian tradition) or total separation (the Cartesian tradition) and account for the mode of being that puts us into contact with the world and yet separates us from it. And there is, of course, such a mode of being, a mode that is grounded in mimesis.

Mimesis is essentially relational in that the imitator has no independent existence outside or separate from the object or person imitated; and yet the imitator is constantly being thrown back on himself reflexively, without ever achieving unity. Thus mimesis offers assimilation with otherness while also drawing boundaries and distinguishing oneself. Animism demands both, and without mimesis the very basis of animistic relatedness is therefore likely to break down. This is not to say that mimesis is identical to animism. We can and do imitate things without being animists for that reason. Rather, what I am arguing is that mimesis is and must be a prerequisite for animistic symbolic world making. Without the mimetic practices of daily life, the symbolic worlds of animism would bear no resemblance to lived experience, and indeed would be nothing but a cosmological abstraction. Mimesis, therefore, is the practical side of animism, its world-making mechanism par excellence. Benjamin's discovery of the importance of mimesis in the modern world is itself a testimony to the surfacing of animistic types of relatedness within our own mass culture. Indeed, much more could be said about the extensive role of animism in modernity, but this must be the topic of another book. The suggestion made here, and for which the Yukaghirs have provided the evidence, is for a plausible grounding—if not origin— of animism in practical mimesis.

Notes

PREFACE

1. Prior to my initial study of the Yukaghirs in 1993 I had undertaken field research among other Siberian indigenous groups. In 1991 I was a member of a three-month expedition to the Evens and Sakha of the Omoloi and Menkera rivers in northern Yakutia. The following year I lived among the Chukchi of the village of Achaivayam in northeastern Kamchatka for about ten weeks. That same year, 1992, I lived as a trapper for six months among Shor and Russian hunters in the northern Altai Mountains.

2. The Jesup North Pacific Expedition was organized by Boas. Its members included Jochelson's wife, Dina Brodsky, who followed him on his expeditions, and his friend and fellow revolutionary Bogoras, who carried out fieldwork among the Chukchi and Yupik (Freed, Freed, and Williamson 1988: 97–104; Kendell, Mathe, and Miller 1997). Jochelson also studied other Siberian groups, such as the Koryak (Jochelson 1908) and the Sakha (Yakut) (Jochelson 1933).

3. During the Soviet period, a small number of books were written about the Yukaghirs, such as Spiridonov's 1996 [1930] short book *Oduly (Yukagiry) Kolymskogo Okruga* [The Odul (Yukaghirs) of the Kolyma Region], Gogolev's 1975 *Yukagiry: Istoriko-etnograficheskiy ocherk* [The Yukaghirs: An Ethnohistorical Outline], and Tugolukov's 1979 *kto vy yukagiry?* (Who Are You Yukaghirs?). However, nearly all of these publications are so severely affected by ideological censorship that the information that is absent often reveals more than that which has been retained. The Soviet authors see it as their main task to determine the Yukaghirs' place within the Marxist chain of sociopolitical formations. For this reason, the contemporary voices of the people themselves are virtually absent, save for overenthusiastic statements about the achievements of the Soviet government. Instead, we are presented with old ethnographic data, provided by

Jochelson and other early explorers, which is used as evidence of "survivals" from various evolutionary stages in the peoples' sociopolitical development. Thus, we are repeatedly told that among the Yukaghirs traits of the earliest forms of religion, marriage, and gender relations (matriarchy) are found. Yet, because of the Yukaghirs' contact with the more "advanced" cultures of the Evenki and Sakha, they have incorporated various features of "class-based" society, such as private property rights to hunting weapons and furs for sale. As Slezkine rightly argues, in Soviet ethnography "the small peoples of the north became one big survival" (1994: 259), and the Yukaghirs are no exception. Only a few works have been published since the fall of communism, but they are very useful. Here I am thinking primarily of the works of the Russian anthropologist Zukova, who has published on Yukaghir religion (1996a) and material culture (1996b). In addition, the Russian anthropologist and linguist Vakhtin (1991) has written a short but extremely useful book about the sociolinguistic situation of the Yukaghirs. Although he does not attempt to analyze his research data, instead providing a purely practical description of the linguistic environment among the various Yukaghir groups, his data have been important in my own assessment of the role of language in the spiritual knowledge of the Yukaghirs. No Western scholars have published work on the Yukaghirs apart from brief sketches within general books about Siberia (see, e.g., Graburn and Strong 1973: 38–49; Forsyth 1992; Bobrick 1992; Slezkine 1994).

1. ANIMISM AS MIMESIS

1. The Evenki are a local reindeer-herding population.

2. Small groups of Yukaghirs also live in more urbanized settlements, such as Zyrianka, Cherskiy, and Shredne Kolymsk, and in the capital of the Sakha Republic (Yakutia), Yakutsk. Moreover, there are a few dozen people along the lower reaches of the Yana and Indigirka rivers who consider themselves to be Yukaghirs, but none of these has spoken the Yukaghir language in their lifetime.

3. Both in the past and more recently, Russian anthropologists have distinguished between Yukaghirs, Koryaks, and Chukchi, who have long been regarded as aboriginal peoples of the northern Yakutia region (Fedoseeva 1980; Erutikov 1990), and groups such as the Evenki (Tungus) and Sakha (Yakuts), who are generally thought to be the descendants of more recent incomers from the south who moved into the region between the seventh and fourteenth centuries A.D. (Vainshtein 1989: 62). The Evens (Lamuts) population is thought to have come into being even later; they are widely described as the product of unions between immigrant Evenki and the local Yukaghir populations (Arutiunov 1988: 36).

4. Communication with the district center today is by car and snowmobile in winter, and by motorboat in summer. The once familiar biplanes and helicopters have ceased to operate altogether.

5. As Tambiah (1990: 49) points out, Tylor made no clear distinction in his theory between animism as religion and animism as magic. Rather, the two were seen as essentially intermixed and interdependent.

6. For a fascinating account of animist ideas and practices in our own Western society see Degnen 2005.

7. Ingold makes this point in his criticism of Guthrie (see Ingold's comments in Bird-David 1999: 82).

8. Totemism is a label for systems of ritual and belief that associate particular social groups, such as clans, with particular animals or other natural entities, such as plants and meteorological phenomena. Totemism is found primarily among aboriginal peoples in Australia and the Americas. For recent comparative studies of totemism and animism, see Ingold 2000: 111–31; Descola 1996: 82–102; Pedersen 2001: 411–27.

9. I take this point from Casey (1996: 15).

2. TO KILL OR NOT TO KILL

1. The elk is found throughout the low forest country, especially where clusters of willow bushes follow the winding river courses. Elk entered the Upper Kolyma region in large numbers only in the 1960s, when it replaced the wild reindeer, which had been the mainstay of the local economy. The only other large animals found are the brown bear, wolf, red fox, wolverine, and lynx. Except for the lynx, all of these animals are common, and all are sought after as prey. Until the mid-1950s the most important fur-bearing animal was the squirrel, but when the sable was reintroduced into the area in the 1950s after having been extinct for more than a century, it became the most hunted fur animal.

2. For a similar experience among the Inuit of southeastern Hudson Bay, see Guemple 1994: 117–22.

3. When a person is buried, people cut a hole in his clothes and break objects owned by him. This is done in order that the *ayibii* of the objects may go with the soul of the dead to the Land of Shadows.

4. For a detailed account of the dangers that an *ayibii* might meet on its way back to the Middle World, see the story "Petr Baerbaekin" in Zukova, Nikolaeva, and Dëmina 1989: 1: 95–115.

5. Every person has, in addition to his Christian name, one or several nicknames, which serve to confuse evil spirits. The nicknames might be in Yukaghir, such as Chu-chu (Eager One), or in Russian, such as Chemodanchik (Small Suitcase), Gitler (Hitler), or Igor Khan (no meaning). Often, the nickname points to a particular unfortunate trait in the person's character or appearance. For instance, "Small Suitcase" is a short fat man with a rather square shape.

6. For further comparative material see, Jochelson 1908: 100–102; Ingold 1986a: 250–51; Fienup-Riordan 1994: 211.

7. Burch (1991: 108–9) has criticized the ethnographic literature on hunter-gatherer societies for neglecting forms of exchange other than sharing. However, while sharing does not necessarily exhaust the repertoire of exchanges among the Yukaghirs, it is the dominant form and the keynote of the value system. In this sense, I can justify giving this form of transaction special attention.

8. An exception is small animals, such as hares and birds, which belong to the man who shoots or snares them.

9. At present the political leaders of the Yukaghirs are struggling to achieve a

higher degree of self-government. In 1998 the Law of the Suktul [Self-govern-ment] of the Yukaghir People was passed in the Yakut parliament, but it has not been implemented to date.

10. Here I leave aside the head of the administration, the rich Sakha I men-tioned earlier, who derived his power not from the community of Nelemnoye, but from the regional administration in Zyrianka.

3. BODY-SOUL DIALECTICS

1. The same holds true for the conceptions of the soul within the Russian Orthodox tradition, in which, as Pesmen (2000) has described in great detail, the soul is conceived as utterly spiritual and unsubstantial.

2. This once happened when a raven led us to prey by circling over our heads. It flew away and then repeated its circular motion over some other point on the landscape. Our hunting leader, Old Spiridon, said, "Look, it wants to hunt with us," so we went to the place marked out by the raven, where elk were hiding. At this point, one of the hunters offered the explanation that it was possible the raven helped us because it was an *ayibii* of ours that had temporarily taken on a bird's shape.

3. Nikolai Likhachev is very old, more than eighty, and has several times been on the verge of death. However, each time he has miraculously recovered, after which some healthy person in the village suddenly died. People are inclined to explain this by saying that he must somehow steal the strength of healthy people to ensure that his own life will continue.

4. This might provide a clue as to why Yukaghirs in the eighteenth century dismembered the bodies of their dead shamans and distributed the parts as amulets among the members of the clan (see chapter 6). Although a person's *ayibii* is said to leave his body when he dies, it seems logical that the parts of the body where the *ayibii* used to dwell would retain some of its substance, and could thus be used as powerful spirit protectors.

5. Nikolai Likhachev claims that once, when out hunting, he fell through a hole in the ground, which led him into the Land of Shadows, or the "Second Moscow," as he called it. "There were houses of every type," he assured me. "Tents, wooden houses, and skyscrapers. People there could not see or hear me; only I could see and hear them. I went into the house of a Yukaghir family who were eating rotten meat. It was awful. After the meal, the family went to bed and I lay down beside the daughter. As I penetrated her with my penis, she screamed, 'My stomach is hurting!' Her parents called a shaman, a woman, but she couldn't tell what was wrong with the girl. Once again, I penetrated the girl, and again she screamed loudly. Then they got another shaman. I recognized him. He was from my village, but had died long ago. As he looked at me, I felt that two rays of light pierced my body. He could see me and asked, 'What are you doing here? You are not dead.' I explained to him that I had fallen through a hole in the ground and all I wanted was to go back. He put a piece of horse skin in his hand and told me to sit on it. The next moment, I was riding a horse. I found myself lying beside the hole in the ground. I covered it with stones, so that no one else would fall through it, and then I returned home."

6. It is questionable if the mirroring of the child necessarily requires the mediation of real mirrors, as argued by Lacan. His "realism" is unfortunate, because it excludes people like the Yukaghirs who, although they possess mirrors, do not habitually place their children in front of them. There seems to be no inherent reason, though, why the child's mirroring must involve real mirrors. Rather, in this logical game it seems likely that anything in the world could potentially function as a mirror for the child, including the child's own shadow, as among the Yukaghirs.

7. For a comprehensive review of the anthropological literature on the self/person, see Spiro (1993).

4. IDEAS OF SPECIES AND PERSONHOOD

1. The Russian word *lyudi*, employed by Shalugin, is the plural of *chelovek*, which means "person." *Lyudi* can thus be translated as either "people" or "persons."

2. I am not entirely sure whether Vasili Shalugin was referring to the master-spirits of rivers and trees or to the entities themselves when he described them as being persons. However, animals, I shall argue, are often conceived as persons in their own right.

3. The Yukaghir word for heart, *cobo'ye*, also means "running" and "motion."

4. In his list of Yukaghir words, Jochelson includes the word *no'do* for "animal" (1926: 330). However, none of my informants who know the Yukaghir language recognized this word as meaning "animal," but said instead that it means "bird." They all insisted that their language has no word for "animal," referring to all nonhuman beings. This is not unusual among groups of hunter-gatherers, who do not set themselves uniquely apart from the world of nonhumans (see, for example, Howell 1996: 131; Morris 2000: 140). Yukaghir hunters know the Russian word for animal, *zhivotnoe*, but I hardly ever heard it used. Generally speaking, they refer to the specific species concerned using allegorical expressions or special terms, since, as we shall see in the next chapter, animal prey cannot be addressed by their real names.

5. The bear's position is rather ambiguous. Sometimes hunters will group it among the predatory mammals as a "dirty" creature.

6. The dogs are a mixture of the traditional hunting dog of the area, the East Siberian Laika, and various European dogs. The latter were introduced with the Russians, and today no pure Laikas are to be found in the Upper Kolyma region.

7. For a fascinating account of the problem of cannibalism in animist societies in which animals are conceived as persons, see Fausto's forthcoming article.

8. According to the myths of the Chukchi and Koryak, it was Raven that brought fire to the humans (Bogoras 1904–9: 40–43; Serov 1988: 242). It might well be that the Yukaghirs have replaced Raven with Jesus. However, none of my informants could confirm this.

5. ANIMALS AS PERSONS

1. It should be pointed out that this story, expressed here as something that happened to the teller, also appears as a common myth. Thus, I recorded a number of similar narratives about how a hunter, while out hunting, becomes able to see the world from the perspective of his prey. We also find this theme in the myths of other groups of northern hunters, such as the Cree and Ojibwa Indians of the Canadian subarctic (Hallowell 1960: 36; Tanner 1979: 136–37; Brightman 1993: 41–48) and the Inuit (Saladin d'Anglure 2001). The theme is also found among hunting peoples of Southeast Asia, such as the Chewong of the Malay tropical forest (Howell 1996).

2. Hunters mainly use metal leg-hold traps, but they also use various kinds of dead-fall traps constructed out of timber to catch wolverine and bear. Until the 1950s, squirrels were hunted with a bow trap, which was made from willow branches.

3. The devil, or Abasy, is said to come from the south, bringing (European) diseases and other disasters with him. The doors of hunters' cabins tend, therefore, not to face south. Because an Abasy has no concept of the past, he cannot turn himself around but can only walk forward. If he should arrive at a cabin, he would be incapable of entering it as long as the door did not face south. He would have to climb over the roof and continue to walk away from the hunters.

4. At the time Jochelson did his fieldwork the Yukaghirs had a whole series of narratives about these cannibal giants. As he writes, "The first place in Yukaghir folklore is taken by tales of the Mythical-Old-People. They are the most genuine Yukaghir folk tales" (1926: 303). Today, however, these giant cannibals have been replaced with *abasylar* as the main characters of these narratives.

5. The Sun deity was traditionally seen as one of the highest of the benevolent beings, and today it is understood by many Yukaghirs to be the same as the Christian God.

6. It has to be said that Viveiros de Castro does explicitly acknowledge the practical aspect of perspectival thinking when he writes, "The animal clothes that shamans use to travel the cosmos are not fantasies but instruments: they are akin to diving equipment, or space suits, and not to carnival masks" (1998: 482). Still, his argument is centered on the essentially symbolic world of shamanism (see Viveiros de Castro 1998: 472, 483). For my part, I argue for a plausible grounding (if not origin) of perspectivism in real-life observations of animals and experiences of hunting. This is not to say that perspectivism is restricted to the hunting context. As a matter of fact, it is present in a great variety of activities, such as in Yukaghir shamanism, as described in chapter 6, and in dancing, in which people imitate animal movements and cries with great vivacity, as well as in trapping, where the hunter tries to think like the sable. Yet the impact of these activities on people's experience of animals as persons with a (subjective) point of view is, I believe, less intense compared with elk hunting, which involves direct face-to-face mimicry and in which the bodies of hunter and prey blend to become one of the same kind. Thus, in my view, hunting is the paramount reality of daily Yukaghir life from which their perspectival thinking ultimately emerges. This may

also explain why it is, as Viveiros de Castro himself observes, that the dynamics of predator and prey are fundamental to perspectivist thinking (1998: 471).

7. As Nelson correctly points out, the elk (or moose) is probably more dangerous than any other creature in the northern woodlands (1983: 166). I have recorded countless stories about elk that have seen through the hunter's trick of imitation and attacked him. The elk will flatten its ears as a sign of aggression, and the hunter must slowly withdraw. Otherwise, he will be trampled to death by the enormous animal.

8. It seems that Feit describes a similar hunting technique among the Cree when he writes, "Au moment où l'orignal entend le chasseur s'approcher sous le vent, il se redresse lentement et se tourne pour faire face, il essaie de percevoir une silhouette ou une odeur, et c'est alors seulement, dans un échange de regards, que l'animal se donne" (Feit 2000: 133).

9. In my description of the mimetic encounter of hunter and elk, I have found great inspiration in Gell's (1988: 118–19) analysis of looking at the Hindu idol, as well as in Hegel's (1971 [1830/1845]: 170–78) famous account of the "master-slave" dialectic. Both confront the same issue I do, namely, the psychological impact of seeing oneself being seen by the person or entity at which one is looking.

10. For another fascinating account of the perceptual experience of seeing and being seen, see Empson's (2006) article on the Mongolian household chest, where multiple kinship relations are revealed at once to the viewer as he looks at himself looking at the image revealed in the display.

11. At first sight this argument might seem to contradict what I said in chapter 2 about the hunter-spirit relationship, which I described as one of mutual interdependence, in which the animal master-spirits freely send prey to hunters so that their herds can reproduce. However, one needs to keep in mind that an animal and its master-spirit are not one and the same person, at least not in any absolute sense. They do not, therefore, necessarily share the same interests. The Yukaghirs themselves are quite aware of this. Thus, I was told that even when Khoziain intends to send his herds of game in the direction of hunters, he never explicitly informs the animals that they are going to be killed. Instead, the master lures them by, for instance, saying to the elk, "Over there, you'll find lots of fresh willow shoots."

12. I use "her" because the hunters tend to conceptualize the elk as a female lover.

13. Even within the European tradition, especially from the twelfth century to the sixteenth, the analogy between hunting and sex crops up again and again in poems and stories. In these writings, as Cartmill writes, "the deer hunt becomes metaphoric coitus, the hunter's arrow a penis, and the stag's death an orgasm" (1993: 69). In fact, Cartmill extends this analogy to include "rape," arguing that "hunters sometimes put forward the same excuse for hunting that many rapists offer for rape: they insist they are not to blame because the victim was asking for it" (1993: 239). This analogy between hunting and rape, however, cannot be extended to include the Yukaghirs and many other groups of hunter-gatherers for whom hunting is generally presented as involving noncoercive relations of sexual seduction.

14. When I first visited the region's center, Zyrianka, in 1993, it had a population of about 10,000; by the year 2000, this figure had dropped to about 3,000. Thus, the scale of the Russian exodus is huge.

15. I take this point from Ingold (1994: 30), who makes it with regard to chimpanzees.

6. SHAMANISM

1. The word *shaman* is of Evenki origin, and although much data about shamanism comes from the Americas and South and Central Asia, Siberia is still commonly considered its "classical" homeland.

2. Slezkine (1993: 15–31) has given a detailed account of the rather unsuccessful attempt of the Orthodox mission to convert the Chukchi and Koryaks to the Christian faith. The comparative success of their attempt to convert the Yukaghirs is, I believe, grounded in the fact that, from the very beginning of colonial rule, the Yukaghirs had much more intense contact with the Russians. It has been estimated that at any given time between the 1670s and 1780s, about 6 percent of all adult Yukaghir men were removed from their communities to serve in the Russian military as auxiliary soldiers in their wars against neighboring groups, especially the Chukchi. Likewise, about 10 percent of all Yukaghir women were living outside their native communities as wives, slaves, or concubines of Russian Cossacks and trappers (Forsyth 1992: 78; Slezkine 1994: 27). All of these Yukaghirs, we may assume, were not only formally baptized, but also adopted elements of the Orthodox faith.

3. One exception is the Yukaghir writer Nikolai Spiridonov (Teki Odulok), who was executed in 1938 on false accusations of being a Japanese spy. However, at that time Spiridonov had left the Yukaghir region and was living in Leningrad.

4. It is interesting to note that the Yukaghir word for the figure with the shaman's skull, *Qoil* (Jochelson 1926: 163), is the same name that the old people use today when addressing the Christian God. That is, they call God *Qoil* without knowing that this used to be the name of the spirit effigy.

5. The child is likely to represent the spirit-owner of each individual animal (*pejul* in Yukaghir), which is sometimes described as a small bald-headed child or dwarf that rides on the neck of the animal.

6. For similar ideas about sexual relations with helping spirits among Inuit shamans, see Saladin d'Anglure (2001: 8).

7. If this is so, however, and provided that Jochelson is right when arguing that the Yukaghirs prior to their encounter with the Russians in the mid-seventeenth century had a patriclan organization (1926: 115–18), it is possible to imagine that the people used to differentiate the social position of shaman much more clearly than they did by the time of my fieldwork. The main evidence we can glean from Jochelson's account, however, comprises few recorded statements about the former existence of a shaman-ancestor cult in which the clan shaman had to be of the same blood as the clan core group (p. 120). Moreover, Jochelson tells us that in the aboriginal Yukaghir society, the positions of shaman and clan elder were clearly differentiated in a social sense (pp. 118–22).

Still, various anthropologists have disputed Jochelson's claim about an aboriginal patriclan among the Yukaghirs. The Soviet ethnographers Stepanova, Gurvich, and Khramova (1964) argue for an aboriginal matriclan, pointing out that Yukaghir grooms used to go and live with the family of the bride (p. 796). Indeed, it would be hard to see how a patriclan could stay together with matrilo-cal residence predominating if it were not the case, as Jochelson reports, that at the time of his fieldwork most marriages took place within the clan (p. 86). The problem is not so simple, however; the Soviet ethnographers point to the fact that most Yukaghir clans during the nineteenth century and until the establishment of Soviet power represented the merging of depopulated clans, and that, according to eighteenth-century marriage records in the archives, Yukaghir marriages had usually been between people of different clans (Stepanova, Gurvich, and Khra-mova 1964: 796). Thus, they argue that matrilocal residence together with clan exogamy would destroy the basis for a localized patriclan and is evidence for an original matrilineal clan organization.

Graburn and Strong (1973: 86–88) take yet another position. Drawing on data provided by Jochelson revealing that ancient legends suggest that it was Yukaghir practice for the oldest son and the oldest daughter to join the clan of the mother (whereas the younger offspring joined the clan of the father), they suggest that the aboriginal Yukaghir clan was a simple bilateral grouping and that descent could be either as in the mode of the legendary ideal or, more likely, according to the situation. That is, the choice could be based on a consideration of the relative advantages and disadvantages of joining the mother's or father's kinsmen, which would allow for the flexibility often necessary in arctic band societies.

Personally, I do not dare speculate on the composition of the aboriginal Yuka-ghir clan. This requires deeper historical research than I have engaged in here. I can only say that, regardless of the aboriginal social structure of the Yukaghirs, within the last two hundred years or more, it has been, in functional terms, a bilateral grouping.

7. THE SPIRIT WORLD

1. In reality, however, many of the children from Nelemnoye did not go to school for more than six or seven years. Instead, they kept running away, back to their parents. In the end, the local authorities gave up on them and simply filled in the forms saying that they had passed their final exams. This kind of local resistance to the Soviet residential school system seems to have occurred across Siberia. In a recent book evaluating the impact of Soviet schooling on the Evenki, Bloch (2004: 102) describes how the people set the school on fire to prevent their children from being taken away. She describes similar cases of unequivocal resis-tance to schooling among the Khanty and Nentsy.

2. For an overview of the number of native speakers among the various indigenous groups of northeastern Siberia, including the Yukaghirs and the Yupik, see Krauss 1988: 144.

3. Bogoras (1865–1936), like Jochelson, was a Russian revolutionary who had studied the indigenous peoples of northeastern Siberia during years of exile. Like Jochelson, he was employed by Boas to carry out fieldwork in Siberia as

part of the Jesup North Pacific Expedition. Whereas Jochelson studied the Yuk-aghirs and Koryaks, Bogoras concentrated on the Chukchi and Yupik. After the expedition, Jochelson settled in New York and was associated with the American Museum of Natural History. Bogoras returned to Russia to become one of the founding fathers of Soviet anthropology.

4. The term *cognitive model* as a synonym for *worldview* refers to what Bloch has called the "anthropological model of cognition" (1998: vii), i.e., cognition as collective representations in the sense of the Durkheimian tradition as opposed to the psychologistic sense of the word. The latter starts from the idea that social and cultural phenomena are firmly grounded in natural properties of the human mind. Later, in my discussion of dreaming and language, I shall draw on findings within this field of developmental cognitive psychology.

5. The statements by Leach and Burr about the influence of language on perception can be interpreted in either the strong or the weak sense. By strong, I mean the notion that the specific structures of a language determine how the speaker sees and interprets the world, as proposed, for example, by the Sapir-Whorf hypothesis (Sapir 1951: 162). This implies that if a people have seven words for snow, they will perceive seven kinds of snow; and if they have no term for blue, they will have no idea of the color. By weak, I mean the idea that language mediates perception, in the sense that there are some identifiable cognitive correlates associated with speaking a particular language. In any case, my argument is that, ontologically speaking, linguistic representations should not be the starting point for analyzing human perception and knowledge.

6. For an example of this attitude toward the loss of Siberian indigenous languages, see Kasten 1998.

7. I had a laptop computer with me in the field, which was of great interest to the locals.

8. The skeptic may find my argument that spirits are like tools problematic, since, unlike tools, spirits are not natural but supernatural, and therefore being-in-a-world cannot include them. The easy way out, of course, is to argue that spirits might not be real to us but they are indeed real to the Yukaghirs, whose worldview is different from ours. I find this unsatisfactory. Later, in chapters 8 and 9, I take up this challenge to address the question of whether concepts of spirits are real or products of cultural and linguistic construction.

9. This can serve as yet another proof that Durkheim's original distinction between "sacred" and "profane" situations and ideas does not pass the test of cross-cultural comparisons. Hunters' rituals that appear undoubtedly "religious" in our ordinary understanding of the term are, as we have seen, not performed in anything like the atmosphere of mystery and awe suggested by Durkheim's description. Indeed, it seems as if the word "ritual" is not entirely appropriate when it comes to describing such practices as feeding the fire. For this ritual does not imply any magico-religious stance on the part of the participants; it is closer to ordinary intentional practical action, such as placing traps or chopping wood.

10. Studies in child psychology seem to support this point: "The affordance of an object is what the infant begins by noticing . . . before the substance and surface, the colour and form, are seen as such" (Gibson in Costall 1997: 80). The essence of things for children thus consists in what they are able to do, or their

functional significance. As Costall puts it, "the child begins to relate to things as an agent rather than a detached observer." (See Costall 1997: 79–80, for an overview of the research on children's ways of relating to objects.)

11. We do, however, find notable exceptions, such as Douglas's work on pollution and purity (1970), in which she suggests that anomalies and ambiguities are necessary as bearers of symbolic meaning in any religious system. However, anomalies become so only because they fail to find a proper place in the overall cosmological order. Thus, for her, as for other anthropologists with a structural bent, it is an a priori assumption that there is structure.

8. LEARNING AND DREAMING

1. This is Heidegger's attitude toward language in his early work *Being and Time* (1962). Later, he takes what Rorty calls a "linguistic turn" (1993: 338) and he begins to see language as the precinct of "being." However, this paradigm shift, which is closely bound up with his involvement with the Nazis and with his attempt to restore the language of the archaic Greek poets—the original speakers of truth—is beyond my concern.

2. Hunters orient themselves in relation to rivers and river currents (upriver, downriver, toward the water, away from the water, etc.). Only places along the riverbanks are named, while the rest of the country remains largely nameless. What is remarkable about the Yukaghir place-names, however, is that they are essentially "ahistorical," i.e., they are almost completely lacking in historical and mythical significance. Thus, in contrast to, for example, the Australian Aborigines, who see the land as being crisscrossed with ancestral tracks (Lewis 1976: 272), the Yukaghir landscape is virtually without historical or mythical sites. Moreover, the people as a whole have very few place-names in common. Instead, each group of hunters gives its own names to places along the rivers where they live and hunt, and the names differ between groups and change over generations. Spiridon and his hunters name places along the Omulevka River after the hunters in their group. Thus, one finds a myriad of places called Ivan's *protoka*, Yura's *protoka*, or Spiridon's *protoka*, for example. To each of these places is connected a personal story. Ivan's *protoka*, for example, is the place where Ivan ate putrid meat and got the runs, so that he had to throw away his trousers. As the river changes its course, which it usually does every fourth or fifth year, its former bed will be displaced inland, and hunters will have to start all over again, naming the various places along its new path. If a hunter is still living and working with the group, his name will be attached to a number of new sites. However, if he has moved to another group of hunters in another part of the country, his name will vanish from the local landscape and from the memory of the people living and working there.

3. The Ilongot are an indigenous group of hunters and horticulturalists in the northern Philippines.

4. My twin brother, Eske, who has also lived among Yukaghir hunters, has given a rich account on exactly this topic. He could not speak the Russian language, but he became familiar with the forest environment simply by going along and doing what the other hunters were doing (E. Willerslev 1995: 50–56).

5. I take this last point from Ingold (2000: 56).

6. I am not revealing the names of the speakers because they asked me not to. I assume it is due to the erotic content of their dream experiences.

7. In Yukaghir, "to dream" is *osyodit tyetuliou,* which means "I saw while asleep." *Ädäbut yo yeio* means "I saw when awake." Therefore, the fact that dreams are taken as real-world experiences is not to be misunderstood as if the Yukaghirs were confusing their dream experiences with those they have while awake, as suggested by Tylor (1929a: 445) with regard to "primitive" peoples more generally. Rather, the point is that the dream world and the world of waking life are seen as one and the same world, but experienced from different perspectives.

9. TAKING ANIMISM SERIOUSLY

1. This, we may speculate, is the condition of the very young infant, who appears to have no sense of differentiation from others and the world more generally. However, for everyone above the age of about eighteen months, the self-other distinction is already cemented and the child is capable of seeing itself as a separate being—that is, it perceives itself reflexively as its own object. Indeed, it is, as we have seen, by means of adopting this perspective of exteriority that the child builds a subjective viewpoint of its own.

2. I take the phrase, "we-ness as sameness" along with the question posed from Viveiros de Castro (in Bird-David 1999: 79–80), who raises it in his criticism of Bird-David's article.

3. I am grateful to Viveiros de Castro for drawing my attention to this point. In a comment on Bird-David's article he writes, "[For Bird-David] all differences are read as opposition and all oppositions as the *absence* of a relation . . . a strange idea which I can only attribute to the guilty supposition that others conceive otherness as we do. Well, they don't: others are 'other' precisely because they have other 'others'" (Viveiros de Castro in Bird-David 1999: 40; emphasis in the original).

References

Altman, J., and N. Peterson. 1991. "Rights to Game and Rights to Cash among Contemporary Australian Hunter-Gatherers." Pp. 75–94 in *Hunters and Gatherers II: Property, Power, and Ideology,* edited by T. Ingold, D. Riches, and J. Woodburn. Oxford: Berg Publishers.

Anderson, D. G. 2000. *Identity and Ecology in Arctic Siberia: The Number One Reindeer Brigade.* Oxford: Oxford University Press.

Anisimov, A. F. 1963. "The Shaman's Tent of the Evenks and the Origin of the Shamanic Rite." Pp. 84–123 in *Studies in Siberian Shamanism,* edited by H. N. Michael. Toronto: University of Toronto Press.

Århem, K. 1996. "The Cosmic Food Web: Human-Nature Relatedness in the Northwest Amazon." Pp. 185–205 in *Nature and Society: Anthropological Perspectives,* edited by P. Descola and G. Pálsson. London and New York: Routledge.

Arutiunov, S. A. 1988. "Even: Reindeer Herders of Eastern Siberia." Pp. 35–38 in *Crossroads of Continents: Cultures of Siberia and Alaska,* edited by W. W. Fitzhugh and A. Crowell. Washington, DC: Smithsonian Institution.

Atkinson, J. M. 1989. *The Art and Politics of Wana Shamanship.* Berkeley and Los Angeles: University of California Press.

Barnard, A., and J. Woodburn. 1991. "Introduction." Pp. 4–31 in *Hunters and Gatherers II: Property, Power, and Ideology,* edited by T. Ingold, D. Riches, and J. Woodburn. Oxford: Berg Publishers.

Barth, F. 1987. *Cosmologies in the Making: A Generative Approach to Cultural Variation in Inner New Guinea.* Cambridge: Cambridge University Press.

Barthes, R. 1990. *A Lover's Discourse: Fragments,* translated by R. Howard. London: Penguin Press.

Becker, A. 1994. "Nurturing and Negligence: Working on Other's Bodies in Fiji." Pp. 100–115 in *Embodiment and Experience: The Existential Ground of*

Culture and Self, edited by T. J. Csordas. Cambridge: Cambridge University Press.

Bird-David, N. 1990. "The Giving Environment: Another Perspective on the Economic System of Hunter-gatherers." *Current Anthropology* 31: 183–96.

———. 1992. "Beyond the Original Affluent Society: A Culturalist Reformulation." *Current Anthropology* 33: 25–47.

———. 1993. "Tribal Metaphorization of Human-nature Relatedness: A Comparative Analysis." Pp. 112–25 in *Environmentalism: The View from Anthropology,* edited by K. Milton. ASA Monograph 32. London and New York: Routledge.

———. 1999. "Animism Revisited: Personhood, Environment, and Relational Epistemology." *Current Anthropology* 40 (supplement): S67–S91.

Black, M. B. 1977. "Ojibwa Taxonomy and Percept Ambiguity." *Ethos* 5: 90–118.

Bloch, A. 2004. *Red Ties and Residential Schools: Indigenous Siberians in a Post-Soviet State.* Philadelphia: University of Pennsylvania Press.

Bloch, M. 1998. *How We Think They Think: Anthropological Approaches to Cognition, Memory and Literacy.* Boulder, CO: Westview Press.

Bobrick, B. 1992. *East of the Sun: The Conquest and Settlement of Siberia.* London: Heinemann.

Bodenhorn, B. 1997. "Person, Place and Parentage: Ecology, Identity and Social Relations on the North Slope of Alaska." Pp. 103–32 in *Arctic Ecology and Identity,* edited by S. A. Mousalimas. Budapest: Akadémia Kiadó, and Los Angeles: International Society for Trans-Oceanic Research.

———. 2000. "He Used to Be My Relative: Exploring the Basis of Relatedness among Inupiat of Northern Alaska." Pp. 128–48 in *Cultures of Relatedness: New Approaches to the Study of Kinship,* edited by J. Carsten. Cambridge: Cambridge University Press.

Bogoras, W. 1904–9. *The Chukchee,* edited by F. Boas. Memoir of the American Museum of Natural History, vol. 7. New York: American Museum of Natural History.

Boothby, R. 1991. *Death and Desire: Psychoanalytic Theory in Lacan's Return to Freud.* London and New York: Routledge.

Bourdieu, P. 1977. *Towards a Theory of Practice.* Cambridge: Cambridge University Press.

Boyer, P. 1993. "Pseudo-natural Kinds." Pp. 121–41 in *Cognitive Aspects of Religious Symbolism,* edited by P. Boyer. Cambridge: Cambridge University Press.

———. 1994. *The Naturalness of Religious Ideas: A Cognitive Theory of Religion.* Berkeley and Los Angeles: University of California Press.

Brightman, R. A. 1993. *Grateful Prey: Rock Cree Human-Animal Relationships.* Berkeley and Los Angeles: University of California Press.

Burch, E. S., Jr. 1991. "Modes of Exchange in North-west Alaska." Pp. 95–109 in *Hunters and Gatherers II: Property, Power, and Ideology,* edited by T. Ingold, D. Riches, and J. Woodburn. Oxford: Berg Publishers.

Burr, V. 1995. *An Introduction to Social Constructionism.* London and New York: Routledge.

Cameron, D., and E. Frazer. 1994. "Cultural Difference and the Lust to Kill." Pp. 156–71 in *Sex and Violence: Issues in Representation and Experience*, edited by P. Harvey and P. Gow. London and New York: Routledge.

Carrithers, M. 1982. "Hell-fire and Urinal Stones: An Essay on Buddhist Purity and Authority." In *Contributions to South Asian Studies II*. Delhi: Oxford University Press.

Cartmill, M. 1993. *A View to a Death in the Morning: Hunting and Nature through History*. Cambridge, MA, and London: Harvard University Press.

Casey, E. S. 1987. *Remembering: A Phenomenological Study*. Bloomington and Indianapolis: Indiana University Press.

———. 1996. "How to Get from Space to Place in a Fairly Short Stretch of Time: Phenomenological Prolegomena." Pp.13–52 in *Senses of Place*, edited by S. Feld and K. H. Basso. Santa Fe, NM, and New York: School of American Research Press.

Cavallero, C., and D. Foulkes. 1993. "Introduction." Pp. 1–18 in *Dreaming as Cognition*, edited by D. Foulkes and C. Cavallero. New York: Harvester Wheatsheaf.

Chaussonnet, V. 1988. "Needles and Animals: Women's Magic." Pp. 209–27 in *Crossroads of Continents: Cultures of Siberia and Alaska*, edited by W. W. Fitzhugh and A. Crowell. Washington, DC: Smithsonian Institution.

Classen, C. 1993. *Worlds of Sense*. London: Routledge.

Collier, J., and M. Rosaldo. 1981. "The Politics and Gender in Simple Societies." Pp. 275–329 in *Sexual Meanings*, edited by S. Ortner and H. Whitehead. Cambridge: Cambridge University Press.

Costall, A. 1997. "The Meaning of Things." Pp. 76–86 in P. Harvey, ed., "Technology as Skilled Practice." *Social Analysis* 41(1): 76–85.

Cox, R. A. 2003. *The Zen Arts: An Anthropological Study of the Culture of Aesthetic Form in Japan*. London: RoutledgeCurzon.

Czaplicka, M. A. 1914. *Aboriginal Siberia: A Study in Social Anthropology*. Oxford: Clarendon Press.

Darwin, C. 1882. *The Descent of Man and Selection in Relation to Sex*. London: John Murry.

Degnen, C. 2005. "On Vegetable Love, Gardening and Genetic Modification." Seminar paper presented in the Department of Social Anthropology, University of Manchester, February 7.

Derlicki, J. 2003. "The New People: the Yukaghir in the Process of Transformation." Pp. 121–36 in *Between Tradition and Postmodernity*, edited by L. Mroz and Z. Sokolewicz. Warsaw: Committee of Ethnological Science, Polish Academy of Science, Institute of Ethnology and Cultural Anthropology of the University of Warsaw.

Descartes, R. 1984. *The Philosophical Writings of Descartes*, translated by J. Cottingham, R. Stoothoff, and D. Murdoch. Vol. 2. Cambridge: Cambridge University Press.

———. 1988. *Selected Philosophical Writings*, translated by J. Cottingham, R. Stoothoff, and D. Murdoch. Cambridge: Cambridge University Press.

———. 1996. *Meditations on First Philosophy: With Selections from the Objec-*

tions and Replies, edited by J. Cottingham. Cambridge: Cambridge University Press.

Descola, P. 1992. "Societies of Nature and the Nature of Society." In *Conceptualizing Society,* edited by A. Kuper. London and New York: Routledge.

———. 1996. *In the Society of Nature: A Native Ecology in Amazonia.* Cambridge: Cambridge University Press.

Descola, P., and G. Pálsson. 1996. *Nature and Society: Anthropological Perspectives.* London and New York: Routledge.

Dillon, M. C. 1974. "Sartre on the Phenomenal Body and Merleau-Ponty's Critique." *Journal of the British Society for Phenomenology* 5(2): 144–58.

———. 1988. *Merleau-Ponty's Ontology.* Evanston, IL: Northwestern University Press.

Douglas, M. 1970. *Purity and Danger.* Harmondsworth: Penguin.

Dreyfus, H. L. 1988. "Husserl, Heidegger, and Modern Existentialism." Pp. 253–277 in *The Great Philosophers,* edited by B. Magee. Oxford: Oxford University Press.

———. 1991. *"Being-in-the-world": A Commentary on Heidegger's Being and Time, Division I.* Cambridge, MA, and London: MIT Press.

Durkheim, E. 1976 [1912]. *The Elementary Forms of Religious Life,* translated by J. W. Swain. New York: HarperCollins.

Eagleton, T. 1983. *Literary Theory: An Introduction.* Oxford: Basil Blackwell.

Eliade, M. 1964. *Shamanism: Archaic Techniques of Ecstasy.* Princeton, NJ: Princeton University Press.

Empson, J. 1993. *Sleep and Dreaming.* New York: Harvester Wheatsheaf.

Empson, R. 2006. "Separating and Containing People and Things in Mongolia." Pp. 113–40 in *Thinking through Things: Artefacts in Ethnographic Perspective,* edited by A. Henare, M. Holbraad, and S. Wastell. London: Cavendish University of London Press.

Eritukov, V. I. 1990. *Ust'Mil'skaia kul'tura epokhi bronzy Yakutii* [The Ust'Mil'skaia Culture of Yakutia's Bronze Age]. Moscow: Nauka.

Faraday, A. 1972. *Dream Power.* London: Hodder and Stoughton.

Fausto, C. Forthcoming. "Feasting on People: Cannibalism and Commensality in Amazonia." *Current Anthropology.*

Fedoseeva, S. A. 1980. *Ymyiakhtakhskaia kul'tura Severo-Vostochnoi Azii* [The Ymyiakhtakhskaia Culture of Northeast Asia]. Novosibirsk: Nauka.

Feit, H. A. 2000. "Les animaux comme partenaires de chasse: Réciprocité chez les Cris de la baie James." *Terrain* 34: 123–42.

Fienup-Riordan, A. 1994. *Boundaries and Passages: Rule and Ritual in Yup'ik Eskimo Oral Tradition.* Norman and London: University of Oklahoma Press.

Forsyth, J. 1992. *A History of the Peoples of Siberia: Russia's North Asian Colony 1581–1990.* Cambridge: Cambridge University Press.

Foulkes, D. 1993. "Children's Dreaming." Pp. 114–33 in *Dreaming as Cognition,* edited by C. Cavallero and D. Foulkes. New York: Harvester Wheatsheaf.

Frazer, J. G. 1993 [1922]. *The Golden Bough: A Study in Magic and Religion,* 3rd ed. Volume 1 part 1. London: Macmillan.

Freed, S. A., R. S. Freed, and L. Williamson. 1988. "The American Museum's

Jesup North Pacific Expedition." Pp. 97–104 in *Crossroads of Continents: Cultures of Siberia and Alaska,* edited by W. W. Fitzhugh and A. Crowell. Washington, DC: Smithsonian Institution.

Freud, S. 1957. *A Metapsychological Supplement to the Theory of Dreams.* The Standard Edition of the Complete Psychological Works of Sigmund Freud, vol. 14. London: Hogarth Press.

———. 1961. *Beyond the Pleasure Principles,* translated by J. Strachey. New York: W. W. Norton.

Fudge, E. 2002. *Animal.* London: Reaction Books.

Gebauer, G., and C. Wulf. 1992. *Mimesis: Culture, Art, Society,* translated by D. J. Reneau. Berkeley and Los Angeles: University of California Press.

Gell, A. 1992. "Inter-tribal Commodity Barter and Reproductive Gift Exchange in Old Melanesia." Pp. 142–68 in *Barter, Exchange and Value: An Anthropological Approach,* edited by C. Humphrey and S. Hugh-Jones. Cambridge: Cambridge University Press.

———. 1996. "The Language of the Forest: Landscape and Phonological Iconism in Umeda." Pp. 232–55 in *The Anthropology of Landscape: Perspectives on the Place and Space,* edited by E. Hirsch and M. Hanlon. Oxford: Clarendon Press.

———. 1998. *Art and Agency: An Anthropological Theory.* Oxford: Clarendon Press.

Gellner, E. 1985. *The Psychoanalytic Movement.* London: Paladin.

Gogolev, Z. V., et al. 1975. *Yukagiry: Istoriko-etnograficheskiy ocherk* [The Yukaghirs: An Ethnohistorical Outline]. Novosibirik: Nauka.

Goodenough, W. 1951. *Property, Kin and Community on Turk.* Yale University Publications in Anthropology 46. New Haven, CT: Yale University Press.

Goulet, J. A. 1998. *Ways of Knowing: Experience, Knowledge and Power among the Dene Tha.* Lincoln: University of Nebraska Press.

Graburn, N. H. H., and B. S. Strong. 1973. *Circumpolar Peoples: An Anthropological Perspective.* Pacific Palisades, CA: Goodyear Publishers..

Grant, B. 1993. "Siberia Hot and Cold: Reconstructing the Image of Siberian Indigenous Peoples." Pp. 227–53 in *Between Heaven and Hell: The Myth of Siberia in Russian Culture,* edited by G. Diment, and Y. Slezkine. New York: St. Martin's Press.

———. 1995. *In the Soviet House of Culture: A Century of Perestroikas.* Princeton, NJ: Princeton University Press.

Grosz, E. 1990. *Jacques Lacan: A Feminist Introduction.* London: Routledge.

Guemple, L. 1991. "Teaching Social Relations to Inuit Children." Pp. 131–49 in *Hunters and Gatherers II: Property, Power, and Ideology,* edited by T. Ingold, D. Riches, and J. Woodburn. Oxford: Berg Publishers.

———. 1994. "The Inuit Cycle of Spirits." Pp. 107–22 in *Amerindian Rebirth: Reincarnation Belief among North American Indians and Inuit,* edited by A. Mills and R. Slobodin. Toronto: University of Toronto Press.

Guenther, M. 1979. "Bushmen Religion and the (Non) Sense of Anthropological Theory of Religion." *Sociologus* 29: 102–32.

———. 1999. *Tricksters and Trancers: Bushman Religion and Society.* Bloomington: Indiana University Press.

Gurwitsch, A. 1979. *Human Encounters in the Social World*. Pittsburgh: Duquesne University Press.

Guthrie, S. 1993. *Faces in the Clouds: A New Theory of Religion*. Oxford: Oxford University Press.

———. 1997. "Anthropomorphism: A Definition and a Theory." Pp. 50–58 in *Anthropomorphism, Anecdotes, and Animals*, edited by R. W. Mitchell, N. S. Thomson, and H. L. Miles. New York: State University of New York Press.

Hallowell, A. I. 1955. *Culture and Experience*. Philadelphia: University of Pennsylvania Press.

———. 1960. "Ojibwa Ontology, Behavior, and World-View." Pp. 19–52 in *Culture in History: Essays in Honor of Paul Radin*, edited by S. Dimond. New York: Columbia University Press.

Hamayon, R. N. 1990. *La chasse à l'ame: equisse d'une théorie du chamanisme sibérien*. Nanterre: Société d'Ethnologie.

———. 1994. "Shamanism in Siberia: from Partnership in Supernature to Counter-power in Society." Pp. 76–89 in *Shamanism, History and the State*, edited by C. Humphrey and N. Thomas. Ann Arbor: University of Michigan Press.

Harner, M. 1972. *The Jivaro: People of the Sacred Waterfalls*. Garden City, NY: Doubleday/Natural History Press.

Harrison, S. 2005. *Fracturing Resemblances: Identity and Mimetic Conflict in Melanesia and the West*. Vol. 5, EASA Series. New York and Oxford: Berghahn Books.

Hegel, G. W. F. 1971 [1830/1845]. *Hegel's Philosophy of Mind* (being Part three of the Encyclopaedia of the philosophical sciences) (trans. W. Wallance together with the zusatze in Boumann's text, trans. A. V. Miller). Oxford: Clarendon Press.

Heidegger, M. 1962. *Being and Time*. New York: Harper and Row.

———. 1982 [1927]. *The Basic Problems of Phenomenology*, translated by A. Hofstader. Bloomington: Indiana University Press.

———. 1993. "Building, Dwelling, Thinking." Pp. 347–63 in *Martin Heidegger: Basic Writings*, edited by D. F. Krell. London: Routledge.

Hobart, M. 1986. "Introduction: Context, Meaning and Power." Pp. 7–19 in *Context, Meaning and Power in Southeast Asia*, edited by M. Hobart and R. H. Taylor. New York: Cornell Southeast Asia Program.

Hoebel, E. A. 1972. *Anthropology: The Study of Man*. New York: McGraw-Hill.

Howell, S. 1996. "Nature in Culture or Culture in Nature? Chewong Ideas of Humans and Other Species." Pp. 127–45 in *Nature and Society: Anthropological Perspectives*, edited by P. Descola and G. Pálsson. London and New York: Routledge.

Hugh-Jones, S. 1996. "Bonnes raisons ou mauvaise conscience: de l'ambivalence de certains Amazoniens envers la consommation de viande." *Tarrain* 26: 123–48.

Hultkrantz, Å. 1953. *Conceptions of the Soul among North American Indians*. Stockholm: Ethnographical Museum of Sweden Monograph Series No. 1.

Humphrey, C. 1998. *Marx Went Away but Karl Stayed Behind*. Ann Arbor: University of Michigan Press.

Humphrey, C., and J. Laidlaw. 1994. *The Archetypical Actions of Ritual: A Theory of Ritual Illustrated by Jain Rite of Worship.* Oxford: Clarendon Press.

Humphrey, C., with U. Onon. 1996. *Shamans and Elders: Experience, Knowledge, and Power among the Daur Mongols.* Oxford: Clarendon Press.

Hutton, R. 2001. *Shamans: Siberian Spirituality and the Western Imagination.* London and New York: Hambledon.

Ingold, T. 1986a. "Hunting, Sacrifice and the Domestication of Animals." Pp. 243–77 in *The Appropriation of Nature: Essays on Human Ecology and Social Relations.* Manchester: University of Manchester.

———. 1986b. "The Significance of Storage in Hunting Societies." Pp. 198–221 in *The Appropriation of Nature: Essays on Human Ecology and Social Relations.* Manchester: University of Manchester.

———. 1992. "Culture and the Perception of the Environment." Pp. 39–73 in *Bush Base: Forest Farm. Culture, Environment and Development,* edited by E. Croll and D. Parkin. London and New York: Routledge.

———. 1993. "The Art of Translation in a Continuous World." Pp. 210–30 in *Beyond Boundaries: Understanding, Translation and Anthropological Discourse,* edited by G. Pálsson. Oxford: Berg Publishers.

———. 1994. "Humanity and Animality." Pp. 14–33 in *Companion Encyclopedia of Anthropology: Humanity, Culture and Social Life,* edited by T. Ingold. London and New York: Routledge.

———. 1996. "Human Worlds Are Culturally Constructed." Pp. 112–18 in *Key Debates in Anthropology,* edited by T. Ingold. London and New York: Routledge.

———. 2000. *The Perception of the Environment: Essays in Livelihood, Dwelling and Skill.* London and New York: Routledge.

Ivanov, M. I. 1999. "The Iukagir." Pp. 152–55 in *Encyclopedia of Hunters and Gatherers,* edited by R. B. Lee and R. Daly. Cambridge: Cambridge University Press.

Jackson, J. 1994. "Chronic Pain and the Tension between Body as Subject and Object." Pp. 201–28 in *Embodiment and Experience: The Existential Ground of Culture and Self,* edited by T. J. Csordas. Cambridge: Cambridge University Press.

Jackson, M. 1983. "Knowledge of the Body." In *MAN* (n.s.) 18: 327–45.

Jochelson [Iohelsonom], W. 1900. *Materiali po izuchniu jukagirskogo iazika I folklora sobrannie v Kolimskom okruge* [Material on Yukaghir Language and Folklore Studies, Collected in Verkhne Kolymski Okrug]. Part 1, *Obrazini narodnoi slovesnosti jukagirov (teksti s perevodom)* [Patterns of Yukaghir Oral Tradition (Texts and Translations)]. St. Petersburg: Peter the Great Museum.

Jochelson, W. 1908. *The Koryak,* edited by F. Boas. Memoir of the American Museum of Natural History, vol. 6. New York: American Museum of Natural History.

———. 1926. *The Yukaghir and the Yukaghized Tungus,* edited by F. Boas. New York: American Museum of Natural History.

———. 1933. *The Yakut.* Anthropological papers of the American Museum of

Natural History, vol. 33, part 2. New York: American Museum of Natural History.

Kapferer, B. 1984. "The Ritual Process and the Problem of Reflexivity in Sinhalese Demon Exorcisms." Pp. 179–207 in *Rite, Drama, Festival, Spectacle,* edited by J. MacAloon. Philadelphia: Institute on the Study of Human Issues.

Kasten, E. 1998. *Bicultural Education in the North: Ways of Preserving and Enhancing Indigenous Peoples' Languages and Traditional Knowledge,* edited by E. Kasten. Münster, New York, Munich, and Berlin: Waxmann.

Kendall, L., B. Mathe, and T. R. Miller. 1997. *Drawing Shadows to Stone: The Photography of the Jesup North Pacific Expedition, 1897–1902.* Seattle and London: American Museum of Natural History in association with the University of Washington Press.

Kennedy, J. S. 1992. *The New Anthropomorphism.* Cambridge: Cambridge University Press.

Kerr, N. H. 1993. "Mental Imagery, Dreams, and Perception." Pp. 18–38 in *Dreaming as Cognition,* edited by C. Cavallero and D. Foulkes. New York: Harvester Wheatsheaf.

Koester, D. 2002. "When the Fat Raven Sings: Mimesis and Environmental Alterity in Kamchatka's Environmental Age." Pp. 45–62 in *People and the Land: Pathways to Reform in Post-Soviet Siberia,* edited by E. Kasten. Berlin: Dietrich Reimer Verlag.

Krauss, M. F. 1988. "Many Tongues—Ancient Tales." Pp. 144–50 in *Crossroads of Continents: Cultures of Siberia and Alaska,* edited by W. W. Fitzhugh and A. Crowell. Washington, DC: Smithsonian Institution Press.

Krupnik, I. 1993. *Arctic Adaptations: Native Whalers and Reindeer Herders of Northern Eurasia,* translated and edited by M. Levenson. Hanover and London: University Press of New England.

Krupnik, I., and N. Vakhtin. 1997. "Indigenous Knowledge in Modern Culture: Siberian Yupik Ecological Legacy in Transition." *Arctic Anthropology* 34(1): 236–57.

———. n.d. "Remembering and Forgetting: Indigenous Knowledge and Culture in Chukotka." Filed in The American Museum of Natural History, Smithsonian Institution, Washington, DC.

Kwon, H. 1993. "Maps and Actions: Nomadic and Sedentary Space in a Siberian Reindeer Farm." PhD diss., Department of Social Anthropology, University of Cambridge.

———. 1997. "Movements and Transgression: Human Landscape in Northeastern Sakhalin." Pp. 143–68 in *Arctic Ecology and Identity,* edited by S. A. Mousalimas. Budapest: Akadémia Kiadó, and Los Angeles: International Society for Trans-Oceanic Research.

———. 1998. "The Saddle and the Sledge: Hunting as Comparative Narrative in Siberia and Beyond." *Journal of the Royal Anthropological Institute* 4(1): 115–27.

———. 2000. "To Hunt the Black Shaman: Memory of the Great Purge in East Siberia." *Ethofoor* 13(1): 33–50.

Lacan, J. 1989 [1966]. *Écrits: A Selection,* translated by A. Sheridan. London and New York: Routledge.

————. 1991 [1953–54]. *Seminar I: Freud's Papers on Technique,* edited by J. A. Miller, translated and with notes by J. Forrester. New York: W. W. Norton.

Langer, M. M. 1989. *Merleau-Ponty's Phenomenology of Perception: A Guide and Commentary.* London: Macmillan.

Lave, J. 1997. "The Culture of Acquisition and the Practice of Understanding." Pp. 309–27 in *Cultural Psychology: Essays on Comparative Human Development,* edited by W. Stigler, R. A. Shweder, and G. Herdt. Cambridge: Cambridge University Press.

Leach, E. R. 1965. *Political Systems of Highland Burma: A Study of Katchin Social Structure.* London: Bell.

————. 1976. *Culture and Communication: The Logic by Which Symbols Are Connected.* Cambridge: Cambridge University Press.

Lee, R. B. 1991. "Reflections on Primitive Communism." Pp. 252–68 in *Hunters and Gatherers I: History, Evolution, and Social Change,* edited by T. Ingold, D. Riches, and J. Woodburn. Oxford: Berg Publishers.

————. 1993. *The Dobe Ju/'hoansi: Case Studies in Social Anthropology.* Fort Worth, TX: Harcourt Brace College Publishers.

Lender, D. 1990. *The Absent Body.* Chicago and London: University of Chicago Press.

Lemaire, A. 1996. *Jacques Lacan.* London and New York: Routledge.

Lewis, D. 1976. "Observations on Route Finding and Spatial Orientation among the Aboriginal Peoples of the Western Desert Region of Central Australia." *Oceania* 46(4): 249–82.

Maslova, E., and N. Vakhtin. 1996. "The Far North-east of Russia." Pp. 999–1001 in *Atlas of Languages of Intercultural Communication in the Pacific, Asia, and the Americas,* edited by S. A. Wurm, P. Mühlhäuser, and D. T. Tryon. Berlin and New York: Mouton de Gruyter.

McCallum, C. 1996. "The Body That Knows: From Cashinahua Epistemology to a Medical Anthropology of Lowland South America." *Medical Anthropology Quarterly* 10(3): 347–72.

Meier, B. 1993. "Speech and Thinking in Dreams." Pp. 58–77 in *Dreaming and Cognition,* edited by C. Cavallero and D. Foulkes. New York: Harvester Wheatsheaf.

Merleau-Ponty, M. 1964. "The Child's Relations with Others." Pp. 96–155 in *The Primacy of Perception,* translated by J. Edie. Evanston, IL: Northwestern University Press.

————. 1998 [1962]. *Phenomenology of Perception,* translated by C. Smith. London and New York: Routledge.

Mikhailov, T. M. 1990. "Buryat Shamanism." Pp. 110–20 in *Shamanism,* edited by M. M. Balzer. Armonk, NY: Sharpe.

Miller, T. R., and B. Mathé. 1997. "Tough Fieldworkers: History and Personalities of the Jesup Expedition." Pp. 9–19 in *Drawing Shadows to Stone: The Photography of the Jesup North Pacific Expedition, 1897–1902,* edited by L. Kendall, B. Mathé, and T. R. Miller. New York: American Museum of Natural History, in association with the University of Washington Press.

Montangero, J. 1993. "Dream, Problem-solving, and Creativity." Pp. 93–114 in

Dreaming and Cognition, edited by C. Cavallero and D. Foulkes. New York: Harvester Wheatsheaf.

Morin, F., and B. Saladin d'Anglure. 1997. "Ethnicity as a Political Tool for Indigenous Peoples." Pp. 157–93 in *The Politics of Ethnic Consciousness,* edited by C. Govers and H. Vermeulen. London: Macmillan.

Morris, B. 1991. "Rights to Game and Rights to Cash among Contemporary Australian Hunter-gatherers." Pp. 52–94 in *Hunters and Gatherers II: Property, Power, and Ideology,* edited by T. Ingold, D. Riches, and J. Woodburn. Oxford: Berg Publishers.

———. 2000. *The Power of Animals: An Ethnography.* Oxford and New York: Berg Publishers.

Nagel, T. 1997. "What Is It Like to Be a Bat?" Pp. 165–80 in *Mortal Questions.* Cambridge: Cambridge University Press.

Nash, D. 1977. "Hallowell in American Anthropology." *Ethos* 5(1): 3–12.

Nelson, R. K. 1983. *Make Prayers to the Raven: A Koyukon View of the Northern Forest.* Chicago: University of Chicago Press.

Noske, B. 1997. *Beyond Boundaries: Humans and Animals.* Montreal: Black Rose Books.

Nuttall, M. 1994. "The Name Never Dies: Greenland Inuit ideas of the person." Pp. 123–36 in *Amerindian Rebirth: Reincarnation Belief Among North American Indians and Inuit,* edited by A. Mills and R. Slobodin. Toronto: University of Toronto Press.

Obeyesekere, G. 1994. "Foreword: Reincarnation Eschatologies and the Comparative Study of Religions." Pp. xi–xxiv in *Amerindian Rebirth: Reincarnation Belief Among North American Indians and Inuit,* edited by A. Mills and R. Slobodin. Toronto: University of Toronto Press.

Pedersen, M. A. 2001. "Totemism, Animism and North Asian Indigenous Ontologies." *Journal of the Royal Anthropological Institute* 7(3): 411–27.

Pesmen, D. 2000. *Russia and the Soul: An Exploration.* Ithaca, NY: Cornell University Press.

Peterson, N. 1993. "Demand Sharing: Reciprocity and the Pressure for Generosity among Foragers." *American Anthropologist* 95(4): 860–74.

Rasmussen, K. 1929. *Intellectual Culture of the Iglulik Eskimos.* Report of the Fifth Thule Expedition 1921–24, vol. 7, no. 1. Copenhagen: Gyldendalske Boghandel, Nordisk Forlag.

Reichel-Dolmatoff, G. 1971. *Amazonian Cosmos: The Sexual and Religious Symbolism of the Tukano Indians.* Chicago and London: University of Chicago Press.

Riches, D. 1995. "Dreaming as Social Process, and its Implications for Consciousness." Pp. 101–117 in *Questions of Consciousness,* edited by A. Cohen and N. Rapport. London and New York: Routledge.

Riordan, J. 1989. "Man-bear." In *The Sun Maiden and the Crescent Moon: Siberian Folk Tales.* Edinburgh: Canongate.

Rival, L. 2002. *Tracking through History: The Huaorani of Amazonian Ecuador.* New York: Columbia University Press.

Roepstorff, A., and N. Bubandt. 2003. "General Introduction: The Critique of Culture and the Plurality of Nature." Pp. 9–30 in *Imagining Nature: Practices of Cosmology and Identity*, edited by A. Roepstorff, N. Bubandt, and K. Kull. Aarhus: Aarhus University Press.

Rorty, R. 1989. *Contingency, Irony and Solidarity*. Cambridge: Cambridge University Press.

———. 1993. "Wittgenstein, Heidegger, and the reification of language." Pp. 337–58 in *The Cambridge Companion to Heidegger*, edited by C. Guignon. Cambridge: Cambridge University Press.

Rosaldo, R. 1986. "Ilongot Hunting as Story and Experience." Pp. 97–138 in *The Anthropology of Experience*, edited by W. Turner and E. M. Burner. Urbana, IL: University of Illinois Press.

———. 1993. *Culture and Truth: The Remaking of Social Analysis*. Boston, MA: Beacon Press.

Sahlins, M. 1972. *Stone Age Economics*. New York: Aldine De Gruyter.

Saladin d'Anglure, B. 1994. "From Foetus to Shaman: the Construction of an Inuit third Sex." Pp. 82–107 in *Amerindian Rebirth: Reincarnation Belief among North American Indians and Inuit*, edited by A. Mills and R. Slobodin. Toronto: University of Toronto Press.

Santos-Granero, F. Forthcoming. "Time Is Disease, Suffering, and Oblivion: Yanesha Historicity and the Struggle against Temporality." In *Time and Memory in Indigenous Amazonia: Anthropological Perspectives*, edited by C. Fausto and J. Heckenberger. Gainesville, FL.: University Presses of Florida.

Sapir, E. 1951. *The Selected Writings of Edward Sapir*, edited by D. G. Mandelbaum. Berkeley and Los Angeles: University of California Press.

Sarup, M. 1988. *An Introductory Guide to Post-structualism and Postmodernism*. Hempstead: Harvester Wheatsheaf.

Sartre, J-P. 2000 [1958]. *Being and Nothingness: An Essay on Phenomenological Ontology*, translated by H. E. Barnes. London: Routledge.

Saussure, F. de. 1959. *Course in General Linguistics*, edited by C. Bally and A. Sechehaye, translated by W. Baskin. New York: The Philosophical Library.

Schechner, R. 1985. *Between Theater and Anthropology*. Philadelphia: University of Pennsylvania Press.

Schutz, A. 1962. *Collected Papers I*, edited by M. Natanson. The Hague: Martinus Nijhoff.

———. 1966. *Collected Papers III: Studies in Phenomenological Philosophy*, edited by I. Schutz. The Hague: Martinus Nijhoff.

———. 1971. *Collected Papers II: Studies in Social Theory*, edited by A. Brodersen. The Hague: Martinus Nijhoff.

Schweitzer, P. P., and P. A. Gray. 2000. "The Chukchi and Siberian Yupiit of the Russian Far East." Pp. 17–37 in *Endangered Peoples of the Arctic: Struggles to Survive and Thrive*, edited by M. R. Freeman. Westport, CT: Greenwood Press.

Serov, S. la. 1988. "Guardians and Spirit-masters of Siberia." Pp. 241–55 in *Crossroads of Continents: Cultures of Siberia and Alaska*, edited by W. W. Fitzhugh and A. Crowell. Washington, DC: Smithsonian Institution.

Sharp, H. S. 1991. "Dry Meat and Gender: the Absence of Chipewyan Ritual for the Regulation of Hunting and Animal Numbers." Pp. 183–91 in *Hunters and Gatherers II: Property, Power, and Ideology,* edited by T. Ingold, D. Riches, and J. Woodburn. Oxford: Berg Publishers.

Shnirelman, V. A. 1999. "Introduction: North Eurasia." Pp. 119–25 in *Encyclopedia of Hunters and Gatherers,* edited by R. B. Lee and R. Daly. Cambridge: Cambridge University Press.

Skinner, B. F. 1938. *The Behavior of Animals: An Experimental Analysis.* New York: Appleton-Century-Crofts.

Slezkine, Y. 1993. "Savage Christians or Unorthodox Russians? The Missionary Dilemma in Siberia." Pp. 15–31 in *Between Heaven and Hell: The Myth of Siberia in Russian Culture,* edited by G. Diment and Y. Slezkine. New York: St. Martin's Press.

———. 1994. *Arctic Mirrors, Russia and the Small Peoples of the North.* Ithaca and London: Cornell University Press.

Smith, D. M. 1998. "An Athapaskan Way of Knowing: Chipewan Ontology." *American Ethnologist* 25(3): 412–32.

Smith, J. 1981. "Self—an experience in Maori culture." Pp. 145–59 in *Indigenous Psychologies: The Anthropology of the Self,* edited by P. Heelas and A. Lock. London: Academic Press.

Spencer, R. F. 1959. *The North Alaskan Eskimo: A Study in Ecology and Society.* Smithsonian Institution Bureau of American Ethnology Bulletin 171. Washington, DC: US Government Printing Office.

Spiridonov, N. I. [Teki Odulok]. 1930. "Oduly (Yukagiry) Kolymskogo Okruga" [The Odul (Yukagirs) of the Kolyma Region]. *Sovetskiy Sever* no. 9–12: 167–214.

Spiro, M. E. 1993. "Is the Western Conception of the Self 'Peculiar' within the Context of the World Cultures?" *Ethos* 21(2): 107–53.

Ssorin-Chaikov, N. 2001. "Evenki Shamanistic Practices in Soviet Present and Ethnographic Present Perfect." *Anthropology of Consciousness* 12(1): 1–18.

———. 2003. *The Social Life of the State in Subarctic Siberia.* Stanford, CA: Stanford University Press.

Stepanova, M. V., I. S. Gurvich, and V. V. Khramova. 1964. "The Yukaghirs." Pp. 788–98 in *The Peoples of Siberia,* edited by M. G. Levin and L. P. Potapov. Chicago: University of Chicago Press.

Stocking, G. W. 1996. *After Tylor: British Social Anthropology, 1888–1951.* London: Athlone.

Strathern, M. 1990. *The Gender of the Gift: Problems with Women and Problems with Society in Melanesia.* Berkeley and Los Angeles: University of California Press.

Tambiah, S. J. 1990. *Magic, Science, Religion, and the Scope of Rationality.* Cambridge: Cambridge University Press.

Tanner, A. 1979. *Bringing Home Animals.* London: Hurst.

Taussig, M. 1993. *Mimesis and Alterity: A Particular History of the Senses.* New York and London: Routledge.

Thomas, D. 1974. "An Archaeological Perspective on Shoshonean Bands." *American Anthropologist* 76: 11–23.

Tugolukov, V. A. 1979. *kto vy yukagiry?* [Who Are You Yukaghirs?]. Moscow: Nauka.

Turner, V. 1982. *From Ritual to Theatre: The Human Seriousness of Play*. New York: PAJ Publications.

Tylor, E. B. 1929a [1871]. *Primitive Culture*. Vol. 1. London: John Murray.

————. 1929b [1871]. *Primitive Culture*. Vol. 2. London: John Murray.

Vainshtein, S. I. 1989. "The Turkic Peoples, Sixth to Twelfth Centuries." Pp. 55–66 in *Nomads of Eurasia*, edited by V. N. Basilov and M. F. Zirins. Seattle and London: Natural History Museum of Los Angeles County in association with University of Washington Press.

Vakhtin, N. 1991. *The Yukaghir Language in Sociolinguistic Perspective*. Leningrad, USSR: Institute for Linguistics, Academy of Science.

Valeri, V. 2000. *The Forest of Taboos: Morality, Hunting, and Identity among the Huaulu of the Moluccas*. Madison: University of Wisconsin Press.

Van Gennep, A. 1960 [1909]. *The Rites of Passage*. London: Routledge and Kegan Paul.

Vdovin, I. S. 1978. "Social Foundations of Ancestor Cult among the Yukaghirs, Koryaks and the Chukchis." Pp. 405–18 in *Shamanism in Siberia*, edited by V. Dioszegi and M. Hoppal. Budapest: Adamediai Kiado.

Vendler, Z. 1984. "Understanding People." Pp. 200–213 in *Cultural Theory: Essays on Mind, Self, and Emotion*, edited by R. A. Sweder and R. A. LeVine. Cambridge: Cambridge University Press.

Vitebsky, P. 1992. "Landscape and Self-determination among the Eveny: The Political Environment of Siberian Reindeer Herders Today." Pp. 222–46 in *Bush Base: Forest Farm—Culture, Environment, and Development*, edited by E. Croll and D. Parkin. London: Routledge.

————. 1993. *Dialogues with the Dead: The Discussion of Mortality among the Sora of Eastern India*. Cambridge: Cambridge University Press.

————. 1997. "Dreams and Omens: Shattered Fragments of a Shamanic Sense of Destiny." Paper presented at the Jesup Centenary Conference, American Museum of Natural History, November 13–17, New York.

Vitebsky, P., and S. Wolfe. 2001. "The Separation of the Sexes among Siberian Reindeer Herders." Pp. 81–94 in *Sacred Custodians of the Earth? Women, Spirituality and Environment*, edited by A. Low and S. Tremayne. New York and Oxford: Berghahn Books.

Viveiros de Castro, E. 1998. "Cosmological Deixis and Amerindian Perspectivism." *Journal of the Royal Anthropological Institute* 4: 469–88.

Wicks, R. 2002. "Death and Enlightenment: the Therapeutic Psychology of the Tibetan Book of the Dead." Pp. 71–97 in *Death and Philosophy*, edited by J. Malpas and R. C. Solomon. London and New York: Routledge.

Willerslev, E. 1995. "Fortabt i Sibirien" [Lost in Siberia]. Pp. 50–56 in *På Rejse i Sibirien: tre danske ekspeditioners møde med Nordøstsibiriens j(ae)gere og nomader* [Exploring Siberia: Encounters of Three Danish Expeditions with the Hunters and Nomads of Northeastern Siberia], edited by I. Asmussen, A. Damm, M. Pedersen, and R. Willerslev. Moesgaard, Denmark: Prehistoric Museum.

Willerslev, R. 1995. "På Rejse i Sibirien" [Exploring Siberia]. Pp. 6–12 in *På Rejse i Sibirien: tre danske ekspeditioners møde med Nordøstsibiriens j(ae)gere og nomader* [Exploring Siberia: Encounters of Three Danish Expeditions with the Hunters and Nomads of Northeastern Siberia], edited by I. Asmussen, A. Damm, M. Pedersen, and R. Willerslev. Moesgaard, Denmark: Prehistoric Museum.

———. 1997. *Yukaghir Stories* (documentary film). Department for Visual Anthropology, University of Manchester.

———. 2000a. *Hunting and Trapping in Siberia*. Foreword by Finn Lynge. Copenhagen, Denmark: Arctic Information.

———. 2000b. "Datsko-Yukagirski pushnoi proiekt" [The Danish-Yukaghir Fur Project]. *Ilken* (August 2) 7(10): 5.

———. 2001. "The Hunter as a Human 'Kind': Hunting and Shamanism among the Upper Kolyma Yukaghirs of Siberia." *North Atlantic Studies* 4(1/2): 44–50.

———. 2004a. "Not Animal, Not Not-Animal: Hunting, Imitation, and Empathetic Knowledge among the Siberian Yukaghirs." *Journal of the Royal Anthropological Institute* 10: 629–52.

———. 2004b. "Spirits as 'Ready to Hand': A Phenomenological Analysis of Yukaghir Spiritual Knowledge and Dreaming." *Anthropological Theory* 4(4): 395–418.

———. 2006. "To Have the World at a Distance: Rethinking the Significance of Vision for Social Anthropology." Pp. 23–46 in *Skilled Visions*, edited by K. Grissini. New York and Oxford: Berghahn Books.

Willerslev, R., and U. R. Christensen [pseud. Igor Kolomets]. 2000. "Kogda vi nam zaplatite za nashu pushninu, Sakhabult?" [When Will You Pay Us for Our Furs, Sakhabult?] *Ilken* (September 22) 8(11): 8.

Willerslev, R., and J. Høgel. 1997. *Time Apart* (documentary film). Department for Visual Anthropology, University of Manchester.

Woodburn, J. 1980. "Hunters and Gatherers Today and Reconstruction of the Past." Pp. 95–117 in *Soviet and Western Anthropology*, edited by E. Gellner. London: Duckworth.

———. 1982a. "Egalitarian Societies." *Man* 17(3): 431–51.

———. 1982b. "Social Dimensions of Death in Four African Hunting and Gathering Societies." Pp. 187–210 in *Death and the Regeneration of Life*, edited by M. Bloch and J. Parry. Cambridge: Cambridge University Press.

———. 1991. "African Hunter-gatherer Social Organisation: Is It Best Understood as a Product of Encapsulation?" Pp. 31–64 in *Hunters and Gatherers I: History, Evolution, and Social Change*, edited by T. Ingold, D. Riches, and J. Woodburn. Oxford: Berg Publishers.

———. 1998. "Sharing Is Not a Form of Exchange: An Analysis of Property-sharing in Immediate-return Hunter-gatherer Societies." Pp. 48–63 in *Property Relations: Renewing the Anthropological Tradition*, edited by C. M. Hann. Cambridge: Cambridge University Press.

Worsley, P. 1997. *Knowledges: What Different Peoples Make of the World*. London: Profile Books Ltd.

Young, J. 2002. *Heidegger's Later Philosophy*. Cambridge: Cambridge University Press.

Zukova, L. N. 1996a. *Religia Yukagirov: iasicheskii panteon* [The Religion of the Yukaghirs: Pagan Pantheon]. Yakutsk: Isdatelstvo.

————. 1996b. *Odeshda Yukagirov* [The Clothing of the Yukaghirs]. Yakutsk: Isdatelstvo.

Zukova, L. N., I. A. Nikolaeva, and L. N. Dëmina. 1989. *Folklor Yukagirov Verhnei Kolymy* [Folklore of the Verkhne Kolyma Yukaghirs]. Parts 1 and 2. Yakutsk: Isdatelstvo.

————. 1993. "Les Ioukaghirs." Pp. 175–90 in *Études Mongoles et Sibériennes*. Nanterre, Paris: Laboratoire d'ethnologie et de sociologie comparative.

Index

Text:	10/13 Sabon
Display:	Sabon
Compositor:	BookMatters, Berkeley
Indexer:	Andrew Joron
Printer and binder:	Maple-Vail Manufacturing Group

CPSIA information can be obtained
at www.ICGtesting.com
Printed in the USA
JSHW051413210722
28374JS00001B/13